GROWING UP

Institutionalized to Globetrotting

Shane Lewis

I would like to dedicate this book to all the people who were so kind and supportive along the way   allowing this all to happen, and for those who were in charge of my care and wellbeing…
For my Noogy who I owe more than I can express!
For my mates who have helped me along the way, you have my love….

PROLOGUE

Playing basketball on a dirt court, barefoot on a small island in Indonesia, I am getting physically beaten up because I am bigger and stronger than my local opponents. This goes on for 10 minutes before I finally let them know that they do not want me to get physical with them. I am trying to play a clean game; please don't force me to get physical.

Their style of play against me does not change. Finally, after being punched in the groin for the 3rd time, I reach my limit. Upset, I decide to play chippy with them as well. A very heated argument about their behavior and mine ensues. I slap a guy in the face letting him know "if you really want to get physical, then we certainly can go there."

Obviously, I am quite the hot headed sports player and always have been. I think it has a lot to do with growing up in 5 different foster homes and 4 different institutional boarding schools where I always had to fight for all I have. Before we played a real game, I spent the afternoon trying to teach them the subtle things about playing basketball, like how to make passes to a shooter in rhythm.

Although I am ultimately a guest, they decide to throw me off the court, telling me they don't want me to play anymore. I'm done with this! I decide if I can't play, then nobody will play. I run, jump up and tear the rim and parts of the backboard off the pole where it was perched. As I land on the ground, I see 20 people suddenly charging toward me. As I back away from this angry mob -- most of whom were not part of the game-- it dawns on me that I'm in real trouble now.....

CHAPTER 1

I was born in a New England town, early 1970's. I do not have many memories of my early childhood. I would like to relate to you the little bit I can remember. My biological parents did not stay together very long. My first memories are of living in a small trailer park with just my mom. Being young I have no idea how hard it is for a single mother to try and raise a child all by herself in this era of American history. Her life has not been very easy up to this point either. Her mother left the family without warning when she was a girl, leaving her to take care of an abusive father. She ultimately decided to leave him at an early age.

When I was 16 years old she pulled me aside on one of my weekend home-visits from boarding school number 3 and showed me the letter she wrote to the Catholic Church to get her marriage with her first husband annulled. It was full of hard times. Abusive stories of how her life was barely livable with her biological father… Since this story is about my life which consists of no parenting, I am going to leave my Mother's life out of this!

At age 6 my bio mother and step father packed up my stuff and drove me to my first boarding school. I remember being so upset that I just sat quietly in the back seat of the station wagon. They did not tell me that I was going to be staying there for a long time until after we drove away from home. I spent some time looking around the car thinking to myself.

"It's ok. There wasn't a whole lot of my stuff in the car."

Upon arrival I realized some of my things and toys were hidden under a blanket in the back of the car. I have little memory of that first day, just the horrific feeling that I was now all alone somewhere very strange, where most of the kids in this school were much older than me. In fact, there were only 4 of us under the age of 8. We were placed in the same bedroom, which had 6 kids in the room. The size of which was 12 feet by 10 feet. After going through the orientation process, the school told my parents that I was not going to be allowed to have any of my toys. I thought to myself, 'Wow, I'm all alone now.' When they finally left, I just cried all night long.

It did not take long before the alpha male troubled kids began to treat me the way they treat all new kids, especially the smaller and weaker ones. They would steal my stuff or that of others, then manipulate the blame on me! My reaction was always the same: angry and violent. I threw chairs and caused all kinds of problems for anybody I could. My thoughts were: hey, if you are going to mess with me, then I'm going make your life difficult. I spent many days and nights sitting in chairs facing corners in those first few weeks. I even resorted to banging my head against the wall with extreme force because it seemed to be the only time people actually responded to me with any kind of genuine concern. As you might imagine, this did not help my cause very much. The powers that be just decided that I was completely unstable.

Troubled kids make trouble for each other. To punish my fellow students for fucking with me at every opportunity, I would run up and down the halls all night long, screaming and throwing things to make their sleeping time just as miserable as they were making my waking time. I felt this was my only way to exact punishment upon my fellow students. This also backfired on me. Soon not only did the assholes fuck with me all day; now the moderate kids decided they would join in the fun of getting Shane going… It was a popular game.

The vicious cycle that never ended went like this: they would upset me, I'd go crazy, throw things, scream and try to break things. Inevitably, I would end up in the corner. Day after day after day.... I lost all personal privileges, sometimes even losing the ability to wear shoes for the risk of me running away. I was often made to sit on chairs isolated from the other students! Educational school took place in separate buildings other than the ones in which we slept, ate, had therapy and performed our social duties.

Students could make some money through work privileges such as cooking or splitting firewood, which might be sold to people off campus! We would use this money to purchase sundries or for our occasional off-campus excursions. The students would go-to the movies or a mall, in an attempt to socialize outside of campus life.

'Oh, how cute! They let us go out and play.' That is, if we could prove we were going to behave ourselves. As you might imagine, I was not often included in these outings.

I created a lot of enemies at this school. The staff hated me for causing trouble, not the least of which I learned was the amount of paperwork required every time I acted up. This created another issue. In schools like this, students are enlisted to help keep the peace and maintain control! Think about this formula: 40-60 alpha male boys in close confined proximity. There is no way 4 staff members on rotating shifts can control everything, let alone have knowledge of all activities that go on. We shower without supervision; play outside without supervision at times. Staff allowed a top alpha male to monitor the students behind closed doors, so to speak. I know this because in the last 2 schools I attended, I was the top alpha male doing this enforcing... we'll get to that later. Staff would actually contract out punishment to unruly kids enforced by 'good' students. It's a strange dichotomy. I was the target of such staff contracts all the time. I would get beat up, picked on, or have my stuff stolen from me. It was fun... I would overreact, blow up and, yes, end up back in the corner again.

I learned to just shut down completely. It was the best way to survive. Educational school was about a hundred yard walk up the hill to another building. For lunch we had to walk back down to the sleeping quarters. A cafeteria was in each of the 3 dorms on campus. There was a main eating cafeteria where we would eat breakfast and dinner, which was also a short walk up the hill and off to the right of the educational facilities. Lunch was in our respective dorms. Since I was in so much trouble for my behavior, I had to have a staff member actually hold my hand and walk me between these dorms. A kind of embarrassment therapy was much more of a burden on the staff members than it was for me. I often missed lunch while waiting for my staff member to come up and get me. The nurses in the educational school would give me a carton of milk just to hold me over until dinner. Meanwhile, other kids got to have lunch in the dorm at the bottom of the hill.

OK it was not all bad. We had an activities night on Friday's in the gymnasium that included shows and comedy skits for example, that allowed the whole school-males and females- to participate. It was actually fun because it was the one time we get to interact with the female dorm. We had talent shows and holiday events there. One Halloween I was pushed into the bobbing for apples in the barrel game. My friends said I would be better at it than the bigger kids due to my small frame. They were right because I won! But when I went back to my room, my prized full collection of the 1972 Yankees baseball cards was gone from its hiding spot! I cried for hours over the loss, and never collected baseball cards again.

There wasn't much interest from the girl students in a 6 year old boy who got as much negative attention as I got. The youngest girls on campus were 8 years old. I did become very good in the 2 years I was at this school playing a board game called *Stratego*. I lost only twice the entire time I was there. The older kids would try to beat me, which was fun because I got the upper hand. We played lots of outdoor sports, like football in the fields to the left of my dorm. Me and three other youngsters would anchor the back line of defense and called ourselves the steel curtain. I am a huge Cowboys fan thanks to Tony Dorsett. It was still a fun time to have camaraderie with students. Long distance running–running miles around the field by myself—became a nice isolated time for me: a solace from the pressure of being fucked with by other kids. It was peaceful just running around and around. There was an outdoor swimming pool above the fields which we got to play in during the summer months. I was actually one of the fastest swimmers in the school, beating kids much older than me on a regular basis. Weekends would have lumberjack competitions, to see who could cut a tree with a saw the fastest, or chop trees etc, etc, etc. I asked to be included but was told I was too young to participate. It looked like fun. I enjoyed the challenge of beating the older kids at anything.

Swimming did not last a long time for me. On one beautiful Saturday afternoon, we all went out to the pool. It had been a quiet fuck-with-Shane couple of days too, so I felt comfortable going outside to activities. We start our swim day, just having fun jumping into the pool –typical boy stuff. I was fascinated by the way the sun beams would change direction as they hit the surface of the water and was trying to figure that out. Quite unprepared, I was suddenly being pulled down under the water! I struggled to get to the surface. Every few seconds I would kick free, get to the surface, gasp for air, attempt to scream and get attention. It's difficult to monitor 40 kids in a large inground pool with 2 staff members. I'd like to think this event wasn't outsourced as punishment. The struggle continues until I become quite frantic, coughing on water while I'm underwater. I realized I was going to drown.

I look up at the beams of light flowing into the water and think to myself, 'Wow! I'm done. It's over! That was a short life.' At this exact moment that I gave up my physical struggle, I was released. I did all I could to get to the edge of the pool and catch my breath. Suddenly, an adult sees me coughing and comes over and asks me what happened. I explained I was being dragged under the water by somebody who was trying to drown me. I was told this did not happen; that something else must have happened. Nobody saw anything. I assure you this was the last time I ever went into the pool at this school. I was a student here for about another year after that. This is also the time I began to completely realize that nobody gave a shit about me, whether I lived or died. It really changed and affected the way I interacted with people for the rest of my life...

I don't have much memory of my therapy sessions at this school. I know we had individual therapy sessions twice a week for an hour. Sometimes more, if you're an asshole like me. I do remember one time in my therapy session which was in the basement of my dormitory that my shrink asked me if I wanted to call home. This was a little strange to me because he didn't often allow me to call home. As I begin dialing the number, the operator tells me that it's the wrong number. I dial 2 more times. I'm now visibly upset and started to cry.

He asks me, what's wrong?

I tell him that the operator keeps telling me that I'm dialing the wrong number.

He asks me, what number are you dialing?

When I tell him, he says: oh, that's the wrong number it has been changed recently.

I'm thinking, why the fuck didn't you tell me this before I got upset or as you sat there watching me get upset and did nothing knowing full well why I was getting upset???!!!
I'd like to think I did not talk to him very much after that moment, but to be honest I cannot remember many days in that office. I do know that my IQ is extremely high which always befuddled my therapists and psychiatrists! Every school to every foster home to every new place I went and getting an IQ test was routine. I was often bored and gave wrong answers all the time just to be creative. At this point, the system owes me a PHD in psychology....lol.

There are a lot of drugs on these campuses, more than you might imagine. The staff organized a hike and asked me if I wanted to come along. I was shocked to be invited that day because I was sitting in the corner as usual. (I often acted up and caused trouble just to be put in the chair or corner. See, if you are in the chair you are very close to the office which prevents anybody from fucking with you. Sure, they said things, whispered things, even threw things; but that's a far cry from being in a place where staff cannot watch you closely. To me this was the safest place to be. I don't think any of my caretakers understood this).

The hikers were a small group so I felt safe. I'm walking in the back of the group to keep the damage at a minimum. There was a rainbow that I recall we were walking toward. Not that we would reach it, but it was fun. The 17 year old boy walking in front of me lights up a smoke. Only it doesn't smell like a cigarette. He tells me to walk closer behind him and breathe in the smoke behind him. Of course I did! It was the first time he ever spoke to me, and I happened to think he was one of the cool kids. In just a few steps, I was lost inside my own head and quite confused. He just laughed. That was the first time I ever got high. It would not be the last....

CHAPTER 2

Home visits on holidays and weekends are standard fare for institutions like mine. Full of anger and hurt, I would tend toward isolated behaviors. Sure I often behaved like a child. Hello! I was a fucking child. My parents expected my behavior to improve. At age 6 I can't remember what I could have done to merit such an outcome as being sent away. In fact when I talk to my friends about this they all look at me in shock. They have kids and say it's hard to imagine putting their kids in such an environment. As a result I cared even less about adults and authority figures. My mouth was so disrespectful, I was swearing at my parents whenever they tried to say anything to me I didn't like. If nobody is going to care about me then why the fuck should I respect anything about you and your social pleasantries. In return parents do what they all do, show physical dominance over you. Send you to your room. Take your toys away. Beat you. My step dad was an alcoholic when he and my mom first got together. I cannot tell you how many times I would hear them fighting arguing and getting violent. On one home visit I heard an unbelievable ruckus outside of my bedroom. I woke up from my sleep while hearing my mother scream amid loud crashes. Agitated, I open up my bedroom door and walk down the hall. Part of the kitchen can be seen from the left of the hallway. I see my mother crawling under the table as my step dad is punching on her and throwing the chairs out of the way to get at her. I scream and they stop, looking at me. They bring me to my room and try to comfort me. "Sometimes adults fight"… blah, blah, blah…

My family didn't have a lot of money. I would sneak out of my room at night to eat cookies and snacks that we really didn't have the money to buy in the first place. For some reason I love sweets. I was beaten and punished for this behavior so many times I lost count. Honestly I don't know why I did it; I just did. It became a joke in my punishment stages:

"Why did you do that, Shane?"

I don't know.

"I DON'T KNOW?" They would repeat incredulously.

Then the standard 'let's embarrass Shane' routine: "I DON'T KNOW" was repeated mockingly back to me. Whenever they asked me anything, they would reply for me. I'm thinking, I'm going to be slapped or hit no matter what I say, so who cares. It was easier to get ridiculed for saying I don't know then to answer by trying to defend my actions which would only escalate the argument further. Seriously, I have no toys. I have no friends. I have no family. I'm in a sleep away school. Does anybody really give a shit about me? Or what I have to say? It's just easier to say, 'I don't know' then get mocked for 5 minutes and move on.

My parents grew frustrated trying to come up with more and more creative ways to punish me! One time on a weekend visit, I upset my mother so much she sent me to my room. She went to the store and bought the largest size diapers, came back and physically forced me to put them on. "If I wanted to act like a baby I would dress like one." She even sent me back to the school with them on, refusing to let me take them off. All I was thinking was shit, if these kids find out I'm wearing diapers I'm dead. It was not easy waiting and holding my bathroom time until late at night, sneaking quietly into the bathroom, taking off my diapers, taking all the trash out of the waste paper can, placing my diapers in the bottom and then putting all the trash back on top without getting caught. Success….

I actually lost all holidays one year, too. No birthday presents, Easter basket, and no Christmas presents. My step Dad's parents were sick of this. I remember being so upset on Easter for not getting any candy. When we went over to my Grandparent's house there was the biggest Easter basket I have ever seen on the table with my name on it. After doing the pleasantries, I went into the living room for the rest of the day avoiding my parents as much as possible.

Another incident occurred on my birthday when my grandfather asked me what I wanted for a present.

"I want a fly fishing rod."

Hey I'm a child that has no concept of economics. Apparently he bought me a very expensive pole. I later learned that he and my step dad did not talk for 6 months because he got me that gift. There was a Christmas that I got up early, went downstairs to get some presents and realized there were no gifts under the tree with my name on it. Going over to the stockings, I discovered nothing but a box in mine. I kid you not: I got a lump of coal in a box for Christmas one year. When I related this to my parents many years later, they tell me I made the whole story up. Seriously, I went back up to my room that Christmas visit and did not come down again until it was time for me to go back to school the next day. I didn't eat another meal at home that visit after the coal incident. My parents often use denial in dealing with me for many things as you will learn in later stories.

In my 7th year, I learned there was no Santa Claus. I was playing with my G.I. Joe guys in bed when I dropped one to the right side of my bed against the wall. I climbed under my bed to get him! There were boxes in my way. Having a complete one track mind, I pulled the boxes out of my way to get my guy. As I was putting them back I noticed the boxes were wrapped in paper with a card 'to Shane from Santa'–a few days before Christmas! I was very hurt and frustrated once again by parental lies!

The next day I went into the neighborhood, which I rarely do. First, we don't go-to the same school; secondly, they usually just harass me. Today I wanted to go around the whole area and tell all the kids I saw that there was no Santa Claus. I even got into a fight with an older kid who didn't believe me. Within hours my parents got a phone call from one very upset mother angered that I was spoiling 'the lie'. A confrontation awaited me at home:

"Why did you do this, Shane?"

My response! You guessed it! *I don't know*. Smiling all the way to my room...

I was removed from the school when I was 8 apparently when my half brother was born. I can even remember the night he was conceived. I was sneaking into the kitchen to steal some apples when I heard all the commotion and noise in my parent's bedroom down the hall. I figured no way they would hear me go into the kitchen. Sure enough they did; opening the door my dad was standing in the doorway all covered in sweat and naked. I just went back into my room, then snuck out 5 minutes later and got my apples. I had no place to throw out the cores, so I tossed them under my bed. Within a day I had fruit flies all over my bedroom. I waited until late that night and opened the window climbed out and threw them into the woods near our house. It was a lot harder to get back in the window than it was getting out of it.

Being removed from school was a total shock for two reasons: I was actually getting used to my surroundings when my parents wanted to try being a family again. Now that my brother was born, 'we were a complete family.' I had no interest or even cared about a family anymore. That desire and need was crushed out of me during those 2 years of my first living hell. Coming back home to a baby brother was kind of weird. He was born early and had more tubes coming and going out of his body than he had body mass.

Finding a school in our town that would take me wasn't easy. My file had grown bigger and my reputation was defiant and impish. In addition, the switch to a public school was in the middle of the school year. Great, now I was the laughing stock again. How fun. Any idea how frustrating it is to constantly be the new kid in school when you don't even know who you are or where you belong? Ok, sure, I was aggressive and become violent at the drop of a hat. To my defense, I was not the initiator but always the responder and not afraid to take it up a notch. At this young age my only recourse to gain respect is to be so out of control that people fear the idea of setting me off. I have very little memory of that school other than being quite fond of punching concrete walls and threatening teachers. It seemed to me the teachers were creating the situation by isolating me in the class and treating me like I'm not even part of the school structure.

I began a daily diet of Ritalin to control my behavior. Kids didn't need much to realize I was medicated since I took my meds during lunch time. I must have gotten into some kind of altercation every day. The principal of the school even brought me into his office and attempted to bond with me by telling me he used to work at the institutional school I just left. At this point I'm already at war in my mind with all adults. Nothing they say or do can affect anything that I feel or think. As long as I still feel as if I'm fighting for my respect I'm going to fight. Sure misguided, but I'm fighting none the less. A few more fights during school and I'm isolated during lunch time as well. Add the fights at the school bus stop and I get kicked off all school buses. I had to walk to this school the last few weeks. I wasn't allowed on the bus or to stand at the bus stop.

As my behavior escalated, so did the stress on my family. I went to live with Grandparents after a runaway incident and some violence between me and my step dad. I grew tired of always being locked into my room, so I climbed out the window one night and ran away and walked into the housing area across the street. I actually attempted to sleep in the trees that night but was afraid of falling out of the tree. So I crawled through a shrubbery and slept there. Listening to my parents call my name as they walked through the neighborhood was kind of creepy.

I stayed with my grandparents for some time. My memory says just a few months. Funny thing is I always did my homework right after school for my grandmother before I went outside–something I never did for my parents without a fight. This could be attributed to the cute little honey I had the hots for up the street. I wanted to hang out with her after school as much as possible. I actually had my first kiss with her and her friend on the beach. I even stole some of my Uncle's playboys and took them over to the 2 girls at their request. We had some fun together on the beach during those days. One of the girls asked me to have sex with her, but I was too scared and unconfident. Hey I'm only 9. I had a horrible mouth at the time as well. She would make me apologize every time I swore. Getting into arguments with her older brother often resulted in swearing at him! We talked one day after school about sitting on the bus together. The very next day I got on the bus, saw that she was alone and sat down next to her. Immediately she screamed at me and embarrassed me for even daring to sit next to her. Lesson number one in the insanity of girls...

The only school that would let me in was the local Catholic school. Great Nuns and uniforms! I hated them. To keep me from fighting during recesses, they asked me to keep an eye on the younger kids during playground time. I really enjoyed doing this. As a result, I hardly fought during recess and broke up more fights than I got into.

My jaw had an under bite–my bottom teeth stuck out further than my top. To fix this I had this red plastic piece attached to my teeth forcing them under the top teeth. Sure that's great, but it gave new ammo for the kids to spin Shane. New embarrassment games started all over again on the bus, at the school, in the classes; before school, after school. I started running through the woods after school because it was safer than putting myself in social settings. Yup more fights again. I even broke that plastic piece a few times during fights. My mother and I argued about that over and over. I tried to explain to her:

I can't just let people harass me so much.

She replied, "Sticks and stones can break your bones; blah, blah, blah."

Ironically, the worst fight we got into about this dental piece breaking involved a school bus incident. I was getting off the bus early, closer to walk the beach route to my grandparent's house. I was trying to get off the bus without trouble. As I got up, some kid stuck his foot out and tripped me. Falling face first, the piece broke flying somewhere on the bus. I had to crawl around the bus quickly to find the broken piece amidst laughter and ridicule. Focused on the piece, I actually found it. Success! Yea! Now get off the bus and on the beach. Breathe; alone; relax. Repeat.

CHAPTER 3

As my brother grew older, my connection to the family continued to erode. Soon the breakdown would be complete, due to my jealous behavior at my mother's unbroken attention for my brother. I'm sent to my first foster home. Somewhere during this time of 8-10, I also lived with my mother's sister. She had 3 boys and would be able to 'whip me into shape.' Funny, she had an entire section of the house devoted to the kids. She cooked only one meal a week for us. We had our own kitchen, bathroom, entrance and exit into the house. If we were caught in the other 2/3 of the house, we did get whipped. In fact, because we weren't allowed into the living room area of the house, we had to walk through her bedroom to get to school which was down a few steps *across her bedroom* into our side of the house.

A game my cousins played was to elbow and punch or scream at the person last in line on the way out the door. The person who woke up my aunt would get whipped by a belt. She actually kept the belt near the bed just to tag us as we went by for waking her up. She worked nights... Since money was tight, feeding and clothing 3 boys was not easy. We all were on a budget. We had powdered milk for cereal and only so much each month. If we used it up my cousins taught me to use cool-aid or juice, instead of milk. It was my first acquired taste experience and not my last.

For most nights we cooked our own dinners. Once, my aunt made spaghetti for everybody. But from the adult kitchen to the kid's dining area was a full flight of stairs. My cousin tripped at the top of the stairs and spilled his meal. She went ballistic for having to clean up the carpeted stairs and told him she didn't make enough for him to get 2 plates. He wasn't going get any food for the night. We all shared our food with him so he could eat.

Sure we definitely were trouble makers. We fought, argued, and more than once broke a window in the house. We played games on each other. One time I got locked out on the second floor patio and my fellow cousins would not let me in. They told me I had to jump to the ground in order to get back in the house. After crying for a while I ultimately did jump.

We also raced each-other into the house from the school bus. Whoever got into the house first got control of the games. Pong had just come out. Plus they had a bumper pool table which was fun. Only trouble was the walkway to the kid's side of the house was up a flight of stairs and across a deck above the driveway, then into the sliding doors. The deck was missing the cross boards, only had the support beams. I'm the smallest and lost these races most of the time. Not this day: I'm winning. Up the stairs first, I'm talking shit to them. As I get closer to the door making careful steps across the gap of missing wood, a cousin pushes me, throwing me off my step pattern. Next thing I know I'm laying on the asphalt driveway. I bounced off the driveway from the fall not really hurt, just stunned! Nice!

The new kid in school! Oh boy, more harassment, more spinning, more kick me signs put on my back as I walk down the halls. This is getting old. It never got old for each new school. I got suspended at least 3 times a month for fighting or causing trouble. In fact, they asked me not to come the last 2 days of the school year letting me and my family know I would not get into trouble for missing school. This is not the last time a public school made this request oddly enough. Oh yeah, once again thrown off the bus, walking to school each day again…

On a bright note I had my first experience of a girl chasing me. At lunch breaks and during outside recess time, we would walk across the street to the candy store. One day out of the blue some girl leaving the candy store called my name. It had been years since I heard a girl call my name in public; I was shocked. Turning to look, not knowing who she was, I saw her wiggle her tongue out of her mouth to me. Later that summer I met her again at her own house where we played tag at night with a bunch of the neighborhood kids. Flirting continued. Unfortunately about a month after that I was sent back home. My aunt had had enough of my behavior after I t-boned my cousins bike during bike tag. That didn't go over very well.

First foster home–oh boy, this is fun– is a home that already has kids living there. Some biological, some adopted. It was ok for a while. I think maybe I got there during the summer time and not during the school year. The family was quite nice. Dinner, video games, movies, they even had a few exotic animals. Strange I thought, in an urban part of the city. Very urban part! So much so there were only a handful of us that weren't black. Great I'm now being beat up for being white. Plus some strange idea got around that I didn't like black kids. I have no idea how that happened. I would never have said this.

When I was 6 at the first school I had a crush on my first girl, who was black. We even peck kissed a few times. Puppy love is so cute. She was older than me, too. I digress, and we have so much to get through.

Back in the foster family urban setting, the after school fighting became so bad that my foster brothers had to protect me. After their school day, they would stand on every corner of the walk from the bus just to keep me from being beat up. This only added to my troubles.

'Baby Shane' has to keep his brothers around to help protect him. Oh boy, that got around fast.

Instead I got more kick me signs placed on my back as I walked down the halls. I got punched in the stomach a few times during the day as other kids blocked the attention of the teachers. I had the wind knocked out of me so many times that I started to do many stomach exercises to build up my muscles. To this day at 40 I still keep 6-pack abs to protect my stomach muscles. Every-time I lapse and see them get weaker I have this horrible flashback of me doubled over in some school gasping for air. That's a motivator!

Here's the beginning of my horror! The father had a friend who was living with the family in the house who was legally blind. He could see, carrying a card and cane. Another foster brother was a little older than me, and the biological son was a year older than him. Within a few weeks, the boarder had me giving him a massage on his sore shoulders outside on the porch as they all played cards. To be honest, I can't remember how that happened. Within a week the foster brother and I were showing each-other our penises. This was a very strange thing to me. The attention I was getting from men, however, was much more important to me than the warnings my stomach was sending me.

I got scared with the foster brother on his bed, we stopped, lying there half naked and stared at the kiss posters on the wall. For some reason the father and his bio son got into fights all the time resulting in things being broken. We soon moved to a state much further up north. I was the first kid in this foster care program to move to a different state. They all told me how hard this was for them.

My second half brother was born during this time. I got a phone call from my parents while I was eating my first fluff and peanut butter sandwich telling me that I had a new brother. I remember thinking:

"Yeah Who cares! I'm 3 states away with no time table of coming home. I have my own problems. Why are you telling me this?"

I hadn't heard from my parents in some time. I was kind of annoyed and shocked at the phone call itself. After hanging up, I'm back to my fluff and peanut butter sandwich. Sorry Shane we just put all the food away. Next time! I just went outside and walked around. We were staying with some family members in a beautiful part of this state. The house was cramped so everybody shared rooms. I slept on the floor at night in the living room. The boarder also slept there. We would watch TV late at night after bedtime. He told me it was ok to stay up and watch TV late. I'm thinking cool, I get special privileges. Then he started sneaking me some candy that he didn't give to others and asked me not to tell anyone. There are like 8 kids in this house now.

Eventually he asked me to sit on the couch late at night with him. We talked about many things, including the girls on the TV! He would ask:

"Do you get a hard penis watching girls on TV?"

While sliding his hand up my thigh, he asked me if he could see! I have no idea how we got that far. Before I know it, mine is outside my pants, and he is stroking it. Even though my gut is fluttering with warnings, I'm thinking:

"Hey, I'm being noticed and getting treated like I am special. I don't care."

Sometime later I'm in the basement looking for something of his in a box stored there. He then pulls out his penis and asks me to stroke it. Not long after that I'm on my knees with it in my mouth. It had a horrible smell and taste, sticky and the smell made me gag. I was so scared I didn't give him what he wanted. I got up and walked up the stairs. He comes up to me later and tells me.

"It's normal. You will get used to it."

He hands me some candy and says it's ok. I'm a quiet person by now; so if you don't ask, I'm not going to tell anybody anything. Hey, I've already lived through a tough life, learned it's only me in this world and nobody gives a shit about me anyway. We go for a hike soon after with him, the foster brother and me. I'm ok because there are 3 of us –until the brother disappears. I'm not sure how that happened or why I stayed, but I did. We hiked up some more. It was a beautiful day. Next thing I know I'm sucking on candy and I'm bent over a rock and he is putting his penis into my ass. It fucking hurt like you wouldn't believe. I was crying and he was telling me:

"Relax. It's ok. Stop screaming."

I was asking God to help me which was the first time I had ever asked that, or even spoke to God. I know he didn't cum because he was very upset, but he was pushing in and out. I cried

19

so much that he gave me like 10 pieces of candy as we walked down, telling me next time I was going to take it all. I'm thinking I'm never going to be alone with you again.

This girl lived nearby, and I did like her. Her name was a month of the year. I didn't see her very often and I don't think she liked me. She was just bored and stuck in the neighborhood. I came down the hill very upset and if anybody had a brain would have seen that instantly in my face. I think she did. Without asking me what was wrong, we just went for a walk and played in the fields around the area. I remember laughing at how when the train went by she and her family had to hold the cabinets and stuff to keep them from falling. I thought that was only in movies. We had such a fun day that afternoon. I never played with her again; never again were we alone. I don't think she has any idea how awesome that afternoon was. I don't think I would have made it another day if not for that afternoon.

There were girls in the house as well, adopted ones and temporary ones. One girl was really confused. She would climb into the boy's beds at night while they slept and tried to have sex with them. It happened so often the guys had permission to physically throw her out of their beds and room. We moved again to another family close by. Things got better. The girls were still crazy. It was still summer and I got to hang outside in the tent with the adults. They smoked pot all night long in those tents. I wasn't allowed to take hits but I was allowed to breathe heavy and stay in the tents with them. We even walked around outside to see the pot plants growing in the back woods of the house. On the way back I saw a snake with a frog half out of his mouth. I felt so sad for the frog I slapped my t shirt against the snake until he let the frog go and hopped away. I almost cried watching that frog get eaten! I had no choice but to let him get away.

I got some food virus or flu, causing me to throw up every night for about 3 nights in a row. Same time every night! Strange I felt great all day long. My foster brother walks up to me as we are going to bed around 11 pm.

"Do you want to throw up tonight?"

No fucking way.

"Walk with me outside."

Sure! I'd do anything to keep from throwing up. He hands me a joint.

"Hey, you're old enough to smoke your own now. I promise you won't throw up tonight."

I'm game!

I smoked my own joint, got high and did not throw up that night or the next night or again for a long while. Yeah, I'm hooked for life. The family knew about the smoking. After 'Turkey Day' one year, I went to steal some pork rind to chew on from the leftovers that were keeping warm in the oven. The first rack I pulled out had nothing but pot buds drying out in the oven. Before I can close the tray, a guy walks in and says.

"Hey, what do you want? I will get it for you."

Ok. I want some pig rind.

That summer I paid for my first movie with my own money by saving change, running to the store for other people. They always let me keep the loose change. *Star Wars Return of the Jedi.* Got high in the parking lot before the movie with my brother!

We would walk to the store by ourselves. Since my time with my cousins, I began stealing from stores. They taught me how to steal, and look for store employees. I taught my foster siblings in this home to steal as well. We went into a store to steal bandanas. The owner catches my 2 sisters and brings us all into the back storage area. He asks me to go up front and get a bandana to see how much they cost (since we all tore the tags off). I take one out of my pants, put it back and get one with a tag on it. The owner asks us to empty our pockets and lift up our shirts. Alas, my 2 sisters had them under their shirts. He sends me home and calls the police. Getting home we all got beat, but my sisters never ratted me out.

The next door neighbor had kids our age. They lived across the street down the little hill. He taught us that if you place nickels just right on the train tracks they squish the nickels to the size of a quarter and with the same weight. You can use them as slugs in the video games at 7/11. It actually did work.

We played with G.I. Joe's, too but by making fires and burning the GI Joes. I was afraid that my parents would see us making fires in the yard so I begged the kid to make them in the laundry area which had a cement floor and walls. The first attempt of burning GI Joes, he pours lighter fluid out onto them as another kid lights the match. Shit! The flame shoots up the fume line toward the lighter fluid bottle. I turn and run for the door and outside, up the tracks so it would look like I was walking down the tracks when the fire started. Actually the kid got the fire out quite easily and never told anybody it was my idea to burn the guys indoors. Though he didn't play with me anymore!

Finally moving to our house! It was quite beautiful and in the middle of nowhere. I had a lot of fun exploring the fields and woods behind the house. It was a small town up country place that has lots of red tape. The street we lived on was paved at the front of it, the middle of the road was all dirt, and the end of the street a mile or so up the road was paved again. Apparently we lived on a street that was geographically in 3 different towns. Too funny! They couldn't organize paving together.

They also already had the school bus path all set up by the time we got there, just no bus to ride. The first few weeks of school we actually had to walk 2 miles to school through the woods with short cuts. We all laughed about this cause of the old timer jokes:

"Hey, Sonny, when I was a kid we had to walk ten miles to school through the woods. Uphill. Both ways. In three feet of snow. We didn't have school buses."

The strangest thing about walking this way to school was a bar along the way that already had people drinking. I thought that was crazy. It really was a beautiful walk through farming fields, apple trees, and horseback riding trails. The kid about my age up the street lived in a green house by our standards today. His father had built the house. It was round. The other cool thing about this kid was his dad had a prescription to smoke pot so I was told. He had packages shipped to him and even had some pot trees growing in the top peak of this strange house built in a dome. We got high every day after school.

A very attractive girl rode horses through the fields we walked across. I asked him to walk me to her house so I could meet her.

Sure he says. We go see her and the horses. First time I meet her she says.

"Do you like horses?"

I hadn't seen any up close before but, yes, I did.

She leaned against the fence; I leaned against the fence and we started talking. I thought things were going well. She walked over to one of the fence posts I was still leaning on and flips a switch. Electric fence! Shit that hurt. Lesson number 2, insanity of girls!

I never went to see her again. I often saw her along the trails; she did ask me if I wanted to ride with her, but I never talked to her again. Her father had this huge apple tree at the end of his field near the road that we had to walk by. We would stop and eat a few apples once in a while, apples he didn't pick or eat. If he caught us, he would ride and chase us on a horse, yelling all the way. Seriously I didn't get it; he didn't even eat them or pick them, just letting them fall to the ground!

Being the new kid in this back country school wasn't easy. Sure there was less abuse, but it's not like it was abuse free. I did get a good shot here because I started the New Year at the same time as everybody else which was the first and last time this happened. I never got in fights on the bus. (After the first few weeks of school, the towns organized the money for a bus to pick us up along the way). Only 2 of us were young enough to go-to this school, it wasn't so bad getting adapted here.

I was even ok in the family. All I had to do was stay away from the boarder, at least not allow myself to be alone with him. The boys started drinking. Because my step father who is still married to my bio mom was an alcoholic and was abusive to me and her, I made it my mission to stay away from drinking. I had many offers. That didn't stop me from beginning to play with other drugs. My first hit of acid was at age 9-10, I think. This time of my life is quite the blur with so many changes from public schools, foster homes, living with Grandparents and Aunt. From age 8-11 is very blurred. Too much too fast happened. I know I can subpoena my file to get all the dates and information but I don't really care anymore. I'm sick of people talking about me and not to me. I know there's a lot of talking about me in there. We'll get to that during my last school ages 17-19.

Late one night as everybody is drinking the boarder comes up to me and the boys and asks if we want to walk down the path to smoke a joint. Sure we begin walking down the path, suddenly I'm all alone with him and I'm scared. I refused his advances and got away that night running back up the path to the house...

He lived downstairs and he would hide his stuff– cigarettes, pot, and alcohol–in a special spot all the time. Someone kept stealing it. He was more upset about the cigarettes and soda than anything. So he takes a bottle of soda to a guy up the street who was a specialist in drilling and making things. He drilled a hole in the bottom of the soda glass and filled it with some x-lax hoping to not break the top seal and thus catching the thief. Oddly enough it was the foster father who spent the second night in the bathroom. More diabolical than this was that every-time something was stolen, the father would somehow find the missing article, of course in his bio son's room. He then would proceed to beat and punish him for stealing while the kid swore up and down he had no idea how it got there. Funny, we thought, how did the father know exactly where the stuff was hidden even though it was different spots every-time? It was a curious thing that we kids talked; we just thought the kid was lying, until the dad spent the night in the toilet. Sadly the boy was beaten many times for stealing soda, beer and cigs. Seriously, the father was stealing from the boarder then blaming it on his kid and beating his kid for it.....

So I go home to see my parents soon afterword and go-to Six Flags with them. Actually, at the end of the home visit I was supposed to meet the foster family at Six Flags and make the exchange of Shane. I love roller coasters. I've always been addicted to anything that feeds my adrenaline. I was only supposed to be home for a week. My brain is thinking about this boarder putting his hands on me and how I don't ever want anything sexual from him again. I'm driving in my step dad's truck and somehow it comes up in my conversation. He is upset at first then seems to calm down. He didn't really ask me many questions. All I got to say was that he was touching my body inappropriately. He never asked if it went any further.

This upset me, as I interpreted it as a lack of caring about the situation. Next thing I know I'm in meetings with my foster care guidance counselors and a shrink.

Oh boy, more fucking shrinks!

I really enjoy having my brain picked by people who are twisting around everything I say. I've been seeing them since I can remember. Child psychiatrists when I was living at home before my first institution, then 3 days a week at my first school; then during my time in the foster home. Seriously I'm sick of this shit. I decided I'm tired of talking to people who know nothing about me that I see once in a while or when I flip out. I mean do they actually care about me? Not in my opinion.

I relate the whole story for the 3rd time to this stranger and I'm tired of having to relive it every time. So I'm aloof, short, not caring just wanting to get back to the foster home. Sure I may not have been having the best time but at least it was much more attention and care than my parents showed me. I'm not visibly upset with this specialist and he doesn't seem to be asking anything about me or trying to get to know me, just endgame questions. I shut down I've had enough.

"Go fuck yourself. I'm done with this conversation."

Sure I didn't say it, but this is my feeling. In just a few years, I would tell every adult in earshot to get the fuck away from me or I'm going to make your life miserable any way I can. My caring shrink tells me to leave the room. Ok fine. Yeah I'm done with this anyway. I'm relieved. They come out maybe 20 minutes later and I get driven back home. Nobody talks to me. I'm not allowed to go back to my foster home. I'm stuck at my parent's house for some time. Not even Six Flags day. Great, another disappointment, you see in my mind my parents have kicked me out of the house 4 times already. Do you really think I want to go back home again to the inevitable "Shane, go away. We don't want you!" I later learned in my mid 20's that everybody believed I had made the whole story up. I've never gotten an explanation as to why. It seems that denial is again my parent's way of dealing with me.

I did get to play with my baby step brother a little. He was much bigger than most kids and a lot stronger, too. I had a hard time listening to his cry all the time. I go into my parent's room early one morning while they are still asleep, and I take him out of the pen. I actually took him out step by step: first placing his hands on the edge of the rails; then moving one leg over the rail, still holding his hands on the rail with my own. Then I get his second leg over the rail and let him slowly slide down to the floor. He tries to crawl away. Quickly I scoop him up and put him back in the pen. Repeat this time holding his hands less. Scoop; repeat. Until he can do this on his own. Surprised he was able to do it on his own, I was even more shocked he could support his weight as he slide down the playpen to the floor. It took me 3 times to teach him how to get out of the playpen. I really hated listening to him cry. Since I couldn't always take him out due to my incarcerations, he needed to learn how to get himself out.

Many years later I hear my parents relating how smart their son is because one morning they watched him step by step climb up and out of the playpen. They were surprised and impressed that he had successfully figured that out.

"I was the one who taught him how to do it," I told them.

They didn't believe me. Then my brother told them he did remember me taking him out of the pen and teaching him how to do this step by step.

CHAPTER 4

I ended up in an emergency foster home until a placement was found for me. Only there a few weeks, this house had a mom and dad, many kids and a few bedrooms that were actually quite nice. Their town's school system did not allow me to matriculate! Instead they sent a tutor to the house every day– all day to teach and give me work. I found this quite odd. But ok, at least no fights in school!

First day I get there, they ask me to take a shower; then the dad walks into the bathroom right after I walk in. He tells me to take my pants down so he can look at me and see if I'm doing drugs. I'm thinking: *"Great! I'm being molested by another man."*

I will admit I did not know that word yet. I was thinking *"C'mon man, do you really have to do this?"*

He threatens me that I won't be allowed to do anything unless I do as he says.

Ok! I do.

He looks very seriously into my penis to *"see if I'm injecting drugs,"* he tells me.

Seriously I'm like 10 years old! He then tells me I can get dressed.

"But I haven't taken a shower yet."

He looks at all my toes and tells me he is also looking for signs of drugs. Even at 10 years old I know what they are. Yes, I've taken acid and smoked some pot, but I had no idea what he was looking for in my toes and penis.

I finally get to take a shower. I get dressed to eat dinner with the other kids. None of the other kids said anything to me that first night. Before I head to bed, the mother pulls me into the bedroom alone and sits me down. I have my first 'birds and the bees' talk. It was not for my education but for the sanity of the house. She tells me:

"If you are going to masturbate, please go in the bathroom and not in the bed. The kids have free reign of the house anytime, including girls. Some of the girls have walked in on guys who were masturbating on their beds –naked and it was a problem once in a while."

I have no idea what she is talking about. I cannot get a hard on yet. I was only in this house for a few weeks memories are short. Not much time later I'm in a new school, new foster home –living on a farm. Milking cows, feeding chickens, geese, ducks, goats, and splitting wood for the fireplace at night! The wintertime was very cold. They are Seventh Day Adventist and vegetarians. I'm a complete carnivore. I have no interest in spending 5 hours a day every Saturday at church. All they wanted was a farm hand. I fought with them all the time. I hated chores, adjusting to a new school and new kids and a new social economic setting. What's more, I've got to go-to school smelling like a farm hand every day. Yup this was fun.

Surprisingly, I didn't have problems in this school — well, not many anyway. No fights with kids, at least. Now I have a new game: I like fucking with adults for fun. In fact, now that I've had so much therapy, I'm quite good at it. With my keen insight and extremely high IQ, I became very good at perceiving what irritated people and then pushing their buttons. I decided to be in control of the drama around me as much as possible. The best way to do that is to make the drama myself. My new mission is to make every adult miserable. I'm pissed and I'm sick of them. The kids and I get along famously. Even have a few girls I like and seem to like me.

My reputation for pissing off any and all adults around me began to grow. It was not uncommon for me to give the finger to any adult who looked at me for too long. I'd tell them to go fuck themselves, with those exact words! I learned to burp quite loudly and with length, which really pisses off adults; so, I perfect my skill, just for fun. Sometimes, however, I would burp even when I didn't want to. So I let one out in class. The teacher tells me if I do that again I'm going to the Principal's office! Yup, you guessed it. Not 5 seconds later I let a louder one rip.

The teacher grabs me by my shirt, walks me out of class and starts to tell me he's going to fix me good if I keep burping. He wasn't finished with his sentence and I'm burping in his face. Laughing as I do it. He picks me up– I can't weigh but 100 pounds–walks me into the stairwell and jacks me up against the wall. He raises his fist to hit me, and I'm still laughing at him. Out of the corner of my eye I see the little rectangle glass window to the stairway all full of faces. He catches my gaze and sees the same thing. Putting me down, he says,

"Go back to class. Don't make another sound in my class today."

Actually I didn't.

Back at the ranch (foster home/ farm), we argue a lot because of all my chores. This goes on for some time. I didn't see my parents very often while at this foster home. One time I was excited about them coming to visit me for my birthday. I get called down to the dining area and was told.

"Your parents are not coming." I got a few presents from them but they never showed. That was the first day I actually went outside and enjoyed splitting wood.

I enjoyed the animals here and got to have a lot of fun with them. Chasing ducks, trying to find where they laid eggs. Collecting eggs from the chicken coup and bringing them to the cold cellar. We had an incubator and I was told that ducks think the first thing they see is their mother. So I go down twice a day to see the ducks hatch, waiting to see if the story is true. It was! He was so cute! He followed me around and I felt responsible for him. When he was a few days old I took him outside to the little pond to teach him how to swim. We went to that pond for a few minutes each day for a week as he was getting older.

I had to feed all the animals, too. The goose pen was the toughest, as they were so aggressive that it scared me to enter. I was bitten by them on many occasions. My observations of the geese reminded me of some school yard experiences.

The geese had chosen a weaker less aggressive one to pick on. They had bitten him so much his feathers were gone from his back. It made me cry watching them abuse one goose for no apparent reason that I could see. I do hate bullying, so when I had free time, I took this goose out of the pen and let him run around in the yard. I even isolated him so he was fed alone. The other geese wouldn't let him eat anything, as if they were trying to starve him to death!

Within a few weeks I watched this bullied goose stand up and defend me vehemently whenever I came into the pen. I thought it odd that he would allow them to bully him, but he never allowed them to attack me anymore when I entered to feed them.

I even had a friendly Guernsey cow that followed me around. The family was vegetarian but they sold the cows to Laotians who came on Sunday and shot them, skinned them and cooked a little after chopping them up into pieces. I was very upset when my Guernsey was the next victim. I never really forgave the father for allowing it to be killed, I begged him to sell a different one to them. He didn't. I revolted with full on disrespect. Constantly fighting him at every angle! Learning how to milk cows was disgusting. It smelled so bad in the barn plus the cows were covered in shit. I got kicked so many times. The father comes up to me one day and says.

"Shane, put this skull cap on. Take the cows tail and pin it to his thigh with your forehead while you milk them. The cow will jerk the tail out of the way before it kicks you. When you feel the muscle twitch and the tail move, just back away and the kick will not get you." Success!

Sometimes I got to go with him to the auctions for the animals. The cow auctions were fun, bidding on cows, raising your hand as the man talked so fast. We would walk up and down the stables looking at them before the bidding started. The chicken farms were the worst. The animals were so thin and scrawny and covered in shit I hated trying to catch them. The ground was so full of shit it was quite slippery. I tried not to fall but it's impossible. I fell all the time, thus smelling awful all day.

I threw up in the first large coup we went into. In fact, I threw up a few times on this farm. Shoveling out the cow barns was my job twice a day. No matter how many times I went into that barn it always made me gag at least once. The cows were locked into stables around their heads so their shit was dropping in the same trough. Cow after cow we would change out the stables as they ate. I did learn that when a calf was born, sometimes the mother won't clean the birthing sack off the baby. If it doesn't clean the sac, the baby will die. Putting molasses on the baby will make the mother clean the baby. I was supposed to learn how to put my hand and arm inside the females to check if they are pregnant, but I told the father I wasn't going to do that. Thankfully, I left the farm before I had to learn this skill.

Chopping a chicken's head off and watching them run around was funny. It took a few tries before I could do it because killing an animal has never been easy for me. But watching a chicken run around with its head cut off is hilarious! I managed to chop off a handful of heads but would get yelled at each time for letting him go headless around the yard. It did make a mess.

The neighbor across the street was a nice guy who lived alone on a property with a small lake. Our ducks often hid their eggs there to keep us from getting them. It didn't take me very long to figure out their spots and collect the eggs. He had a 3 legged dog that I really loved. We got along so well, he would follow me around all day long sometimes walking through the 100 acres for hours!

The neighbor even took me to the movies once to give the family a break from me. We went to see Tarzan. Tarzan was ultimately shot while up a tree. This really upset me. It seems in our world, if anything challenges us or is different from what we want, then either we cage it, sedate it, or force it to fit into our ever growing smaller societal boxes. The smaller these boxes get, the more people will fall outside them.

I wanted to learn to play the guitar, so they hired the school music teacher to come to our house twice a week to teach me. I was having fun in school and learning the guitar. Although the kids still did harass me, I didn't get into many fights. Just normal hazing stuff! My first day in the school I was in a bathroom stall taking a shit, when some kid stood up on his toilet, looked over my stall and started to tease me. It would be years before I ever got into a stall in a public bathroom with somebody next to me. In fact, I got into trouble for asking to use the bathroom after the bell rang knowing all the kids would be in class.

My foster father and I started to wrestle a little bit. He had this tactic of pinching very hard the inside of my thigh whenever he wanted which caused extreme pain. Sometimes this happened when he was angry at me. I related this to my case worker who asked to see the bruises. I said

"It's just fun. We're not really violent or getting in big fights."

I was starting to get used to my chores and the life I was living here. That Tuesday, my music teacher came over to teach me the guitar. Before he came over I was told I was being picked up the next day to go to a meeting with my case worker.

I knew it would be my last day in the foster home and I told everybody it was.

Even my guitar teacher said, "No, not true. If you want, keep the guitar as proof that you are coming back."

I told him not to worry that I wasn't coming back and he should keep his guitar. I was enjoying the instrument– even getting used to the painful calluses on my fingers, learning some chords. Sure enough as I get to the new foster home I'm not there 10 minutes before they inform me that I'm staying there and not be going back to the farm. At first I just looked at my case worker who just spent the last 3 hours lying to me. Then I just cried not realizing that all my clothes were already packed and in the trunk of the car.

Beautiful! New home! New school! Great!

I was just getting used to the other one. I'm upset. It took them an hour in a 'therapeutic meeting' to tell me something I already figured out in a minute: this would be my new home. I went off to my room to cry for a few hours until they called me down to dinner. They like to build puzzles on the table in the living room. It's a quiet sort of anti social activity that feeds my bored brain.

The first thing I discovered was their 2 German shepherd dogs. I loved those dogs, one male, one female; Purebread dogs originally acquired so they could breed. Oddly enough the male was sterile. He was a beautiful dog. Their back yard was attached to some town land that had paths and trails in it. We took the dogs for walks twice a day. Those dogs were so smart! During the winter season I would go outside 15 minutes before they did and climb trees to hide from them. Then they were let out.

"Go find Shane."

In a few short seconds, they would be barking at the base of the tree in which I was hiding. I even tried to jump to other trees close by. They still barked at the base of the tree I was in. Amazing.

They owned a house in another state up North that was attached to a farm. The farm owner did not care if we drove snow mobiles on his property during the winter. I really wanted to learn how to ski. Looked like such fun during the Olympics. I was removed from the home in just over 1 year. Never learned how to ski!

During the summer months we would go up to their second home. There was a river close by where we would walk the dogs. The dogs really enjoyed catching the rocks we would skip past them. The male would even bite the rocks in his mouth and crack them in half. The mother asked me not to skip big heavy thick rocks so as to avoid breaking his teeth. I was amazed that he could even catch the rocks. I'm quite good at skipping rocks. I loved those dogs so much. They often comforted me during my saddest days.

It was not easy getting used to this very strange place. The foster parents were new age hippy types with existential views on life, society, and philosophy! Ok I'm game; sounds interesting. No religion anyway. I'm tired of that. In fact, I'm so sick of it that I told my real parents that if they wanted me home during holidays I was not going to dress up for the church services.

If they insisted on it, I would not come home anymore for the holidays.

Since I'm such a trouble maker, the town had a PTA meeting to discuss if they were going to allow me into the public school. This would not be a problem except that one of the parent's sons was the bully of the school. Apparently she went back home and discussed the meeting with her family. Great, that was a fun first day of school at a new place. Sure I have no fear of adults or kids but getting food thrown at you during lunch every day is tough. Getting tripped in the halls, more kick me and punch me signs on my back. Yeah. Sounds like so much fun.

I moved to the town at the end of the school year, with just over a month left. It was elementary school and the last year before junior high school! I enjoyed playing soccer during recesses. I was the only kid brave enough to go airborne and make headers. I enjoy being tougher than the other kids! For once I felt special instead of being beaten down. I actually had some fun that month.

During summer I met a kid up the street who was quite friendly. We hung out a lot. He was allergic to bees. I covered the newspaper route while he went on vacation. There was this very large hill that I had to walk up. I got lazy after the first few days and didn't deliver the papers. Instead, I threw them into the woods nearby, saying I didn't get enough papers to cover the whole route. He told me this happens sometimes. So, I used that excuse to not deliver the papers. We played often by the river or in the ponds on the golf course nearby, catching the baby turtles.

That summer I got my first migraine headache. Wow. I was so sick, I couldn't stand up. In fact if my body got more than 3 feet off the ground I just threw up. So I would crawl out of bed to go-to the bathroom. It was a struggle to get up on the toilet. After the 4th day I was taken to the hospital, X-rays etc, etc, etc. They said it was just a bad migraine. I went home and it did go away after 10 days. I cried many hours in bed while this was happening. My friend and I were getting bullied while we walked to and from the candy store and some other areas of town. We would cut through the high school fields where the football team was practicing to get across town. Some of them would chase us across the field to the river, up the hill and threaten us all the time.

During my doctors visit for my headache I saw an empty needle in the trash. I know if I inject air into the body it kills people. I think I'm going to take this and the next time they chase us and steal our candy I'm going to stick this kid with it and no more bully. I plan it out beautifully. We get chased and run across the river start going up the sand hill. This time the kids were waiting for us, so I'm ready I've got the needle in my hand. I'm ending this today.

As we get closer to the top of the hill I tell my friend to keep running.

"I will let them catch me so he can get away."

I stop, turn around, pick up a handful of sand and throw it in the kids face. He can't see. His friend catches me by the arm; takes my candybar – a Charleston chew – and throws it into the river. I reach into my pocket for the needle to stick him with it. For some reason, he stops his assault on me and walks down the hill, just swearing at me:

"Next time I'm really going to hurt you."

I'm thinking, *"Kid, you have no idea how close you came to being killed today."*

After he walks away, I sit in the sand at the top of the hill. Alone with my thoughts, I decide I don't wish to kill anybody. I throw the needle as far away as I can into the woods. Not two days later, the doctor's office calls up my foster home looking for the needle. I lied at first, and then told them what I did. The family was so respectful to me that I had a hard time lying to them. We drive to where I tossed the needle. I can't remember if we found it or not. Just the long talk on the short ride home!

The beginning of the new school year as a Junior High school student! The school decides to put me in the SPECIAL ED program. What the fuck. This is not going to make anything better. Just a new reason for kids to tease me and make fun of me! The first time I found a punch me sign on my back at this school I was leaning over to drink from the fountain. Somebody punched me very hard in the stomach as I was drinking. Got the wind knocked out of me, now I'm gasping for air on the floor in the middle of the hall while the classes are in switch. Everybody was laughing at me as I struggle to get my breath back! Getting up, a teacher takes the sign off my back and shows it to me.

From this day forward I begin to watch and listen to every single conversation that is going on around me. No matter what public setting I'm in, I can tell you what everybody around me is talking about as well as the conversation that I am having! Making sure I know what everybody is talking about around me so I'm aware if anybody is attempting to harm me or get in behind me with any close distance. This is still a tactic I apply today. If the conversations around me are loud enough for me to hear I am following it, no matter how many different conversations there are, I am following every single one I can hear. I'm now 40 years old. While being seated in restaurants, I position myself so that nobody can get behind me and I pay close attention to my exit points. In fact, I do this in every situation –no matter what it is – even if I'm going to a $200 dinner!

Do you have any idea how awful it is to be in class with students who are mentally slower and/ or with physical issues when you are as able and intelligent as I am??? I tolerated this for about 2 months. I then informed the school that if they did not put me into main stream classes I would not do anything in school but sit there and look retarded. Surprisingly they did switch me. My bio mother later told me that if she was in control she would never have allowed me to tell adults what to do. Yeah for my mom having my back!

I was having so many problems with the kids every day because I was in special ED classes it wasn't helping. I also refused to take Ritalin. Told them don't bother I won't take it and if they want to throw me out of school so be it. Wouldn't be the first time! It was still very hard starting school in the classes after spending the first 2 months in special Ed. The kids all knew this and thanks to the PTA parent telling her son all she knew. The whole school knew everything. I got in many fights. Sometimes when I got suspended I would run up and down the halls screaming and slamming doors until the staff caught me and put me in I.S.S. I spent 5 days a month there.

I got kicked off the bus again. The walk to school wasn't very long and it went through the golf course it was a pretty walk. One day when it rained really hard and I got to school all wet. The guidance counselor bought me this light weight rain jacket to stay dry. It was the first time anybody bought me anything worth using in a very long time. I didn't know how to handle such a thing. After about 5 months of this torment I began to stand up for myself even beating up my bullies. This was fun. I began to get harassed less and less. But the damage was already done. The school system was tired of my behavior and I got suspended for breathing wrong.

My friend up the street borrowed some of my G.I. Joe toys. I had this off road truck that my parents bought me that was my pride. I loved it. I would play outside all day long in the pine trees debris of my front yard. Sure you can use them even the truck I loved. I just asked that he not break the truck. He did break it and I asked him to replace it. He just gave my foster parents the money to buy a new one. They didn't make that model anymore.

The next time I went to school, the entire school knew about it and teased me so badly. How can a kid my age make somebody pay for the toy? I got in a fight during music class over it. Great! 4 days of I.S.S. with the kid too! My foster parents didn't have much money so they made my lunch each day for me. The first day in I.S.S., I open up my lunch sandwich, took a bite and find maggots in my lunch sandwich. Last time I ever ate a lunch they made for me. I'm in this I.S.S. with a bully who loves teasing me. So I had to act like I wasn't hungry and hide this information from him. Not easy, but successful. Especially since the kid and our teacher are asking me how my lunch was and why didn't I eat after the first bite.

Computers were just starting to become popular. The school had the TSR 80 and a computer class we had to take. I showed some insight with working with computers so I got into a before-school class that taught us how to do programming. Another friend of mine was brilliant. We would spend hours designing simple games and programs. I actually had a lot of fun with them. At the house they had one as well but that was apple. I got some cool pc games and played them whenever the father wasn't using it. I asked for a joystick to play other games and get faster reaction time. They wouldn't buy me one. Not until they realized I was wearing out the functions of the keys, then I got the joystick.

I later learned that all these homes would get money just for having me in their house. Plus, they would receive money to buy me clothes and stuff. I found this information quite entertaining since every time I asked for something, the response was always we can't afford it. Not even new shoes or clothes. Years later I thought,

"Where did the money go? Thanks so much for taking care of my needs."

New clothes would have seriously alleviated some school stress since I was always getting teased for my old non-fitting clothes!

I enjoyed the computer games. The father even got this telephone modem to link with other computers across the country and/or world if need be. Wow cool. I actually hacked another computer in California, it was easy and simple. I turned the computer off, took out my games and decided that day I didn't like where computers were going to lead. I never used another computer for many years after that.

On Saturdays we went to an apple class to learn the new language. They even brought in a robot for us to play with. It was about 4 feet tall, rolled around and even spoke. But he didn't speak correctly. You had to spell the words you wanted him to speak in phonetic form or he would mispronounce them. I found this very curious since it's all just programming issues. When they weren't looking I walked up to the main terminal controlling the robot, got into his programming and began to isolate his voice programs, I begin to trouble shoot the program and see the problem. But before I can make any adjustments, the tech guy walks over and turns the computer off without informing me he was turning it off.

He then tells me, "Don't touch it anymore."

Geesh! I'm trying to fix your robot....

The family packs up the car and says:

"Hey! Shane! We're going for a ride; would you like to come? We're going to another state, taking a picnic and having a good day."

Sure. New scenery is always appreciated.

We drive for a few hours as we get closer to our destination, I'm informed were going to a special kind of therapist. Great more fucking shrinks! I'm already in 'fuck you' mode as we walk in the door to meet some slight looking women. She had a nice house with lots of dark wood and mantles and statues all over the living room and reception area.

We talk for a few minutes about how this therapy is supposed to release repressed anger issues. My anger issues aren't repressed; they are fresh daily for a multitude of reasons.

"Want to know what makes me angry? I despise people who do not respect me and fucking talk for me. I hate you fucking shrinks who think you know me and this is the first time we met!" That's what I wanted to say but swallowed the words.

I mean I've been dealing with this crap on my own for so long now. I'm not sure that it will ever end, and so I just don't care anymore. This is my life! It seems the whole world is never going to take the time to attempt to get to know me and my motivations for my behavior. Worse when I do speak they don't seem to care or listen. When it became apparent to me that my views were never going to be valued, I just stopped offering and caring to offer them.

So this living room had an empty adjacent room except for a blanket on the carpeted floor plus a tripod with camera on it. I also noticed spotlights facing the center of the room. Ok interesting, but not alarming. I'm then told to lie on the floor and relax as they begin to ask me all kinds of questions relating to my relationship with my parents.

The 'therapy' continues when two large well built guys come down the stairs and hold each of my legs and hands. Next they tell me that my foster mother is going to lie on top of me. My first thought,

Are you really going video tape me having sex with my foster mother?

Wait! They change the order. Now my foster dad lies on top of me and the mother lies on top of him. That's a lot of weight on top of me now. The guys are holding my hands and feet out in stretched form. I'm trying to relax. I'm still being drilled about god knows what subject. My focus is getting out of this fucking strap down.

I squirm. I struggle. I attempt to wiggle out.

"Relax, (I'm told). It's all part of the program".

Now the questions revolve around my mother. I tried to tell them that my mother and I didn't have violent issues and we didn't have any inappropriate behavior. They don't believe me and continue to drill me. Now I'm really getting upset, it must have been about 35 minutes of this crap so far.

I'm still being pinned down and I'm still trying to get out. I've had enough!

"Get the fuck off me!!!"

Swearing, screaming, I trying to get loose! I've even spit in every direction to get them to turn away so I can attempt to twist out using balance. No luck. I'm still fucking pinned down. I'm really upset! They continue to drill me about my mother. Ok! I desperately try to analyze the result they want to hear so I can get out of this fucking mess. I've decided the only way out of this fucking day is to play along.

I'm exhausted, I'm sweating. The spot lights are hot and bright. I'm facing up; my foster father is facing down to me. His wife is lying on top of him facing down as well. I'm still being drawn and quartered by 2 guys. I told them whatever I thought they wanted to hear just to get the situation over with.

After a couple of hours they do finally let me up. I'm in and out of consciousness. I just remember waking up and having no type of pressure on me and I could move my arms and legs. Yeah it's over.

The whole time being in the house was just over 3 hours. I saw the clock on my way out. Again I'm the consummate analyst of my surroundings. We leave the house get into their car and begin to drive away. They say something comforting to me and ask me what I want for lunch. My head is saying you fucking people will never get any information out of me again.

I started immediately a plan to run away in my head. About a week later, the plan was executed! I went to a friend's house; his parents let me stay one night then sent me back. I just gave the family hell every second of every day from that day forward and refused to talk to them about anything that wasn't related to daily activities. A couple of school suspensions later and I get kicked out of the home. Did they expect that I wasn't going to rebel in every way possible?! I'm just thankful that I didn't have to experience that hell again.

CHAPTER 5

Now the real fun begins. At 12 years old I will see no more foster homes. From here on out I will attend 3 different institutional boarding schools! School numbers 2-4 each have a full campus! The educational building is down the hill from the dorms. Everyone eats in the cafeteria except on the weekends. On weekends we eat in our own dorms, where we are separated by age groups! There is even a day school section for kids who can't behave themselves in a public school setting but have no problems at home.

Arriving in the middle of the year, I find the adjustment difficult. Each room in each dorm can hold between 2 to 8 kids. We have dressers but it's rationed out for one drawer per kid. We have standing closets that are shared with two students. My dorm has a hallway which is set up like a wing. The room door can and is locked during the day so we can't go-to our rooms.

All these schools have some sort of level system: if you are good and play their game, you get privileges which then are taken away depending on your behavior. Kids began to push my buttons relatively quickly. We all have group therapy twice a week after breakfast before classes. Everybody knows each other's issues and problems. It would not be until I was in my early 20's that I realized the whole world isn't alpha males and females. I had a hard time adjusting to this realization once I was free from being institutionalized.

People steal each-other's stuff. I had a collection of comic books that I accumulated from home to home to school. My roommate stole the entire collection and sold it to a store where he lived, on one of his home-visits. I never got them back even though the school said they would make him pay for it.

I also got in a lot of fights with the kids. I'm not one to take abuse and harassing from anybody. I don't harass people or fuck with anybody just for entertainment. This point seemed to be lost amongst my therapy sessions.

"Why are you out of control?"

I'm not! You fuckers don't get it. People fuck with me; I retaliate.

My retaliation may be more violent than the initial response. Thus I end up in the corner sitting on a chair for hours in front of the staff office. I often got into so much trouble I would lose the privilege of wearing my shoes for weeks on end except for classes and meals.

I got in a fight with a kid at breakfast and threw him across the table. He was covered in eggs, syrup and pancakes! Eventually I was restrained by two adult staffers. I love being held down and pinned by 2 staff members. I actually enjoyed learning their techniques and trying to get out of them.

I learned a limitation at this school. I can't physically attack adults anymore. I got sick of being pinned down. As you can imagine when you are as big an asshole as I am, the staff have no problems taking cheap shots on you during your violent rage moment. I would often get elbows in the jaw or head that were not part of their soft restraining classes.

During school time I still got in fights and arguments. I spent a lot of hours in the time out rooms. The man who ran the time out rooms was large and didn't play games. If you fucked with him once he just took you out quickly. You couldn't move. On the other hand, he was a very respectful person. He treated me like a real person, once I got to his space I never created any trouble for him. He talked to me like a real person, got to know me. He didn't just talk at me or ignore my reasons. He was one of the few people who deserved his position and wasn't just collecting a paycheck. Most of the staff didn't care about who or what we were. This was never lost on us sleepers. After a while I became very good at understanding and reading people. I have an insight into people that is uncanny. We'll get to that in the 4th school where it became a game.

I'm doing everything I can to get on the inside crowd. I'm tired of being bullied and fucked with. I begin to get straight A's. I've decided that the only way out of this hell is to get great grades and go to college. I want to become a lawyer and fight for the injustice of this world. Sitting in class one day we were talking about who has cavities and what not. Most everybody has them.

"I don't have any yet." I said out loud.

"I don't believe you," one kid says. "Come over and show me."

I open my mouth and he spits down my mouth. I get up attack him and spend the next week in the time out room 7 hours a day. The whole class tells the teacher.

"He didn't spit down Shane's mouth." They have no idea why I attacked him. "Shane is crazy."

We continue this battle in the dorm later that day. He puts me in a headlock and punches me in the face about 10 times before I can get free. Ok. He can kick my ass so I'm staying away from him forever now. We never fought again but we did exchange verbal wars often. I'm still scared to use the toilets when people are around so I take a piss outside along the building. Great! The biggest kid in the school catches me and tells the staff. I'm publically embarrassed during the next day's morning dorm group therapy session.

My male hormones and sexual desires emerge. I began masturbating which is hard to do privately in this setting. Soon I get caught and my nickname became "Spanky." A few fights ensue over this and I'm back without shoes again. When this happens you get to stay in a 10 × 10 room just outside the staff office, while everybody else goes outside and plays soccer or softball or goes on the swings! I had to eat the weekend meals all by myself.

We also did our own laundry. In fact, I've been doing my own laundry since I was in my first institution at age 6. A couple of the foster homes would do my laundry; others just showed me where the machine was and said "You are on your own."

Laundry wasn't that difficult because I didn't own much. From the time I was 6 until mid 20's all I owned could be put into one duffel bag, the kind you check in on a plane when you take a trip. I learned to not care about possessions. My clothes were completely out of style which contributed to ridicule. I figure nicer clothes would alleviate one source of trouble.

This school refused to give me any real money to go shopping: $25 for shoes and $50 for clothes each season! In protest, I bought the ugliest clothes I could find just to say.

"Fuck you. I will embarrass you when you take me off campus."

Funny how those high level privileges were rare.

Some staff members would take me out on trips even though I did not have the privilege for it. They earned my respect those days. I was put in this arts and crafts class as some kind of therapy. I never got it. They all thought it was working. It didn't work. I was just sick of being isolated and the kids in the class didn't have the mean streak in them that caused me to react in violence.

We also had a cool gym teacher. He started this outdoor activities club with some of the other hard cases. We would go on hikes, learn to use a compass and go camping. We had so much fun. Nobody got in fights; nobody harassed each-other. No drama. We even got to sit around the fire and smoke cigars. He said day one:

"If you fight; if you disrespect each-other, then you will all lose this thing. No matter who starts it; no matter how."

So we must learn to work and respect each-other. To my surprise, kids I fought with didn't fuck with me during these outings. We got closer as a group. We even stopped fighting during the normal school functions. He let us talk any way we wanted without restraining profanity. I'm sure this was for me. My vocabulary as a 13 year old kid included swears every other word in general conversation.

During a meal in the cafeteria I heard a familiar last name of a friend from the first boarding school. He and I were one of four younger students. I don't see him and ask to have this kid pointed out to me. I rummage through my limited belongings on the next home visit, looking for the paper that has our 2 names in it. The article discusses how we were the only kids in the school that could run a full 5 miles. I show the kid the paper and he then admits that his brother went to the school. At first he denied having a brother and having a brother that went to that school. Hence the reason I went and got the paper on my next home visit.

I get to go home every once in a while. It's not a long train ride to get to my parents house. I am less and less interested in going home. Every week or so there is a meeting with my therapist the head school psychologist and my parents. It's always a bad session because I'm always in trouble. I'm told years later that my parents went out for drinks after each meeting.

Within a year I'm not even talking to them very much anymore. All my mail communication is screened before I get to read it. One year I lost a package of fresh plums that my mom sent from her tree. Because it was a holiday, they rotted sitting in the mail boxes waiting for my therapist to come back from the holiday.

I go home with another kid who lives quite near me. We take the train together. Arriving at the train station, his parents are not there to pick him up. I ask my mom to drive him to his house. It was cool, I even walked up the road 2 miles that weekend to get to his house to hang out, figuring we could bond outside of school and become friends. It was a fun time.

Not two weeks later he deliberately breaks my leg during a soccer game. Snapped both bones on my lower leg and shatters the ball of my ankle. He just came in and jumped on it with the intent of breaking my leg. He said,

"It was an accident" only to avoid getting in trouble.

I was in surgery for 16 hours: two screws and a cast for 4 months. I was in the hospital for a week. I had a top bunk during this time, but they moved my bed right in front of the office. This allowed them to both monitor my leg, as it was a complicated surgery, plus make sure kids couldn't really fuck with me since I was on crutches and couldn't climb into the top bunk easily.

My time in the hospital was fun. Nobody was fucking with me. This beautiful girl down the hall would come in and push my wheel chair. She helped me get in it so I could go-to art class and other activities with the kids. I saw a kid who had no arms in the class. My first reaction was to cry just looking at him. Then I saw he was and still is the best sketch artist I've ever seen. Since I've travelled to over 70 different countries around the world I've seen a lot of street artists and professional artists. He is still the most detailed artist I've seen –and, he drew with his feet.

I had a TV in my room but had to pay extra for it. My parents didn't want to pay for TV, even though the school covered all the hospital bills. My mom did come to see me. She drew a smiley face on my big toe sticking out of the cast.

The staff member who taught me not to fight with adults any-more actually paid the bill for my TV:

"Do not to tell anyone."

I found out when he stopped by. He asked to change the chan-nel and watch something he wanted to.

No! I said.

"Hey! I paid the bill."

I never told anyone. Besides who would believe me anyway?

I never got to say good bye to that girl. She checked out the day we were supposed to exchange addresses and such. It was ok. She made my week there very fun.

The first time I tried to stand up after surgery I just fell on my face. The nurses in the room didn't expect me to be so unstable and weren't prepared for my fall. No worries. The hardest part was that I didn't have a cast yet, just this drainage tube sticking out of my leg with a ball at the end of it full of nasty liquid.

On one of my visits home I read a letter that was on the office table in my parent's house. As I walked into the living room, my name at the top of the page caught my eye. It said

"The state I lived in was now my legal guardian."

Hmm. My parents and I did not have this conversation. This motivated me to turn down home-visits. At the next 2 boarding schools, I volunteered to stay and turned down many trips home. I called home very infrequently.

The school denied a vacation with my parents that first year I was there. My parents set up the itinerary for me. I love roller-coasters! We were supposed to drive down south to Disney and stop by a park along the way that had a lot of coasters. I had asked the school to let me go. There was a meeting and ultimately decided that it would not be in my best interest to go. This really upset me. There was nothing I could do about it though. I told the school I would not say a single word during the 2 weeks. Not to anybody. It was a protest of mine.

The hardest part was the first two days. After that it got easy. The only issue was some of the asshole staff wouldn't read my notes. There were times I had to communicate: early in the morning we have to ask a staff member to check our room before we are allowed to leave. Bed has to be made; clothes put away. It takes time, you get up, shower, get dressed, clean your room, vacuum it. There is a rotating schedule for vacuuming the rooms and cleaning the dorm.

The early staff would not read my note so I could get my room inspected so I could come out and watch cartoons before breakfast. They just left me in my room.

"We don't get paid to read your notes."

No problem. I just sat quietly on my bed until breakfast. If they didn't clear the whole dorm, then one of them would have to stay back from breakfast and sit with me. They never did. They want to eat too.

I even fake slapped one of them, inches away from her face clapping my hands together. I don't think she ever liked me anyway. She contracted out beating me up a few times to kids.

During one stretch when I was playing nice with the school I got some upper level privileges. I was allowed to stay up late and watch Saturday night live. This is reserved for upper level only. In a week or two, I will be allowed to walk off campus alone and buy stuff at a nearby mall.

One rule is when staying up late you can't cross the imaginary line past the doorway that is usually locked to the hallway of the bedrooms. If you do, you are not allowed back into the living room. If you cross and come back you lose a level right there. It's supposed to prevent loud playful chasing at night.

One kid who does not have upper level privileges comes out to talk to her.

"I don't feel good." He says then walks by, smacks me and runs down the hall!

I stand up to chase him and before I can stop my momentum, literally cross the line by 1 foot. She is standing right behind me and busts me down a level right there as soon as I cross back to the living room area. I would not play nice again.

The no talking did affect my grades though which upset me. They tried to play this power struggle by having me read the chapters of the book that we are learning in English class. I still didn't read.

After 5 days, they brought this special therapist in from another state to meet with me. I just laughed.

"You don't get it. I'm not talking until the end of the two weeks." I wrote this on a piece of paper.

"I am not going to read it", he said.

They thought this only counted for the day to day activities not therapy. No response.

"If you are not going to read it, then I'm done talking/writing."

Twenty minutes of silence, with unanswered questions. They sent me back to my dorm. In fact, they don't even schedule another therapy session during the 2 week period. It was a relaxing time for me. My nickname was motormouth (given to me by my cousins) because I could never stop talking. I got in very little trouble those 2 weeks except for the staff fucking with me and me fake slapping them every day.

The next day one staff person even tried to step into my fake slap and get me to slap her. I laughed...

I wasn't even watched very much during this time. I could walk almost anywhere I wanted, without staff breathing down my neck. I was walking to school one morning, when the gym teacher and outdoor activities / camping leader caught me in front of the gym steps.

"I heard of your protest. Are you ok?"

Out of respect I did reply to him. *"I really wanted to go-to Disney and have fun. I didn't know any other way to say, 'You are fucking assholes' without tearing up the place. Would they rather I destroy shit and go off?"*

To his credit we chatted for maybe 50 words. Starting talking again was difficult. He didn't say or act like we were talking when anybody was within range. He really earned my respect that day.

The next year, they took the whole school to Disney. They even bought 2 extra tickets for a student and a staff to come home early in case a student acted out. I was told by my gym teacher in a private conversation between us before we left that those tickets were for me. I would be assigned to his group.

He asked me, "Can you behave yourself?"

If I'm not fucked with then there will be no problems.

"Come to me first, if anybody starts fucking with you and we'll try to sort it out amongst the group before there was trouble."

Agreed!

A prize for the best behaved kid was awarded during the week. The kid having to use the tickets was not me. I also got many votes for being the best behaved kid, too. My whole group and the 3 staff in charge of our group voted. I didn't get it. Guess they couldn't give it to a constant trouble maker. The kid who won was always a good kid.

I'm starting to get a real good understanding of the human mind; of how it operates and how to analyze people. One time this kid in the dorm is putting shit on people's pillows during the day somehow. He does this to 4 different pillows before he gets caught. At a house meeting after the 2nd incident, I tell my friend,

"Give me a day– I will figure out who it is."

Later that day after thinking about it, I tell him who it is.

He says, "No way! It can't be that person."

Sure enough: when the culprit is revealed, it turned out to be the guy I predicted. My friend just looks at me and smiles.

If I am going to be honest about everybody else's behavior then I must also point out my own. This book often paints a horrible picture of my own actions. This is the first time my memory can clearly discuss my appalling behavior.

For example, I started to wipe my boogers on the walls of my room. I was placing them all around the room not just by my bed, so I couldn't get caught. They became quite gross and there was a huge house meeting on the subject. After a few days of trying to find out who was responsible, I admitted it. Surprisingly I didn't get into as much trouble as I thought and my fellow roommates helped me clean the walls, wearing gloves of course. I never did this again anywhere.

Near the end of my time there, I got into a huge fight. I was so frustrated that I just walked up to my house and into my dorm. The 'fake slap' woman tried to stop me from getting into my room. I just pushed by her; she followed me up the hall. I grabbed a 4 foot glass picture off the wall and threw it down the hall toward her. The hallway was only 6 feet wide. As soon as I let it go I realized it was a great throw. It flew down the hall toward her and didn't clip the walls on the way by. I thought

"Oh shit! It's going to hit her."

At the last second it clips the wall and shatters, strewing glass all over her.

I also told another kid that a staff member and I had some 'physical activity'. Though she did allow some boys to actually grab her ass and get a little too close with her, she never did this with me. He went to the director of my house out of jealousy. He was Spanish and so was she. I had to admit that I lied at a house meeting. Tough but hey, it's a healthy tough moment.

I became involved with a teacher. We were flirting, sending notes and even getting quite physical. I found out she was having a real affair with an 18 year old day student. He got caught in her shower. She lived with 2 other teachers. He –a 'Fonzy' type –was much bigger than I was. If you touched his leather jacket he beat you up. We actually became friends, or so I thought.

He confidentially told me he loved this teacher and was going to move in with her. I mistakenly told him about me and her and asked him not to fall in love with such a girl. He must have gone right up to her and asked her about it.

After school I was walking up the hill to play softball. I saw 'Fonzy' standing there looking at me, so I walked up to him. He grabbed me; I grabbed him back and tried to throw him to the ground. Fail! He got the better grip. He wore cowboy boots. I got the shit kicked out of me.

Later that week he knocked over his own leather jacket, I just happened to be getting up from my chair right next to him. He beat me up again for touching his leather jacket! After lunch the next day he came after me with real violence; I could see it in his eyes. Oh shit. A teacher grabbed him and jacked him up against the wall and told him to stop. 'Fonzy' was not bigger than him...

The next therapy session my shrink tells me that she was in the basement of the school looking at old files. She discovered that my biological father was in the same school many years earlier with some of the same problems I had! Isn't that a shit? My father attended the same school and had similar problems with kids, with staff, etc. I made a decision that day that I was not going to have children ever. I was cutting the line off right there with me. No more tortured kids in this hell. Today at 40 I have no kids.

This same therapist often brought me news that would alter my experience. About to go on another outdoor activities club weekend, I see my therapist walking across the yard on a line in my specific direction. I can tell she has nothing but bad news. We meet and she tells me that in a week I will be removed from the school. Great! Where to next?

CHAPTER 6

Time to grow up! I became a man at this next school. I learned how to fight. Started drinking and smoking pot on a regular basis; became the B.M.C.; lost my virginity; had free roam of the campus; learned to play basketball; and, oh yeah, got kicked out again. What a surprise.

Within my first two weeks I get drunk for the first time. The best way to get rid of a hangover I learned is to chug a beer first thing in the morning. I'm 15. This institution is an old mansion from the 1800's—a massive complex. Buildings are made of brick. Huge main staircase with split upper staircase! Tennis courts, gym, school buildings are all a short walk away. The ages of the kids are fairly close in range. Maybe because I'm getting older the dorm rooms seem smaller and have less people in them. The most people in a room that I saw was four and only a few of them had that many. This dorm had 3 floors. You were not even allowed on the 3rd floor unless you were part of the B.M.C. (Big Man on Campus) crew. I didn't get to go up there for a year.

I arrived at the school with no money and very few clothes. I asked about getting some soap, deodorant, shampoo, laundry detergent! The laundry machine was in the basement and we had to wash our own clothes. There were times I was so depressed I would go for weeks without washing my clothes or my hair. A bad case of athlete's foot changed that and I started to care. My clothes smelled so bad I couldn't stand them. They told me you need money in your account in order to get sundries from their supply. Apparently I didn't have any money yet. They said it usually takes a couple of weeks to get funds from the state. They knew my legal guardian was the state. I found out that I could go down the hill and help split wood with a staff member at a robust $3 an hour. He sold the split wood to local people for firewood. I spent that whole day down there. He even stopped off at CVS so I could buy sundries. I actually liked the guy for some time, until I saw the way he treated the black kids. He was a ball breaker; we clashed every day.

Most of the kids were on break my first two weeks there. When they came back I went to the main dorm. The girl's dorm was about two miles away. The whole campus–boys, girls, off campus day students– ate all meals in our dorm Monday through Friday. Our dorm housed the middle teenage kids.

During the first day's dinner, I expected the typical 'let's test the new kid' stuff. I wanted to stay out of everybody's way until I figured it all out. A kid with a name close to mine who was actually there for murder which he committed when he was 13 (he is 17 at this point) tells me to go get his dessert!

I'm thinking: *"OK. Here comes the first fight."*

These kids are bigger than I am so I'm intimidated. I don't get his dessert. I just get up and walk out of the cafeteria. He confronts me later and grabs me.

"The next time I tell you to do something, you better do it."

Ok. That was a harmless exchange. The staff here have a better understanding of how this alpha male group thing works. There seems to be a level of respect between staff and kids I have not seen before. Maybe this school isn't so bad.

Shift change is at 11 o'clock. The night guard duty consists of one guy: a 3 tour Vietnam vet. It took me 2 years to find that out. He never talked to us, but sure as hell caught us in everything we tried to get away with. He was so good that we never acted up on his shift. He slept on the chair downstairs with his eyes open.

Creepy. If we made a noise, he would be right behind us before we knew it.

"Mr. Lewis, why are you out of bed?" From two feet behind me! Suddenly and quietly. We all feared him.

Within the first month I discovered that a select group of kids got to play basketball in the gym long after it was bedtime but only up until the 11 PM shift change. I decided

"I'm tired of being the bottom guy. What do I have to do to get inside the cool kids circle and stop getting beat up and harassed?"

Step one. Grow the balls to walk into the gym. I'm taller than everybody else and they noticed. They even made some comments already that I should play basketball. I walk in alone. Everybody else was already playing. Two staff members are playing, too. Nobody said a word.

"Can you play?" Someone finally asked.

I said, 'No'.

"OK. We'll teach you."

It wasn't long before I won every game of 21 simply because I learned how to tap in rebounds for baskets. I won so often they changed the rules.

"You must take back all rebounds to the free throw line!"

It took six more months of daily basketball before I began to win again. My dribbling skills got better. My long arms allowed me to play great defense. Then they changed the rules again.

"Shane must use his left hand to shoot and dribble."

It took six more months before I was ambidextrous with dribbling. No one could beat me again. No matter if I got double-or triple-teamed. In fact, when I left that school I didn't lose another game of one on one until I was in prison in my later 20's. I even played in the cities with the ghetto kids because the style of basketball is more to my liking. I didn't learn to shoot jumpers until I was 19. I loved taking it to the basket. Right at you! I could jump, even spent an entire year working on jumping and by the time I was 17 could do 360 dunks, leaners, and double pumps. It was fun.

We started to play basketball against other schools around the area. We went to the local youth lock up and got beat by 100 points. Another school came to see us in our gym and things really got out of hand. What started off as a very physical game ended up in a full scale fight between the two teams. Even the coaches got involved.

One of my friends was fighting a member of the other team, when their coach stepped in and picked him up. Turning I punched the coach right in the side of his face as hard as I could. He dropped my friend and covered up. We finally got corralled into our locker rooms. The other team left on their bus. Many consequences ensued from this little riot. We lost privileges and basketball games!

On an occasion close to my arrival, we had a brawl with the school down the road over some girl who later took my virginity. This fight occurred in the yards of the surrounding neighborhood. With assorted damages, blood was left on the sheets and clothing hanging on the neighbor's clothes lines. The entire school was put on house arrest for two months. Nobody who had upper level privileges was allowed to leave the campus. We ultimately had to invite the local town to a dinner with us so they could see we were not animals, just kids who got too wild one night.

As I was beginning to be included inside the cool group, I was still called 'Spanky.' I don't understand how that nickname came with me. One staff member was calling me that often. I was sick of it. So as I walked by him, I slapped him in the back of the head right after he said it in front of everybody! I took off running!

I ran out the side cafeteria door, out into the yard, across the campus into the tennis courts. He finally caught up to me but was too tired to do much. As we stood on opposite sides of the net,

"If you ever hit me again, I will beat the shit out of you."

Stop calling me, 'Spanky.'

At night we had a snack time where the staff would open the kitchen. Scooter pies, chips, soda, we pretty much got whatever we wanted. Only our dorm had this privilege, since the kitchen was in our house. This was great! Since we were high most nights, we could use some snacks. Our own closets had private keys. We snuck food and sodas into our rooms, passed the staff and into our closets for late-night-after-getting-high snacks. We somehow managed to get a copy of the kitchen key and broke in all the time. (Technically, it's not breaking in if you use the key, right)? We never took too much; just enough to keep us happy. We decided to steal a case of steaks and burgers but when we saw that the box said 'Grade D meat' changed our minds. I decided not to eat meat there anymore.

The salad bar was excellent. Breakfast was the same style. We could get anything we wanted if you could get out of bed in time to eat it. One kid ate 6 fried eggs every day. You could get omelets, bacon, muffins, French toast, waffles, or cereal. We had a mini-war when the new box of mini cereals came out! Who could collect all the frosted flakes?

I didn't win that war often. In fact, I never got up. I slept my time away, often missing first period of school and getting in lots of trouble. The school operated on a point system.

"Oh, boy! A point system!"

Stay up late: lose a point. Skip a class: lose a point. Skip after school activities: lose a point. Swear at a staff member: lose a point.

If you lost four points a week you would effectively have no off campus privileges, i.e., no mall, no movies, no Saturday parks. Some old war parks were very close by. Since I slept through first period classes every day, I lost five points right there. Sometimes the staff would come in and flip my bed over to wake me up. I would just sleep right there on the floor. During winter they would strip my blankets off the bed, open my windows and freeze me out. I just used the plastic coated mattress to block the cold and slept anyway. I often hid in my lock-in closet to sleep there as well.

My first roommate had multiple personality disorder. I've had many dealings with this since including some girls I dated in my 20's. For a while I concluded it was my lot in life to be around such people. Again, where is my complimentary PHD?!

I admit that I beat him up once in a while. He cut a circle hole out of his mattress and filled it with shampoo and fucked his mattress at night. Drove me nuts!! He had a TV though and we would watch *Duck Tales* and other animated programs after school every day. He let me borrow the TV on Sundays to watch football.

I actually borrowed another kid's TV and watched all the games. The 2nd TV I borrowed was from this kid who we thought was truly crazy! He shaved half of his head, and made severely disturbed mix tapes and blasted them. Everybody feared him like he would slit their throats anytime any day. He had a private room – the only one on the 2nd floor. So I imagine staff felt the same. We actually got along. I treated him with respect and very cautiously. I would knock on his door when I wanted to talk to him even if the door was open! I met my roommate's mother once when she came by to drop off his care package. She was a total nut job. After I met his mother I never let anybody ever fuck with him. I even stood up for him. Sometimes you just don't know what shit people have to deal with.

The school would get new kids all the time. People would come and go. My new best friend came. Some Greek kid from the capital! He was a heavy pot head and always had it on him. Between us, we had all the drugs and power of the 2nd floor. The powers that be decided to put the 3 of us in one room— me, him and the acid kid. I was thinking,

"Are you fucking kidding me! You are putting all us trouble makers in the same room?"

What's more an extra room was adjacent to ours. The only way in or out was through a door in our room. We got a master key for every door on campus from a former student who came on campus one night and met us at our party spot. Apparently things don't change much!

The room became our smoke house. Sure staff would come in once in a while and bust us. One time they came in when five of us were in the room, smoking a 4 foot bong. They demanded that everyone in the room come out from our hiding spots. There were old mattresses lying against the walls; stacks of boxes all over. Some came out; some didn't. They took our drugs and bongs, locking them up in the safe! They often left the safe open, however, while working in the office. All files were locked in it.

We would stage fake fights in the main room and then get the smallest kid to climb in the window and steal back our stash. We succeeded a few times.

They even had a drug czar come in who mandated that some of us attend N.A. (Narcotics Anonymous) meetings a few times a month. The first meeting the facilitator pulls out rolling papers and teaches us how to roll joints properly. We didn't have the heart to tell him we prefer bowls and bongs, easier to hide.

Twin brothers attended this school. Their story was that some kind of accident killed both parents; they had millions in a trust fund waiting till they turned 18. Stuck with us until then, they were split up but one was in my dorm. Their voices sounded like *Elmer Fudd*. I got high and went into their room just to laugh at them. They were hanging with their click but didn't kick me out. They asked to get high once in awhile.

"Sure. OK I can oblige that."

We would have floor fights with the fire extinguishers all the time. They had the water ones so they shot very far. We emptied them out so much they changed them to chemical ones. That didn't stop us. The chemical ones made a huge mess.

Being contracted out by the staff to control the kids was fun. Sure beat the other way around by a long shot. I am the BMC of my floor. One new kid came in and attempted to start a fire in the lobby by the payphone. It was late at night just before shift change; a quiet party night, too. Most of us were sleeping.

By the time it was noticed the fire was burning up the wall of the porch area. It was not a real threat to burn the school down, but it was still an arson event. Later we were all called into a smaller room with couches lining all the walls.

"No one is going anywhere until someone admitted doing it."

Students have an 'Us vs. Them' mentality. Nobody rats on anybody. We may know who does everything, but we don't tell staff anything. It's an unwritten rule. We're still sitting there waiting for staff to come in. I'm reciting the last few chapters of my latest book which is getting laughs. Making some jokes!

Staff walk in. "Tell us what happened!"

I didn't know what happened. I was woken up from sleep. Most of us were sleeping!

"The three BMC's would have been killed if the fire got out of control. Tell us. We are not leaving until somebody admits to starting this fire."

We already knew who did it. We talked before the staff got in the room. A few kids and I even walked out to talk about it before the staff arrived. We did get yelled at for leaving the room.

The lead staff looks at me and the other BMC's and gives us the look. He says, "I've got to go to the bathroom. By the time I get back somebody better say something."

He walks out the door; we wait about 10 seconds. Then the 3 of us jump up and beat the shit out of the kid who did it, no facial hits. Leave him in the middle of the floor curled up bruised and crying. We all sit back down. The staff walk back in and he admits it immediately. He asks,

"What happened to him?"

Nobody said a word.

One of the dorms off the main campus did catch on fire. It suffered so much severe damage that by the time I was kicked out of the school was not yet repaired. I don't think we ever found out how this fire started. It occurred at night with 90% of the kids sleeping. Many of the kids would have died except that one boy who had severe cerebral palsy– he had to use crutches to walk around and often fell while using those –He woke up the whole house, climbing up the stairs multiple times to make sure all the kids got out.

We had class trips, proms etc... We went to Six Flags as an entire school and got to run around and have fun. While on some spinning ride, to my horror I espy sitting on a park bench the foster father in whose home I got molested. My whole body shakes. He's looking right at me with leering eyes.

I get off the ride and realize he is starting to follow me around the park. I look to my friends and tell them the story of who he is. I asked them to keep an eye on him.

"If he gets too close to me, I'm going to kick his fucking ass."

To his credit he does not come closer than 100 feet. His wife, however, came up to me while I was playing video games and said "Hello! How are you?" We talk for a few seconds and she walks away.

I got my first girlfriend at this school. I was scared to lose my virginity. She slept with everybody on campus but me. When I found out I confronted her and slapped her for it which got me suspended from school and sent back to my room for two days!

I didn't get in much trouble during school hours except for missing classes. I often skipped my therapy sessions and lost more points. I got so sick of therapy that I made up stories: "I had killed someone while on a home visit." That drove her nuts! I got in all kinds of trouble for that. Another kid and I felt she was staring at our crotch during sessions and we told people. He got a new therapist. I didn't. I really hated that therapist. I cleared her desk once as I walked out and told her I'd never go back.

I finally met a girlfriend that I really liked. We learned sign language together so we could talk and communicate secretly. We communicated important information like where we would meet after hours and fuck, drink, and smoke pot. It was fun watching the staff try and catch us. We could go missing for 45 minutes without getting into real trouble. Anything longer than 45 minutes was called AWOL. AWOL caused a lot of paperwork for the staff, which cut into the things they wanted to do like talk to girlfriends on the phone in the office and play basketball in the gym. None of us got to play ball until the paperwork was done.

They let us get away with certain things for the sanity of the school and honestly for their own. In return, they got no headaches and got control. I learned this the hard way.

The first time I violated this 45 minute policy I just got back from fucking my girlfriend. I was high and walked into the kitchen to get my snacks. As I turned the corner to get to the BMC section of our snack area – anyone not part of BMC was not allowed into the back area. I got punched in the chest by the head staff. My body lifted off the ground, my feet and hands stuck straight out dropping all my food everywhere. He then looked at me and explained,

"You have 45 minutes. Next time when I'm the head remember that! Teach this kid the rules..."

That really ruined my high and spilled my snacks. I never got in any trouble while he was the head guy again.

We had yearbook and photography classes during the summer and regular school year. I only joined so that me and my girlfriend could hang out in the dark room and get sexual while the red light was on. One of the photos taken for that first yearbook created some eerie results. The photo featured four girls on campus. Within 8 months all 4 girls were dead.

It became a sort of cult thought process for us, making many jokes about the whole ordeal in an effort to balance the awkward losses. One girl robbed a gold necklace from an ex boyfriend on a visit and had her head blown off with a shotgun. Another girl killed herself. Another girl was killed by a turning tractor trailer while on a moped on her way to an abortion. The 4th one died in a car accident. It was all kind of strange because after the 3rd one died we were joking with the last girl that she was next. It was just a joke until it happened on the next home visit.

Our group of kids was very eclectic. One kid was actually born at Woodstock and he never took showers. I hated sitting behind him in English class because the door that alleviated the summer heat blew his foul stench right into me. There is somebody for everyone though, because a girl who was also just as unhygienic began dating him. The school supplied birth control for the girls even though relationships were forbidden. They tried to control the level of physical contact between us. I guess you have to choose your battles, because we did just about whatever we wanted with girlfriends.

Some kids had more money than others and we would give our extra money to the kids with less. The smokers needed it, begging each other all the time for smokes. We told one kid if he had sex with the fattest girl in the school, we would give him a pack of cigarettes. Not only did he have sex with her, he got her pregnant. Since she was so overweight the school did not supply her with the pill. We gave him a carton of cigarettes.

I did go home to my parents once in awhile. I went to Disney with them one week, which this school allowed. I wonder if they read about my reaction last time in a file.

Many years later I told my parents that I got drunk on my 16th birthday on that Disney trip. On a later trip while watching a house next door burn late at night, I talked to my step dad about how I hated the taste of southern comfort. He was not as pleased with that admission as the 16th birthday story.

I stopped going home after that trip. Something my step father said to me while I was talking to my oldest half brother outside helped me decide that this is not the kind of people I want to be around anymore. For my 16th birthday I asked for a video game system. They got me a car. Like I can ever use a car! I'm stuck in an institution probably until I'm 18 at the minimum. I'm aware of my 'incarceration.' The car didn't work anyway and they got it for free. I was really upset by this though. The video game would have been more of a functional gift. Something I could actually use.

Two things helped change my 'odd man out status' I felt I had among the guys. I lost my virginity, and we started smoking pot together. After the 3rd floor boys beat me up so much, I learned how to fight and grew in my physical awareness! Then I started to hang out on the 3rd floor. That 2nd year I got high 3 times a day and drunk 3 times a week. Every-time we had a home-visit somebody would come back with an ounce and some acid. A kid from New York was a rocker. He had acid all the time. It was a struggle to get him to share it though. I did get some once in a while. Every-time we went to the mall on a night outing we would pool our money together and buy pot. We usually got $20 per person each time we went out. We all had accounts for money that our guardians would give us.

One of my friends who is the BMC of the 3rd floor had a girlfriend too. She cheated on him and gave him an STD. I heard this from my girl. I told him and he asked me to keep my mouth shut. I got really drunk and high one night and told some people about it. As the end of my time at the school approached, it seemed that everyone hated me.

In fact, my girl told me often she wanted me to have sex with somebody else to see if I really loved her. At first I thought she was crazy. I'm thinking no way. There were some girls off campus who loved to hang out with us. We all had some sexual fun, smoked, drank and just had laughs. One of them really liked me and wanted to have sex with me. I refused for a while, but finally caved in thinking.

"OK! I will do what my on campus girl wants."

Some boys I fought with told her about my escapade. She broke up with me because she didn't like the girl I chose to have sex with. Hey she told me to do it! We had many talks about it. Another lesson in the insanity of girls.

I stopped going to class because I was very upset about losing my girl. I got in fights all day, Had to isolate myself just for safety, being monitored by staff all the time! Every-time I got into a fight, there would be kids coming out of everywhere to beat me up. I lost all privileges and all friends!

One night as I sat in my room just watching the window, I hear a conversation about the crazy therapy that I experienced with the people holding me down. Apparently some kid there had the same experience. I walked outside and said,

"I know everybody hates me. Please tell me about this because I went through it, too."

It's called the holding. He had it much worse than me. When he acted up, the school and police even had permission to administer this therapy to him. Strange world! As the conversation ends, they all walk away say stupid things to me:

"It's time to go now, Shane, before you get your ass kicked."

As they walk away some kid picks up a rock the size of my hand and throws it at me. In the darkness of night I didn't see it until it lands about 2 feet from me. Wow that was close. I look up and see two more coming at me from the boys as they walk away. I just watched them and moved out of their way, not turning my back to them until they were gone.

Later that week as I'm practicing basketball by taking my 500 jump shots a day, some kid walks up to me with brass knuckles in his hand in their proper position. He notices that I see them and doesn't seem to have the balls to start the fight. I'm running through my mind how to avoid the first swing and take his fucking head off. I even tell him:

"You have one shot. If you miss, I'm going to kick the shit out of you."

I have no fear of anybody, especially when it comes to fighting. I got it into my head that I would be dead by the time I'm 18 years old. So, I'm not taking any shit from anybody. Once I learned how to fight it was a no brainer. My level of violence was so much more intense than my attackers.

One time I beat this kid up bad. He was trying to build his rep by fucking with me. He went and got a fire extinguisher to slam against me. I walked right up to him turned around and told him:

"Go ahead! Take your shot. But if you don't knock me out, I'm going to kill you."

He didn't have the balls to do it.

My file rightly says I am violent; but I still restrain myself from reckless violence. During my last few days, a kid attacks me and we get in a fight. I pick him up and think to slam him against the tree. I see a broken stick protruding out of the tree. As I pick him up and begin to push him toward the tree I'm thinking:

"I can slam him against the tree and this stick will go through his body. Good."

At the last second I turn him away from the stick and throw him to the ground. In return, he eventually beats me up with help from some others. I'm removed from the school the next week. OK! Where to next?

CHAPTER 7

I spend some time at home in between schools only to be greeted with the same shit.

"Shane, you're a loser. You are fucking up your life. Why can't you work with the program? You've been kicked out of another school? You are going to end up with nothing."

Hello! I've gotten nothing from this family since age 6. With no chance of being anything since that day! Nobody who grows up like me is ever anything but a serial killer or a suicide victim.

To get out of the house I walk a few miles down the road to play basketball. Basketball is the only thing I love doing these days. I play every day.

On one occasion this girl walks onto my court and starts to shoot around with me. We start talking about who I am, what I'm doing and why I'm not in school. I tell her some stuff. We meet again the next day to shoot the ball and shoot the crap. Then –OMG –we realize we're related. She is the daughter of my biological father's brother. Strange fucking world we live in. Crazy things happen that Hollywood can't even write.

I walk back home with her to her house. Walking in I met her dad, who recognizes me instantly. We talk a little about my parent's divorce court hearing, and my early years. He knew me until I was age 2. Two days later I have dinner with my biological dad whom I have not seen since I was a child. I know I briefly met him at a school but I didn't remember what he looked like. This brief meeting happened because my therapist found his file and must have contacted him. One day while walking up from school, I ran by to say hello to her. Later she told me the guy standing next to her was my bio dad. She told him that he could say hello but he couldn't say who he was. I have a real hard time remembering people's names; I've met too many people. I do not tell my parents about this, until a family meeting at my next school.

My case worker flies me up north to some small town and a new school. I'm in 'fuck you' mode already. The school is in the middle of nowhere – heavily wooded area, very pretty. We begin the initial interview meeting, the one with the standard questions, blah, blah, and blah. I put my feet up on the table in passive defiance. The woman sitting in front of me tells me in such a manner as to take my feet down. She looks me right in the eye and we just stare for a second. I take my feet down.

The meeting is less than 20 minutes. Some questions later, she stands up and says,

"I will take him. We were going to put you in a different dorm but I want this kid in my house."

I said something sarcastic and she laughed. I'm told there is no room for me right now but the second a spot opens, I'm there. Two weeks later I'm on a flight back! *Oh boy, back to that bitch who likes provoking me!*

My mother hands me some garbage bags to pack my clothes in for the plane ride. It's not my first flight. I'm almost in tears at the idea of walking up to board a plane with garbage bags instead of a suitcase. Finally, she takes me behind the local grocery store and says,

"If you don't want to use garbage bags, then climb in the dumpster and get a few boxes out. You can place your stuff in there."

When my social worker picks me up, he has a few duffel bags with him. "Your mother told me she wasn't giving you anything but garbage bags." We switched my stuff from the boxes to the duffel bags.

I arrive and settle into my dorm room by emptying the clothes from the duffel bags. Everybody is playing softball. There are three dorms on campus: one for street tough kids; one for younger and other problem kids; the last one for highly intelligent kids. Nobody in my dorm has an IQ under 130. It would not be fair to put anybody in this dorm that was not equipped. They would not be able to adapt to the level of mind games we all played. New thing for me, I've never been able to use my brain. Just constantly fighting for myself! In fact, at the last school my vocabulary was so poor and my reading level so low that my friends made me read books before I could smoke pot. They asked me to recite what I was reading to them.

This school has intense therapy, group, social, and private. There is a level system just like the others and based on how well you cooperate. You can't even talk to anybody who is in trouble. If you are caught, you get a dealing group. You can't talk to anybody who is at a low level, if you are at a low level, it is called building a contract. The only way you can have these conversations is if somebody is monitoring these talks.

If you break the major rules you get put in the corner or worse, isolated into a small room with a person sitting there watching you at the same time, until your sentence is over or until you get dealt with. No sex, no drugs, or violence. Any violation of these and it's an instant group meeting where you get dealt with. A dealing group has the one being punished in the front of the house; every person then gets up in your face and screams at you all at the same time. It was not uncommon to have 20 people in your face screaming at you.

No physical contact between boys and girls. You can shake hands once in a while but only on a special occasion. All conversations between boys and girls must have a high level 3rd party witness. There is a head count made every 15 minutes during the day and night showing where everybody is all day long.

Education school is at night for 4 hours. Some kind of group or social therapy happens during the day. No walls in the dorms.

All rooms are connected by a long hallway with rooms off to the sides. Girls on the opposite side of the hall! There is a wall and a full hallway separating the girls and boys, but once you enter any of the boy's dorms you are in another hallway.

If you break the violence rule you get put into a circle with boxing gloves and you get to fight another kid who is bigger than you. Everybody stands in a circle holding hands so you are stuck in this circle for 2 minutes. If you beat him, they will put another kid in there until you lose. Your room is inspected everyday and your bed has to be made a special way. If it's not, you get dealt with. If your space is a mess you get dealt with. The kids get to be the security, kids are making the headcounts and kids monitor the exits. In order to leave the building you need staff permission, and that permission is followed up on before you get let out. All of this is written down in a shorthand log. At night the kids are also the security to make sure people don't run away. This short hand log is then written long hand and filed into a cabinet. All dealt with incidents are logged. All personnel activities are written down.

There are groups that deal with daily activities. The kitchen group gets the food for meals, then sets the tables, clears the tables, washes the dishes. These meals are held in our private dorms. The food is picked up in the main kitchen where kids cook our food. Each dorm supplies three kids for kitchen duty. There is a cleaning group, often made up of the kids who have been given some sort of punishment. Plus the supervisory level of the group. These places change depending on your position in the house. Moving from one group to the other is common as well as up and down the positions in said groups depending on your levels. The program lasts 18 months on average. I was there 23 months before they kicked me out.

It was a mentally intense program. Everything you say and do is monitored so closely that you learn so much about yourself and others. The first thing they do when you arrive is strip you down, break you down and destroy all false bravado and self images. Girls aren't allowed to wear makeup, for months. Boys lose all tough guy clothes and image stuff. I had my long hair cut off short. I actually cried that day. An outside barber came in once a month to cut hair. If she wasn't so sweet and nice about it, I might have refused. She just told me it will grow back.

We were not allowed to talk to our parents for the first three months. No mail. No phone calls. Nothing! Then we had this meeting with them and our support person. Then a weekend visit in town. Group meetings are crazy. If you have any issues during the week or day, you drop an anonymous note in a box with your reason and who you're confronting! Twice a week we're split up into groups according to these issues; the staff and upper level kids decide which issues are worth dealing with. A kid is always present during these organizational meetings. All staff members have advanced degrees in social work, therapy, psychology etc. By the time I got to this upper level I had learned so much about the mind and psychology. Again, my PHD please…

CHAPTER 8

We sit in our chairs in a circle of only 10 feet diameter. One staff is assigned to each group. My dorm was broken up into 3 groups of 10 or 12 each with mixed sexes and ages. We are all around 16. The moment the group opens, the fun begins. Grab your chair and hold on; unload at the top of your lungs. Anything you want to say to somebody who has caused you some sort of angst is fair game. Wow! What a shock. We can say anything we want in any form, any language. Only you cannot scream over another person; one must wait their turn. We deal with one issue at a time involving two persons at a time. Once all feelings are dispersed we move on to the next pissed off couple. Once this is all done issues are resolved calmly. What fun!

I don't even know the rules until after the first week. I get in more dealing groups because I talk to anybody I want to. There's a beautiful red headed girl that I keep trying to talk to which only gets me in trouble.

"This school will straighten you out," one girl says while we're at the beach. (Though I can swim, I don't have a bathing suit yet. There is a lake down at the bottom of the hill).

This unknown-to-me girl is just sucking up to the director, who sitting not 10 feet is away listening to her crap. She is also in a low level because she is a bitch.

My response: *"Honey, I've destroyed every school I've ever been to. This will be no different. Give me time; this is what I do best."*

A year later when I became high level in this school, I would have dealt with anybody who said such an arrogant thing so quickly and swiftly they wouldn't dare speak like that again. I have no idea why the director didn't deal with me that day. (She was my 'shoes on the table-stare me down'- lady from the first interview! Lol).

I sat at a table later the next day bragging about why I was kicked out of my last school. I gave some antagonistic quotes just to get responses. Within seconds the director gets up, and says at the top of her lungs:

"Can I have Shane knocking in 20 seconds."

What the fuck does that mean? I am escorted down the hall and told the order of my next experience. Ok done and done. Four people sit in chairs yell at me one at a time. Each person has a topic they focus on. That was fun, off to clean the bathroom as a punishment!

I remember a person sitting in the corner facing that corner. *"Why is he there?"*

He refuses to work in the program.

I'm so confused. A 20 page thesis would only begin to explain how this place works. Within a week, I'm standing in the middle of the dorm with my house director standing on a chair poking me in the chest! She later told me that my file said I was so violent; she wanted to find out how violent. She realized that I wasn't violent in that moment.

I'm now getting screamed at by everybody in the dorm, I'm trying to keep from crying. After the first salvo, I'm in complete 'fuck you' mode. She asks,

"How do you feel about women, Shane?"

I'm trying to piss her off. *"I hate them as a species."* It sounded good at the time. Oops!

Next thing I know, all the girls are screaming in my face. The director puts the two highest pitched, loudest girls on each side of me to yell in my ears not 5 feet away. It would be a few minutes before I could hear clearly again. Great, now I'm cleaning toilets on my hands and knees. That's my punishment. I get to clean toilets with brushes and cleaning supplies, I've again lost the privilege of shoes and I'm cleaning bathrooms all day long for like 6 hours a day for 3 days.

I get some privileges back eventually and now it's time to deal with my mouth. I still swear every other word. So I am told I have to make this cardboard sign that is the size of my body. The sign reads

"Please ask me why..."

Then I have to add the sentence that will cause my classmates to ask me why I swear so much.

"Hell, no! I'll sit in the corner."

I last 3 days then I break down and ask for my sign so I can circulate back into the society. I wear that sign for a month. The string that attaches it to my neck broke a few times. I had to rewrite it over and over again. Most signs last 10 days. Mine? 4 weeks! It would be the last sign I would wear.

Sometimes two or more people will contract and agree to get things accomplished together, like having sex with someone or smoking a joint or getting alcohol on campus. It works like this, we are watching a movie as a house. The kid doing the headcount comes up to me and tells me he can't find one of the girls and one of the guys. The movie is almost over I ask him to go through the dorms to see if any of the screens are broken, indicating somebody jumped out. He comes back nope all intact, I look down the hall-way to make sure the security kid is sitting at his post near the exit door. The movie is almost over so I'm not gonna stop it and call a house meeting. When the movie ends if those 2 don't come to the living room as we prepare for bed then I will investigate further. In reality what happened was the security kid is sitting in front of a closet that holds all our cleaning materials. The guy and girl in question are inside the closet having sex. He covered for them, hiding their location for 2 cycles of our 15 minute headcount. It normally takes 2 to 3 ppl to get something like that accomplished. This would eventually be found out because "when you break the rules in one manner, you break the rules in other ways" as well. Stop making your bed nicely or stop being productive in the system indicates usually that something is awry. If you pay attention to the little details, you will find out the root of it all. It all comes out in the wash, is a slogan at this school.

The first parent's meeting was designed to allow the open expression of my feelings toward them. I soon began to swear and get loud. My step-dad says,

"You can't swear at your mother like that."

What I find quite interesting about this is many years later, my step brother who is still living at home in his late 20's, swears at my mom, even calls her a bitch right to her face. Apparently she simply didn't buy the right kind of food he likes. He does not pay rent or help with bills. His father says nothing and does nothing.

In that first parent's meeting, he physically threatened me for saying similar things. I always remember this moment when I hear him treating my mom in a similar manner in front of me. It's one reason why I stopped going to family functions during my later years. I neither could handle the violent drama of his treatment toward my mother, nor the general disarray in which he would leave the whole house during holidays. I preferred to travel out of the country for all American holiday weekends.

I look to my staff members in the room and they didn't seem to back me up. I back down for a second but shortly I'm loud and screaming again. I told them about seeing my biological dad. We talked after, went on a weekend visit at my uncles cabin nearby. I didn't go home very often from this school. I volunteered to not go home during holidays because there had to be some upper level kids staying to watch the kids who were in that 3 month period of no family contact. I told my family that I lost the 'draw straws' contest. In fact, I volunteered so that some other kid who had a much better family life than me could go home.

I signed up to go-to this basketball camp that hosts scouts from all over the country. The school had set it up for me. The week before I was supposed to go, I got a letter saying that we didn't pay for the whole week yet. Just the deposit! I was assured that the program costs would be paid.

I was very upset. I was trying to get myself to college and out of this fucking hell I've lived in so long. I don't know anything else. I just walk out of the phone conference with my guardians and caseworker! In about 20 minutes the staff came out.

"We are going to pay for the rest of the bill."

It was a fun week of basketball. I do have mad skills, plus I am the only kid there who could dunk at will. Some scouts came over the first day and asked me what school I was from, But the second I told them the school name, I was no longer the topic of interest. Apparently, they attempted to take another athlete from this same school years earlier; this kid just became violent and had to be arrested from the *juco* school. They weren't going to take another chance on me.

This was a huge disappointment. After the first day's games, I was the talk for about an hour then they lost interest. The camp became my forum to prove myself. Unfortunately, my aggressive style –often attacking kids and staff on the court with my game –did not benefit me! Later that week I blasted "Two Live Crew" outside my window so that everybody could hear it. One staff came into my room and physically threatened me right to my face! That was progress for me, because just two years earlier I would have just kicked the shit out of him as a simple blind reaction to his threat. I just laughed at him, turned the radio off and said I was sorry.

I was the dorms entertainment each night. It was a college campus and my stories from all my time in schools and foster homes were the subject of great entertainment for my dorm. They were so popular that my room was packed each night with kids standing in the halls marveling at my life stories. In the interest of this book and its length, I'm not just writing school stories for entertainment's sake. Maybe I will write another book just of 'Stories from Schools and Foster Homes along the Way...' Someday.

The day I was leaving for my week long basketball camp, a kid was scrubbing the same four one foot square tiles in the middle of the living room. He was a huge run away risk so he had to be monitored. Since I was now the top student in the dormitory, I was privy to the staff meetings. The staff often asked for and respected my opinion when it came to the way kids are broken down and built back up again. The director of my house even gave me her outline of her PHD thesis and asked me to give her my opinion. After restructuring it a little we talked; she actually agreed with my ideas. I really enjoyed this process.

I have so much experience and knowledge into people now. In a good mood, I felt this kid after 3 days could handle doing something other than spending all day on his knees in the center of the living room. I call him off to the side to ask him

"How do you feel? What is your next course of action going to be?"

I'm satisfied with his response and, although I did not give him his shoes back, I did allow him more interaction in the house. I then call over a lower lever kid who has been trying to work hard to move up the ladder. He has no real responsibilities and so I drop the responsibility of watching this kid all day long to make sure he doesn't run away.

"Just keep an eye on him when the house is busy, so he doesn't run away."

When I return from basketball camp, I find out he ran away on the second day and was still missing. Within a week or so, we find out that his body was found in the woods a few miles away. Apparently he had met a local girl who sort of adopted him. She gave him shoes and fed him while he hung out around her house. He had a .357 bullet put through his chest. The father was the prime suspect but, strangely in these country towns, you can get away with just about anything. This particular town had a bunch of unsolved murders in it. It was a small town. I cannot shake the feeling even to this very day that I cost this kid his life by letting him have some privileges back instead of leaving him scrubbing those 4 tiles until I got back from camp.

A game we called, 'Watch and Write' became a very fun pastime amongst me and my friends. Because of my vast experience dealing with people– especially troubled kids, I'm the best profiler I've ever met. When a new kid arrived, boy or girl, my friends and I would sit in a table in the back and observe for 5 minutes. After watching I would begin to write everything I thought about this person. Whether they were molested by a man or woman; whether they were violent, or used drugs and which kinds. What type of relationship they had with their parents. What types of siblings they had and how they got along. What birth order in their family of origin. How intelligent they were. What types of games they would play in the house to get themselves established. Who they would become friends with!

It was fun until the director of the house caught me! My punishment was an upper dichotomy student knock. Since you are only allowed to knock in front of your peers, my knock was an all PHD staff giving me a verbal reprimand. It was so loud the whole house heard it.

As insightful as I thought I was, these adults were much more. The game was now forbidden. I will add, however, that the reason this game became so popular was because my accuracy was above 90% correct– with just 5 minutes of watch time. The game was around before my time and probably rises up again from time to time. The director frowns upon it; she even took one kid's chess set away from him for doing the same thing just a few months before my arrival. Smart woman... It wasn't long before I was running the house. I would keep track of all the kids and learn how to psychologically build people up in the proper manner, working with both families and staff. My fellow students felt I was power hungry; who knows? Maybe I was.

Applications for college were due and I really wanted some guidance from my staff. I didn't get any which bothered me a lot. I asked more than once. I ultimately lied about sending my application in to a local school and said I got a letter of acceptance back. I told them the acceptance was sent to my parent's house. Nobody really did a follow up. I did notice that my graduation date corresponded with the first week of classes in that college. When they finally pressed me about the letter, I had to say I lied. This was the beginning of the end of my time at this school. In addition to all this, I eventually broke down the physical barrier with a girl. This came out at the same time as my college lie blew up. I got busted down to nothing, and then reacted as usual –by trying to destroy all that was around me. I got sent to a corner in another dorm and was kicked out of the school after 23 months.

CHAPTER 9

My family comes to get me. The plan is to move back with them after so many years away. I get this bullshit story about how we are a complete family and how they are so happy I'm home. We talk about how I'm going to get half of the downstairs for my bedroom with my own entrance into the house. They have a raised ranch with a garage entrance. Ok! Getting my own space for once will be nice.

I apply to the local college and actually get accepted. I'd like a chance to play ball at college even if it's just for fun at a d2 school. I have no idea how to relate to my step brothers or my parents. Within a week my room size gets reduced down to the size of a shoe box. It's so small I can't even get a normal desk. I have to get a corner desk. My bed is really tiny, too. The room was like 6 feet wide by 7 feet long. The twin bed barely fit in the room. This really depressed me. There was no discussion letting me know I was getting a smaller room. I was done that day with this finally and the 'real family' crap.

Additionally, my mother made me feel so guilty about not having a job. I had no choice but to take a job working at McDonald's on the highway where they could accommodate a flexible schedule. All I really wanted was some time to collect my thoughts, go-to college and play some basketball; to have some kind of normal life.

The women who ran the last school warned me.

"Shane, you are going to have a hard time relating to people your own age when you get out. You've experienced more than most people will ever experience in their whole life. You won't be able to relate to people until they catch up to you. Life will be better for you when you get to your 40's."

I was only 19 at the time.

She was the one who taught me to use my intellect instead of my physical size, telling me "It's time to learn how smart you are and stop reacting like a child."

She often gave me books to read with special topics and scheduled movie seminars for us. It wasn't long before I realized, yes, I am brilliant and somebody does care. Actually she was the best female role model I ever had.

She walked into the dorm one day with a huge handful of files. She throws 10 files on the table and one file next to those. The 2 piles were the exact thickness, one file versus 10. She says:

"Shane, come here. These are 10 people's files stacked together. The other file is just yours alone. Notice yours is as thick as the pile of 10 people." She continued her admonition. "You need to develop your intellect so people can stop talking about you. I've been dealing with you for almost 2 years now. It's quite clear to me that no one ever took the time to actually get to know you. This is the shit you have been dealing with your entire life. In one part of this file it says you're a complete sociopath."

(To date I have not killed anybody, only a few chickens on a farm).

The local college began with a freshmen orientation weekend and, unfortunately, I had to take two days off from work to attend. I drive this old mustang car that starts hard but is cool and fun to drive. I really wanted a jeep, but my dad controlled the purchase so that's what I got. The weekend orientation was very hard for me; nobody really talked to me at the BBQ lunch and dinner. In the dorms my roommates didn't talk to me either. I just cried in my car alone that day.

The words of the director came back to me. She was right. First, I didn't realize that the whole world was not alpha males. Secondly, my thoughts during the mini classes we had did not impress my fellow students. I got ridiculed for some ideas I expressed. My teachers really loved me and took an interest in me. They asked many things about me when we were walking in and out of these little sessions.

I didn't want to go back to school after that weekend. I never felt so alone in such a long time. During the tryout session and some practices the team becomes friends. The center for our team has a baby brother who was in the school I just left. I just laugh at this knowledge like: Are you kidding me?? The world couldn't be any smaller! I played basketball with his brother all the time. He arrived just a few months before I left...

My parents were on my case about getting more hours to make more money from work. I just gave up on basketball which made me even more depressed. I ultimately had to quit basketball, because I couldn't juggle work and school and home and basketball at the same time. If I wasn't at work or at school, I was sleeping in my room. This gave my mother more ammo that only made me feel worse. She would tell me how much a loser I was – just sleeping all day. What was worse is when I went to class I just walked into the library and slept all day too.

During the first few months at college I did make an effort to go to classes. I was excited about learning and the chance to have control of my life. I enrolled in all the required freshmen classes including Biology 101. The first day of lab we are scheduled to dissect animals. As I walk into class I see cats all strung up on the desks. The teacher says, "Anybody who is uncomfortable dissecting cats can leave the room. However, the next time we have this type of class, you will not be able to leave class."

Since I'm in depression mode I take this chance to leave the class. I walk out of class and head toward the staircase exit when I see 'Fonzy', the guy who beat me up for telling him his love was cheating on him with me in the second school I went to. Our eyes meet and we recognize each other instantly.

"Don't say anything stupid," I say to him, *"because I'm not as small as I was then. I will kick the living shit out of you in seconds."*

He is making out with some girl, standing against the wall pressing his body against her. To his credit, he didn't say a word. I would have unloaded 14 years of anger on him. Soon after full blown deep depression hits and I sleep my first college experience away.

I met a great girl while working at McDonald's. We got along so well. She was sweet and kind and made me feel like a normal person. We went to movies and had some fun at work. I drove up a few times to see her at school. I got in a bunch of fights with my parents; it never even occurred to me to tell them I was going to my girlfriend's house for the weekend. I've never had to check with anybody what where and how I do things since I was 6 years old. I just did it, most of the time. This didn't go over very well.

"Get out, Shane. Get your own apartment."

Ok that's good, because I don't want to be here anyway.

I was even willing to give up on college and get a full time job. McDonald's offered management classes. I asked my parents to co-sign a loan for a new reliable car.

"Nope. We can't take that risk for you." They did for my brother just a few years later.

My old car eventually broke down. I was living with my girlfriend after she graduated college. She lived in an apartment owned by her father. She was in fact, quite wealthy which I did not know for almost a year.

I went back to college to start over since I failed out the first attempt. As a part-time student I took just 10 credits a semester. But I did get straight A's. I was taking law and political science classes. I wanted to be a lawyer.

I took a test home to my parents– my first straight A's grade. My parents looked at me and said, "Your girlfriend made that up and she graded it."

Nice. I just laughed and walked out of the house.

My girl's family had a summer house on an island near the coast where I lived. The single house - single island could only be used during a few months of the year. I spent a lot of my summertime there. Being there was a necessary way to refresh myself and recover. I really enjoyed my time in this place, and being around the family.

The second year dating her I learned her mother had a multiple personality disorder. As she moved back closer to home to get her Master's degree in education, her personality changed. She developed a multiple personality disorder as well which was triggered by proximity to her mother. I didn't notice it very often the first year. I saw it a lot during the third year and we started to fight more. The first 2 and half years we never had an argument. It was nice to be around her. As our relationship deteriorated so did my school work. I had an internship with a local congressman, having some fun, when it all unraveled!

I didn't handle the break up well. I told my advisor my dad died and then dropped out of school. I traded my mustang in for a jeep. I got a job waiting tables just to pay my bills and to stay close to my girlfriend. I tried to keep my relationship! We did get along for a while, and even got engaged. In retrospect, I realized she felt sorry for me more than she loved me.

I got a second job at a grocery store to make more money and work a lot more. I was actually making good money. For some reason no matter how I try – and it's been this way all my life – either people love me or hate me. There is no in between.

The ones who don't like me always seem to have authority over my life in some way shape or form. I am not as nasty a person as people try to make me out to be. For example, I got drunk one night at a party in my apartment. I wasn't on the schedule so I didn't go to work. The schedule had been penciled in and changed after being printed on Friday. I wasn't working all weekend so I wasn't going to come in until Monday. When I got there Monday I was fired.

"You didn't show up for work. We don't care that you looked on Friday and the schedule was changed between then and Monday. You missed a scheduled work day."

I took my anger out on a boss at my next job when the parking policy was changed over the weekend as well. When I parked in the same spot I've parked in for a year, I got a ticket.

"Why did I get a ticket? Why did my boss call the cops on me and give me the ticket?"

He just looked at me and laughed. I got in his face, cussed him out and threatened him badly. I trashed the break room, walked out and was without a job all in a 24 hour span! I had to move back in with my girlfriend. She does let me but I have to sneak in and out and keep looking for a job.

We move into another of her father's apartments. Things are going well between us. I get another job; start to make some money again. Things seem to be going ok. We talk about getting married. We tell her father we are living together. The family puts pressure on her about me. Within two weeks of telling her father we live together, she looks at me and says:

"You have to leave. You have 2 weeks. You don't fit the lifestyle of my family. I can't date you anymore." A huge fight ensues. I punch the wall, walk out and I get another apartment.

I start to party and drink more with a college buddy of mine. He has a great apartment but is leaving to go-to college down south. He arranges with his landlord to let me rent his place. The apartment complex is full of bartenders and local band members. It's a fun scene: parties, drugs, girls, free concerts, and back stage passes.

I move in get settled and the girl is gone. One of my homeless friends gets arrested for credit card fraud. He asked me to help him out. Using the title of my jeep I bond him out. Not 3 months later he jumps bail and the bondsman takes my jeep. No car, no job and not long before I'm homeless.

During one night of drinking, in an attempt to get rid of a girl, we tell her I'm HIV positive. I didn't deny this. Before I know it, everybody thinks I actually am. I got so much attention from it that I didn't bother to correct anybody. We used to make all kinds of lies trying to pick up girls. If a guy said he went to the best college in the area that usually got him laid all the time.

I start to spend time with a girl who goes to one of the universities nearby. We met at the local coffee shop just hanging out. I go see her on campus and spend a few nights in the dorm. It's over the summer so nobody cares. As the school year starts we continue to see each other often. The R.A. calls the cops on me for spending too much time in the dorm. The cops pick me up and give me a warning.

The next day I go down to the President's office and find out the policies on visitors. I'm told non students can sleep over 4 nights a month; if not sleeping-over, non students have to be off campus by 1 a.m. I show her a copy of the lease on my apartment proving my address. I promise her I won't be on campus other than when I'm allowed. Ok we shake hands and she even apologizes for the misunderstanding.

The next night I go on campus to hang out, walk in and sign in properly. I tell the R.A. about my conversation with the dean. No problem, be out by 1 am. We walk up to her floor and the floor R.A. sees me. Apparently the floor R.A. and my girl don't get along very well. In fact, they hate each-other. The dean didn't communicate our early conversation to her, the head R.A. of the dorm.

I get flat out arrested; spend the night in jail for trespass. I'm let out the next day, on a PTA court date. Not bad. I'm pissed. I go down to the Dean's Office and ask her why she didn't tell her head R.A. I spent the night in jail and have a court date after I did everything I was asked to do. She calls the cops. They don't arrest me just tell me I'm not allowed back on campus ever again.

After losing my job and my car I began to lose everything. I'm homeless and need to get a life again. I go back home to my parents who found out I'm 'HIV positive'. They challenged me about being HIV positive and I'm forced to admit the lie. Not a good time. But hey, it all comes out in the wash. It was a destructive lie. When I became homeless I had to go back and beg for help. There was a lot of yelling and screaming and having to admit it all. My parents just bought a house as a rental property so I worked for them every day. My mother kept a log of how many hours I worked each day. Eventually when they got renters, I would get money for the apartment and get myself settled again. So I worked.

I started to use the gym down stairs in the basement. By now my small room walls were all gone. I shared a room with my bother sleeping on the top bunk. I was working out on a regular schedule. Staying away from everybody as much as possible knowing this isn't going to last long before it all blows up again. We will never get along for very long.

Soon I see my dad driving by the apartment each day in the company truck he uses. My mother drops me off each day on her way to work. They check my progress each day, making sure I am working. I was and did work hard on the renovations of this house. The first tenant moves in with her very attractive daughter. I flirt with her and we talk sometimes. Her mother is a nice woman and we get along, too. Sometimes I stop by after work before I go home just to talk. I was allowed to use the family truck some days. Other days I would walk or get dropped and picked up. It was going ok. I was just trying to make money, get sorted out and then get my life back on track.

I started to see my child psychiatrist just to keep the peace in the family. My mother made it a demand for letting me back into the house. It was really weird to go see the same guy I was seeing when I was 4 years old. We just talked. By now I've had so many therapy sessions in my life it's like a broken record. It was nice to talk to somebody who was actually listening to me even if he was being paid. In my experience nobody ever asks me or tries to talk with me; instead, they just make suppositions about me and then talk about those suppositions. I concluded there's no point talking to someone who isn't really listening to you.

Most of the time everybody is twisting my words around against me, adding things and telling me I said and did things without ever asking me or including me in the conversation. This infuriates me and lets me know people can't be trusted to care, so why bother telling them. When I was 14 I started to spin my therapists just for fun. I know all the jargon, all the motivating psycho analysis of every walk of life with motivating factors. I enjoyed working my therapists over, setting them up with stories and thoughts over weeks of therapy. Then without warning I would change the story all up again! It became my only joy in these sessions. I was very good at it.

The trick I learned, since all staff had some kind of degree in varying forms of child behavior, is to make the daily staff think something totally different. So during the staff discussions with our therapists nothing would match. I even got very good at making my facial expressions and body language say the complete opposite of what my head and heart are thinking at the same time causing even more confusion!

STOP fucking psychoanalyzing me, people!

By the time I was out of schools, I had had 16 years of intense therapy on many levels.

It wasn't long before the accusing and arguing began at home. I got my first body piercing. I invited the girl to come with me to get it done. She blew me off and after, I stopped by to say hi. She was pregnant and I wanted to make sure she was ok. It was not mine. Her mother was the only one there. I wanted to hide the event from my parents as long as possible. I parked down the street when I came back and walked up to the apartment. My dad was still there working on it. When he left he saw the truck. That was a huge fight when I got back home.

"Shane's sneaking around again."

I didn't say a word. As usual better to get yelled at for the not talking and playing dumb, then to have to deal with follow up questions until I can't keep my eyes open anymore. Besides I'm so used to being yelled at and in trouble, it doesn't faze me anymore. Just blame everything on me. Nothing I say or do will ever change this fact, Shane is always the cause of everybody's problems – somehow someway! I think it's comical.

Sometime that week my dad drives by while I'm on the porch talking to the girl. Actually she asked me to help build something for her that her mom just bought. Seriously I was on the porch for about 5 minutes before he drove up. So he walks up and begins to accuse me of spending all my days talking and not working. I give him the "whatever."

He gets in my face to yell at me and attempt to intimidate me. This is not going to work with me. After all I've been through not having any parents for 80% of my life. Nobody intimidates me. He grabs me and I just laugh at him. He then slaps me.

You got to be kidding me. Now you want to play dad?

No chance! I slapped him right back. He tried to grab me. I spun him around and threw him off the porch. I was actually surprised he didn't fall over. He comes at me again and tries to escalate the violence. My memory of the day that I watched him as an alcoholic being abusive to my mother –when he was punching on her in the kitchen as she crawled under the table– flashed through my mind. This is my chance for payback.

I grabbed him, pushing him up against the company truck.

"Do you really want a piece of me?" I pull his shirt over his head and raise my fist to hit him in the face. I chose not to. *"You're too old to try this with me. Next time I won't hold back."*

He says," You are done."

He turns and walks into the unfinished apartment and locks the door on me. Solid door. No matter. Four punches and I punch right through the door. (He had done the same thing to me many years ago but through a hollow door. I locked him out of my room after I got suspended from school causing them to remove my locks after that). I walked in, got my stuff and walked out. He picks me up walking toward home up and informs me: "It's time to move out."

Yup, got that right.

During this transition time I'm not allowed to use the weight system anymore in the basement. A few weeks later and I land a job at a pet store and find an apartment. My job is on the busline so I don't need a car. I found out there was a birthday party for my 18-year old step brother at my parent's house. My youngest step brother had his own phone line and we talked sometimes. He asked me if I was coming to the party. I did not know there even was a party. They scheduled it on the weekend of his birthday and not on the actual birthday.

I take the train to my parent's town and walk to their house. I bought a gift for my brother. My step dad is visibly upset that I am there. When he questioned me how I found out, I told him the other brother told me about it. Apparently I ruined his plans for his son simply by showing up! I find out some time later that the brother who told me about the party got grounded and lost the privilege of his phone line for a month, even though he paid for the line with his own money......My family.

CHAPTER 10

I got a nice apartment and began my new job. Before long I ran into a guy with whom I used to work. We started smoking pot every day. Doesn't bother me. I love playing basketball while stoned! Pot makes me sleep easier, too, but it does spend my money of which I don't have a lot.

I start to get along with the owner of the store- even talk about possibly being a manager. I can make some extra money; get a car maybe start chasing girls again. I worked there for about a year. I got a few more piercings but by now they don't feed the addiction the way they did at first. So I start getting penis piercings. I love them! I got a little carried away and got 10 of them in my dick. My boss then disrespects me. I was hurt and frustrated at the way I was being treated. I set up his entire fish cleaning system with special UV cleaners and even showed him the distributers. For a few years I worked while I was in college. I set up 2 new stores for him, and then all of a sudden I was at the bottom of the totem pole again.

I moved to a new job working for a Non Profit organization doing fundraising which required canvassing towns in the area. It was fun but not what the job had advertised. I was frustrated and bored. I go-to these houses in the city; it's our neighborhood for the night. I go to a door, give my spiel to the women who answers it and she says

"My husband is not around. Come back another time if you can."

I walk away head to the next house give my spiel get a donation. Next house, repeat. As I go to the third house, I see a man who is following me listening to me at each house. I finally turn and ask, *"Hey what's up?"*

"You are very good on your feet", he says, "and you're a smart thinker. Your spiel is good. I work on Wall Street. You could do what you are doing now and get paid a lot more money." He hands me his business card. "If you want to talk give me a call."

Yeah, ok. Whatever! I've got work to do.

At the end of the night the kid in charge of our office is kind of a jerk to me. I walk outside, find a pay phone and call him. Sure I'm game what do I have to do?

He gives me an address and says, "Show up Monday at 9 a.m. That's your shot."

Dressed in a suit, I show up to a room with 15 other guys dressed like me. Geesh! I hate being ordinary. They give their pitch and then say each of us will get a 5 minute interview and see what happens. After waiting, my turn finally arrives. I am escorted across the floor and into his office.

"What did you think of my pitch", he asked me?

I tell him. You need to improve your tactic and the style of the approach. I give him some pointers. He listens.

"That's not what I meant."

I told him it's the same thing I was doing for a nonprofit organization, and I wasn't making any money. If the whole world is only after money and there isn't any justice, if it's all about who has the money and power, then I want my slice.

He says, "Come back tomorrow and you can start working."

The company approach for the sales staff is cold calls. I make an average of 400 calls a day. I attempt to get information from people about what and how they invest in the stock market. Later, my boss will follow up and try to sell them stocks. It's fun and I'm very good at it. I find it easy to break down people's walls after what I've been through. Four weeks later and I'm taking classes run by the firm to study for my Series Seven license.

This lifestyle is insane. Drugs are everywhere on Wall Street. If they actually did a drug bust, there wouldn't be enough people left to ring the bell the next morning. Yet my boys get arrested all the time for drugs and dealing. I learn another lesson in life. If you're making the system money, the rules don't apply anymore.

We would go-to bars after work and do coke lines in the bar on the bar. Pop pills and drink drinks. I even got paid to whip out my piercings in 'broker only' bars. Expensive suits and we have to smoke a joint at lunch just to calm the nerves down. Pills and speed for breakfast; downers after lunch, and coke for the early evening! No joke! It's that crazy.

The secretaries all dress like prostitutes; the owner of the firm who flew to work in a helicopter has a former stripper for a secretary. They even want to fly me to their favorite brothel in Vegas to let the girls get a hold of my piercings.

After a night of partying and a few too many drinks, I miss the last train. I'm stuck at the station waiting for the morning train. As I sit there among many people in a similar predicament, I read my book passing the time. A smoking hot woman walks by with a hickey on her neck. She is hot, I don't care about the mark. I wait for my chance.

When we are let into the station, we all wait near the tracks. I strike up a conversation with her. We sit in the same seat on the train. I enjoy watching her try to cover up the hickey. I'm sick of stupid girls so I drilled her on topics that have nothing to do with material possessions. She passes. I give her my work number. (I can't afford a real telephone number in my apartment with the rent and the monthly train passes. Plus I smoke pot quite often).

We go out the next week. She sleeps over and that's it: we don't spend another night apart for many months. I ran out of money feeding my pot need. My rent wasn't getting paid and my train pass was running out. I forged a train pass to get my ride in and out of the city. I get caught and I can't think of anybody to call except my new girlfriend. By morning I'm bailed out.

Because I never went to my other PTA, I have two cases pending now.

I head off to work after missing a few days for this mess. They find out about my arrest walk up to me ask for my key card and ask me to leave. Crap! Only two weeks before I take my Series 7 license. Now I have nothing, again.

The girl and I get an apartment; for a while I'm just living off her while trying to find a job. We have lots of fun together. We go-to beaches, smoke pot, go-to concerts and play a lot! I even teach her to play basketball! We had pit seats to see *Rage Against the Machine* with *Wutang*. Her first and only pit!

We also saw U2, our favorite band with bus tour tickets for the best 50% seats of the show! Our bus arrived first in the parking lot. Remember, my *modus operandi* is to sit in the back so nobody can get behind me. Lol!

I'm watching the guy give out tickets from a stack he has In hand. Each packet has elastic bands around them. I realize each elastic pack has specific seats in them. At the bottom of the stack is a very thin pack with an elastic band around it, too. I grab my girlfriend and tell her to wait until we're the last ones off the bus. She doesn't want to listen to me so I actually grab her shirt from behind and explain to her my observation.

"Those bottom tickets are probably front row seats or very close."

The 'ticket master' is black as is my hot girlfriend. I tell her

"He isn't going to give front row seats to a group of more than 2. Since we're just 2 people, we're getting off last. He got on our bus first. He might give us front row seats if you quietly ask him for tickets off the bottom of the stack."

'No way,' she says.

I then pinch her and tell her: *"I'm not black and I'm not hot. Trust me. He will give you great seats."*

Apparently I failed to tell her about my prowess at Watch and Write from boarding school. She does what I ask. He then pulls the stack off the bottom which only has 4 tickets. He hands us two tickets and I tell her, *"Don't even look; just walk."*

Another passenger who got off already saw our quiet exchange and asked for great seats, too. He says "I don't have any more, I gave you tickets already."

We got front row seats for the show at Giants stadium. It would not be our last front row U2 concert. The next two shows, our tickets were for inside the circle. Amazing shows! Anybody who wants to experience a great concert with lots of energy won't be disappointed to lose a day's sleep and wait all night after buying General Admission seats to a U2 show to go inside the heart / circle.

We would get really high once in a while that would inevitably result in nasty arguments. Some of the arguments ended up in physical fights. Sure I'm bigger and stronger but by no means was I the only one being physical! We fought about once a month. I never punched her but I did slap her a few times, even leaving bruises on her legs from it. If I've been smoking frequently and I am not high, I get really moody.

I got a traffic ticket from an accident we had; I went to court to protest it. I was arrested; no bail.

CHAPTER 11

The family policy about arrests is that kids, if arrested are on their own. The family might visit us, but we would have to deal with the consequences on our own. I'm sitting in the cell thinking everything I do and touch turns to shit. I'm just sick of it always crashing around me.

I sit down and pray, "God if you save me from my lifestyle, I will serve you for the rest of my life." Later I'm sent to the bigger jail house. No problem. I get sent to the holding cells for processing. The last one called out of the cell, I get a photo taken and sent to the shower for a full body strip down and shower.

"WTF are those? You can't have body piercings in your body while in jail."

I have to remove them all. Ok, not easy but doable. Now on to a block which is not a real jail just the city processing block where people stay until their sentencing. After 3 days I see the kid I told I had felt up that staff member that ultimately ended in a house meeting, with me explaining myself. He tells me he got arrested for putting a shotgun under somebody's chin and robbing them. I laugh a little at the thought of the similarities of it all: this block and my years in boarding schools!

I'm telling a kid the story of my prayer and he tells me I should get on my knees and make the same prayer to Jesus specifically.

"What am I supposed to pray?"

He tells me anything that I can remember. The only thing I can remember is the Lord's Prayer. Ok done with that. Now let's deal with my cases.

I get 30 days for the trespass case. Once sentenced I get sent out of the holding block up state. Fun bus ride in chains and lots of people! I'm just telling jokes to lighten the mood. Not everybody here is comfortable; you could see it in their eyes. This is old news for me.

Upon arrival we take off our clothes and get jail clothes. I can't even remember what they looked like. I just remember having to lose my clothes and get unfamiliar stuff. This is a level 4 jail with people who are working their way out. But, yes there are rapist and murderers in my block. It's a dorm setting; no walls, 8 blocks in total. Each block is isolated and can be locked down; 90 people per block. I'm trying to stay out of everybody's way until I sort out the rules– written and unwritten.

My first task is to get strings in my piercings holes so I can keep them, I take apart some of the strings in my blanket. Done, though everybody thought I was jerking off. I'm not there 4 hours and I'm being offered coke, heroin, and pot. It's all in the block, anything I want. A guy hands me a pair of shower shoes and says you'll need these. My first thought was, what do I owe you now? Surprisingly he never spoke to me again.

I first start by not saying anything. My bunkmate is getting out in a couple of days on some form of good behavior. He puts toilet paper in both his nostrils at night and even covers his mouth while sleeping.

"Why?" I ask after the 2nd night.

He informs me: "The day before you get out, you get a urine drug test. The other inmates often get jealous of you leaving, so they will put coke in your nose or in your mouth while you sleep so you fail the drug test."

Nice.

Late at night people take a shit in the toilet then sift through it with their hands looking for drugs. The drugs come in to prison during visits this way. When a visitor comes to see you, you go through a full strip search– naked with a bend over and spread your ass cheeks for the guards to look. Then you get one kiss with your visitor, usually a girlfriend who visits. This kiss isn't supposed to be tongue, but it is and it's not stopped. The females will pack balloons with drugs and tie them off. When they kiss their men, the men then swallow the balloons.

Since the visitors aren't known criminals, they can't be searched. They are not allowed to bring in any loose items. I found all this out from my girlfriend who came to visit me often. My parents didn't visit; even after my girlfriend went to their house to drop off my stuff and told them where I was. A few years later my brother gets arrested for passing counterfeit money in another state. My parents wake up the family lawyer at midnight and get him out of jail. He didn't spend one day in jail, proving once again that the rules for me are very different than the rest of the family!

Meals caused fear for me; I didn't know how they would go. I was asked to sit with some people. Unlike my movie induced stereotype, it was not as racially segregated as I thought it would be. Ironically, the person's crime was judged more harshly than the person's race. For example, one kid was in there for burning his son's hands on a hot electric stove. He was South American Spanish. He never lasted more than a day out of the infirmary before the other Spanish kids put him back in. They beat the shit out of him every time he got out, usually the same day. Apparently child abuse is not accepted even among murderers. Farting and walking by somebody else's bed is called a drive by. You will get beat up for this.

I decided I wanted to find out how good I was in basketball. Hey! I'm in prison and all they do is play basketball all day. I go out and start to play with the big boys. They can't stop me! Admittedly I couldn't dribble around them; they have fast hands and, being 6'5" my dribble is high. When I got in the block, however, or even the high post, they couldn't handle my spins and pumps. I have a 32" vertical leap. I can elevate and change directions. I'm actually very good, the only white guy on the court most of the days.

I also went to the library every day and got a few books. Hey why not read as many classics as I can. In fact, I read 42 books during my 2 ½ months in there. Greek philosophy, The Rise and Fall of the Third Reich, Alice in Wonderland just to name a few.

That my girlfriend was black caused a huge shock. Since I'm bald everybody thought I was a skinhead. When my own dorm mates saw how beautiful my girl was I got mad respect that day. A normal visit is 45 minutes in length. The guards take the slip with the visitor name and put it on top. When they get a new visitor, they take the slip put it on top, and then take the bottom slip and declare your visit over. On this Saturday, my visit lasted 2 hours. I realize the guard took my slip and moved it up as his shift change occurred, giving me another hour. Cool, I slickly told him thanks on the way by to the outdoor court.

Another crazy aspect of life in prison is everybody gets the same soap, unless you have money to buy separate stuff from commissary. They train the dogs to bark at the smell of the soap. So when the poorest ghetto bangers walk by the dogs bark at them all day long. I never went to the weight room unless I needed a hair cut! Not a safe place for me.

The showers are not communal; this was a surprise to me. We had curtains and private stalls with a rubber grate on the bottom. The toilets had walls that were only 4 feet high but no doors. So the C.O. could look down the hall from behind their glass room and see the bathroom area. A side note to all this topsy turvy world point of view. One of the C.O.'s coke and heroin suppliers was in the block. She was quite nice to him.

I watched Jordan's last title run from the common TV room. I actually got a front row seat because I was so good at basketball, one of the top 3 in our block. We played games every night in a league. After my first day at rec they realized how good I was. All I had to wear on my feet were the boots I came in with.

One day when I was working on Wall Street I wore my boots because I was going to party after work. As I was running across 8th avenue to meet up with my fellow lunch smokers, a taxi cut into the bus lane and was heading right at me. There was not enough room or time for me to get out of his way. I turned my body so that when the taxi hit me I would slide up his cab and toward the windshield. Allowing my legs to be taken out, I jumped slightly as he hit me so my feet wouldn't be planted on impact! My back faced toward the impact so my legs would bend with the collision. I slid up the hood of the taxi and waved at the driver! After he hit his breaks, I just slid off, landed on my feet and kept on running across the street in one motion like it never happened. (Just like in the movies)! This story got around the firm very fast. From that day forward I started to wear 10-hole boots thinking if I wasn't wearing them that day I probably would have broken my legs. One of my fellow inmates let me borrow his sneakers so I could play basketball during these league games. It was a proper gym and no scuffing shoes were allowed on the court.

I had to return to court to receive my second sentence. I was woken up at 3 a.m., sent to the main area, and put in feet and hand shackles attached at the waste. We sat in a bus that drove all over the state picking up other inmates going to their court sentences. Some inmates were dropped at one court house where their case was filed. Then the bus moved on to the next courthouse for other inmates.

At noon, my body is so sore sitting on a bus in these shackles. No food or water! Another hour and we're at my court-house. We get one bologna sandwich and water. Another hour sitting in a cell! I did not sit, Instead lying on the steel cot just to get my muscles and body to stretch out. They walk us into the courtroom, sit us on the bench in the order in which we are to be called.

The Spanish kid who told me he was arrested for shotgun robbery was actually arrested for domestic violence, slapping his girl a few times. He skipped his court date. You get to hear all the cases being read aloud while you wait. It's my turn to get up in front of the judge and they want to postpone my case! Before they ask me anything, I say,

"Stop! I want my case settled today!"

They tell me the only way to do that is to get another sentence. My original case got me 30 days. The prosecutor looks at me and says "why would you do that?"

"I don't want to spend another 10 hours in shackles just to hear you say your case is dismissed."

She tells me that if I take another sentence it's on my record; if I come back, it will probably be dismissed. It's a small case and with my time served will probably be dropped. I told her and the judge, "Your honor, I'm not a real criminal: just stupid. I'm not planning on coming back to prison again. I cannot handle another 10 hour day in these shackles as a 6'5" man."

The judge says, "I sentence you to another 45 days."

That's ok with me. My girlfriend is looking for an apartment for us. This gives her more time.

My last week behind bars, I found many 6-leaf clovers in the yard. They reminded me of the days my mom and I would just look in the grass after school for 4 leaf clovers. On our way home from a pick up from one of my schools, we drove by this pond. She told me she heard lots of frogs in the pond. My mom was a bit of a tom boy and wanted to try to catch a big bull frog. I hated it at first but after being covered in mud and catching a huge bullfrog it became my most memorable and fun day. In fact, my mother doesn't even remember my favorite day with her.

Sometimes we would stop by fields of shrubs and bushes. She would hand me a basket and say, "Go crawl through there, pick some berries and I will make a pie." Blueberry and raspberry, we would go a few times those years. Funny! Years later as we were driving back home I saw that all those spots had been turned into subdivision housing. What a shame.

The week before my release the library was closed for some reason. I had to just sit and wait couldn't do anything to occupy my mind. Since I'm actually serving out my sentence, it doesn't matter if they put drugs in my system at night. One guard doesn't seem to like me; he's been fucking with me all the time. He's mad that my girl is so hot and I'm white. He gives me shit for it all the time.

He tells me on Friday, "You can go-to the library today; it's open just for a few hours."

I walk out of the locked door while everybody is going to the yard and start to walk around the circle toward the library. I'm stopped by a guard who asks me

"Where do you think you're going?"

I was told the library is open.

"No, it's not open. Who told you that?"

I pointed out which guard told me that the library was open for two hours only. He walked me over to him, but he denies he ever told me that. We argue. He looks at me and says,

"Hey! I can put you in the hole for just talking back to me."

You can do anything you want; I discharge on Tuesday. No early release; I'm out.

He says, "Yes, you do. But I can transfer you to a maximum security branch of the prison complex. How long do you think you'll last there?"

I didn't say a word. The second guard looks at me and says, "Go back to your block and keep your mouth shut until Tuesday."

Agreed!

Tuesday comes; they call my bunk number and let me walk out. I have to go around to the different departments of the jail to get signatures saying I don't have any overdue library books or unpaid commissary bills, etc. ,etc. I get to the outer building where I was processed and ask for my clothes. They tell me after 30 days, they don't keep clothes for inmates. I tell them I have nothing to wear. They open up a room off to the side. In it is a pile of clothes enough to cloth 100 people in any kind of style you want. I pick out some really baggy jeans and a shirt and walk out to my girl. My parents never once came to visit me.

CHAPTER 12

First things first: After any stint in prison, certain priorities take precedence: French fries, ice cream and sex, for example, though not necessarily in that particular order.

We (my girl and I) have an apartment but most of my stuff is at my parent's house. When we arrive there, I am met with a pleasant surprise. They hand me $150 and my step dad offers me a job in the trade he has been in for years, union. I decide this may be the last chance I get to make some real money and have a career, so I take the offer.

From May until fall when school starts I work for him learning the trade. That summer me and my girl go camping and hiking a lot. I need nature around me after that jail experience. We hiked up the highest mountain in the area up north; my girl actually slept in a tent and hiked it. After the jail bit and because she came to see me so much, I decided to ask her to marry me at the top of the mountain.

It was quiet, no 'on my knees' proposal. I just held her as we looked at the view and whispered in her ear, *"Will you marry me?"*

Yes.

We plan the wedding while we drive way up north to another country and decide to add the wedding to the trip. The location is a famous place with real famous books written about it. It was beautiful. I was truly pumped, I even got a speeding ticket on my wedding day. Too funny!

I didn't tell my parents this idea for some time. Since we had one car, my girl would drop me off at my parent's house on her way to work and pick me up after her work. I would read a book waiting for her just to minimize the interaction between my parents. Less interaction meant less chance of fighting. I work for my father's company which is frustrating because he is constantly treating me like a child. I'm not allowed to do anything without him breathing down my throat, telling me how to do it. All I care about is making some money and spoiling my girl a little. I planned our first cruise, nothing special.

We move to a nicer area away from the ghetto. I'm still working for my step father and school classes at night are fun. Stuff is boring though. I'm a Christian now and I don't swear or drink or get very angry for many years. My fellow classmates go get drunk after classes often. I get picked up by my girl, go home and sleep.

Peace doesn't last long; everybody makes mistakes and so did I. I fought with my boss almost daily, so I began to avoid him as much as possible. The tension builds between us every day. My foremen got yelled at all the time. In fact, one of them even says,

"Every time Shane comes here, you guys show up and treat me and him like assholes. You really should deal with this and not include me in this bullshit."

I happened to walk into the job trailer during this conversation; as I opened the door that is what I heard. I closed the door, walked out and talked to my foreman after my step dad's partner left. Eventually I asked for a transfer. I tried my best to keep the peace all the while being treated poorly.

I tell my parents I'm getting married. We are going to elope in a small place up north. Nothing special, we see no reason to be in debt for 5 years just to have one day. Weddings in this culture are insane. I watched my aunt go ballistic at her wedding because somebody ate a cookie off the Venetian table before she did. Seriously people, thousands for a dress; thousands more for a reception and church rental? The average couple is still paying for their wedding 10 years later.

We decided to include the wedding on a week holiday. Save money and go on a European vacation for 16 days instead of rings and dresses. No debt. The honeymoon was amazing. We flew into Athens for 3 days before the cruise departs. On the day we attempt to get from Athens to the cruise port, all taxis are on strike! We had 5 bags of luggage! It took me a few trips to learn how to pack. The concierge finds a taxi that would be willing to break the lines. He got food thrown at his taxi the entire time we drove through the city. People even spit on his taxi! I gave him all the Lira I had left in my pocket for being a good guy.

The cruise was awesome. We went to all the places I ever dreamt about going to. Egypt, Rome, Pompeii, Athens, Malta, some Greek islands! It was fun. I was not a very good husband in those first years of dating my wife nor was I a good husband on this trip. I got flirted with by some beautiful women and yes, I did return the flirtations. My wife and I fought about this on the cruise. It would take me some time to figure out how a husband is supposed to treat his wife. By the time I figured this out, however, she was gone and we were divorced. I am truly sorry for my behavior in the marriage. I could tell all the things that she did to drive me nuts and create stress in our marriage, but this is not helpful. I failed my wife. Plain and simple!

I got the travel bug but she didn't! From that point on all I wanted to do was travel around the world.

We also started investigating different churches and religions. Looking for the truth isn't easy, as there's a lot of shit out there. We start with the Mormon religion and almost get baptized into the church. As we got further into their dogma, we realize it's not following the bible and makes up its own versions – adding things to it that aren't in the original text. This book would be thousands of pages long if I were to launch into my opinions of religion. Suffice it to say, we didn't get baptized into this religion. After months of searching and attending services, our apartment neighbor tells us about a church nearby that has a reputation for maintaining a responsibility to the text. So we go.

During this time my wife and I travel often. She worked for a corporation that gave just 2 weeks vacation. We try to add a day or two to the normal weekends off – 4th of July, Labor Day, Memorial Day, and New Years Eve. So we go to Venice and Rome for a full week! We go-to Paris for our first year anniversary. My wife had told me many times that she tried to go to Paris and it somehow fell through. I wanted the trip to be just for her. So the entire trip was about her wishes and desires while I let my wishes and desires remain unsaid. (No readers, that is not a sexual statement).

I only asked her to do one thing: walk next to me – side by side. We fight about this all the time. She typically walks in front of me. If I slow down, she speeds up; if I speed up, she slows down. Supermarkets, book stores, grocery stores etc etc. So for the whole week in Paris, she doesn't walk next to me. I ask for one thing! Why is it so difficult? I waited until the last night and then blew up at her.

We traveled to many Islands. I also got involved in missionary work with the church we attended. We went to the Czech Republic for an 18 day mission trip. I participated in a planning weekend in Holland with other church leaders from several countries who were organizing the Czech experience. After landing in Amsterdam, we took a train out to a southern Dutch town, one of the most beautiful train rides I've ever taken. To see the dikes along the way and how people and couples will take small boat rides though the dikes the way Americans take drives in their car was really cool to witness. My first thought was,

"I've been a pot smoker for almost all my life, and my first time in Amsterdam I don't even smoke pot anymore." If anybody doesn't think God has a sense of humor they are not paying attention!

My wife wants to go see Ireland and we take a bed and breakfast tour for a week around southern Ireland. The Ring of Kerry is beautiful. Did you know Ireland has palm trees? That really surprised me. I mean, palm trees on Caribbean islands ok, but in Ireland? That's really cool!

On a side note my fellow travelers, do not kiss the blarney stone. I have some mates who live in Ireland and they have informed me that the locals piss on the stone then laugh while you pay them to take a photo of you kissing it.

The next year we went to Dublin for St Patrick's Day week. The fire works on the Liffey were amazing. One of the things that bothered me about cruises was the lack of quiet time at any given place. This created a preference for traveling on my own. I wanted to spend more time in a location and get a chance to soak up my thoughts, ideas, and the local aura without mad tourists all over the place infiltrating my brain with noise, noise, noise. I read in a travel magazine about backpacking travel. I'm game.

CHAPTER 13

During my mission trip to Czech Republic I meet a woman who amazed me. Not in a physical manner but her style of personality was so impressive I wanted to find out if her home was the kind of culture that inspired such people or if she was simply unique. We get along so well. She is from Iceland. I go see her the next summer for 8 days.

From my first breath of fresh air outside the airport I was higher than if I had smoked a joint. The oxygen is so pure it requires some acclimation. With 24 hour daylight in the summer, she tells me to go nap and relax before we go out exploring.

Her husband comes home drunk that morning after partying all night. They have 3 girls. I love those girls. If I were to have a daughter I would name her after Asa, pronounced Ausa. We drove all over the southern part of the island. I went ice climbing on a glacier. On my hiking trip with my wife, the day I asked her to marry me, somebody suggested I should see how beautiful the mountain is during winter. That next year I begin to get gear and hire a guide learning to climb ice. I love it. Of the extreme sports I do ice climbing is the one real passion. My climbing guide for the day was amazed at my photos of climbing ice with trees in the background even using them for belay stations and anchor set ups.

My friend tells me that they have never been to the blue lagoon. We immediately plan a family trip to the lagoon with my friend and her daughters. Her husband didn't want to come. It was weird seeing her youngest daughter extremely nervous. We finally got her into the cave and even had her place her hand print with silica on the wall.

On my way home the flight is overbooked. I get bumped off and receive a voucher for a free flight to anywhere *Icelandair* flies. I immediately decide to go back to Iceland in the winter to see the northern lights. It's a dream of mine to see the northern lights. Finding out it's quite cheap to fly to Iceland in the winter, I bring my wife to meet my friend, her girls and the northern lights.

We rent a wooden cabin in the middle of nowhere. I even begin to learn the language, amazing. First night we get to see the lights as we drive. They were so mesmerizing. I was driving along a dark road with no lights in a snowstorm trying to follow another car in front of me with my head hanging out the window looking up at the sky. Watching the lights like a dog hangs his head out. It was a scary way to travel!

Iceland has very few trees and the ones they have are usually short. There is a joke there that says, "If you're lost in an Iceland forest, just stand up."

Driving during the winter months is almost impossible. Wind-blown snow creates blizzard like conditions. Short trees do not stop the wind from blowing snow for miles and creating total white out driving conditions. No street lights exist once you get outside of town. The entire 4 days we see the lights every night after the sun goes down. I taught them how to make shmore's which they had never even heard of. I brought them purple and green ketchup and colored gold fish snacks. The kids just laughed at them; 2 of the girls wouldn't even eat the strange colored foods.

"Hey! The lights are coming in. I'm going to walk up the path a little way to get a pure view."

I hear my wife walking up behind me; we lay in the snow just staring up at the sky. She doesn't like cold weather at all. We went shopping to get really good clothes for her to stay warm during the week.

Later back at my friend's house, after her husband went out drinking, my friend and I started a conversation about our spouses. I know she wasn't happy with her husband. She asks me how my marriage is. I'm a very emotional guy who needs emotionally engaging attention. I tell her that if I had known my wife wasn't going to be emotional – in fact, she is quite cold to me – I wouldn't have married her.

My wife, awake in the next room, comes out and yells at me. I was just about to say,

"Even though she didn't feed my emotional needs, she is still my wife and I'm glad for her!"

That didn't happen, she was understandably upset and said, "This was your chance to say you loved me." Again I was not a good husband.

We all went to the blue lagoon the next day and I got a massage. Nowhere else in the world can you see black beaches covered in swans, the northern lights, and walk on a blue glacier all in the same day!

I did not use the travel voucher for this trip. I wanted to save it for a trip to Germany during the summer. *Icelandair* flies to Germany, and I can stay over in Iceland for up to 5 days with no charge. Cool. I get to go to Germany and Iceland without paying for the airfare.

I spent 18 days backpacking through Germany and another 10 days through Russia. Since childhood I wanted to see Russia. The idea that it was so bad to America when I was a kid in school, just made me want to go see the place. Why was it listed and taught as the monster of the world? I found a company that flies to cities across Europe for a nominal fee. I pack up a backpack and for the first time plan a month long trip to Germany, Iceland, Russia, Lithuania, and Estonia.

I arrive in Frankfurt to get my transfer to Lithuania. Upon boarding my flight, I'm seated next to a basketball team. I teach them card tricks during the flight. I land in Vilnius and get buses to my hostel. I loved the castle in the middle of the city. So far it's the best castle I've seen, much better than anything I saw in Ireland. Getting around is difficult as it's my first attempt at this sort of trip. I walk through an island part of town that is connected by a bridge. I thought it was so quaint when I saw it from the top of the castle; I had to go check it out. At first I thought it was a historical landmark but soon realized it was a place where people lived shopped and worked in. I got coffee along the river, and really enjoyed my 'European' afternoon!

Traveling provides diverse experiences and exposure to varied customs for common and ordinary events. One might be surprised to experience the bathrooms and customs of other cultures, for example. This was the first place I had seen that doesn't let you put toilet paper in the toilet when you flush it. A trash can next to the toilet posted a note that asked you to deposit the toilet paper in it instead. This may have been my first 'strange to me' bathroom experience, but it would not be my last.

I am very excited to head off to Moscow. To stand in Red Square and just think for a few minutes was my dream. A tough security check at the airport with very stoic guards who size me up with scrutiny welcomes me to Russia.

I pay for a taxi to take me to the hostel. It's raining hard. Because I hate people serving me and treating me special, I sit in the front seat of the taxi. Although the driver and I can't speak each-other's language, we have a great talk about how many bad drivers there are on the road. We have many laughs and hand gestures.

I checked in and I hired a tour guide to take me around the city the next day. The Kremlin is a must do, as is seeing Lenin's body. A policy of the hostel is to run your passport through security. In fact, I had to get a visa for the trip to Russia. The Russian Consulate wanted to know what hostel I was staying in and when and what museums I would be viewing. I even had to pay the hostel to send me a fax of a special form inviting me into their hostel. This bureaucracy is weird to me. But ok, I want to go.

While waiting for the women to bring down my passport so I can go-to bed, I sat in the common area, talking to another kid who speaks English. He has been in Russia for 4 months now and just wants to speak English. He is German and has been studying there in school. As we sit talking, 5 girls walk up the hall wearing almost nothing. They lift their skirts showing what they have underneath: no clothing. We just laugh, both aware of the high level of prostitution that is among girls under 25. Not anything that we are interested in but, hey, if you're showing, then I'm going to look.

It was nice to have a tour guide because I wasn't prepared for the lack of English speaking people or print. Everything was written in Cyrillic. The subways in Mockba are famously talked about. I decided to use it for my transportation to and from the city the next 3 days. The subway decor truly will take your breath away: chandeliers, Mosaic walls, and manicured floor tiles. As the busiest subway in the world, I thoroughly was impressed. NYC in comparison is a mess. This place was so clean and shiney, you could eat off the floor. Along the walls is no spray paint or graffiti; it's lined with paintings and frescoes easily matching anything I've seen at the MET or the Louvre. It was like walking into lobbies of large hotels that have multiple sets of elevators on different parts of each floor. Just imagine the elevator doors being doors that open up to subways. They open and you step in to your subway line. You can't see or even really feel any other part of the subway. All you know is the door opened in a concrete wall letting you board.

I tripped and fell on the stairs walking up to the street. The steps are very short. I got trampled on by a few people before I could get up. All I was thinking was that I'm glad I am as big and strong as I am because if not the people might not have let me stand back up –it was that busy and packed full of people. Like a scene out of Metropolis. The German kid and I find out that were going up to St. Petersburg the same day, not the same train but the same day. I learn a few things about Red Square. It's not named Red for Russia. When the Mongols ruled these lands, they rode swiftly with horses and very little artillery. After they burned Moscow a couple of times, the Czar had the trees cut down around Red Square at the maximum distance the Mongols' arrows could fly. The loss of trees gave them no hiding ground as they invaded and attacked the Kremlin walls. Ultimately never getting inside again!

The stones used to place over the dirt and make the square were red. Hence Red Square! It was also funny to learn they were removing a hotel just outside the square that is mainly for wealthy tourists because it takes up too much view of the square. They even built a mall underground so they could get tourist shopping but not obstruct the view of the square. They made plans to move a bridge away from the main entrance, because it also obstructs the view. Wow, a culture that isn't subservient to its wealthy consumers. I'm thoroughly impressed.

The cheapest coffee in the city is at McDonald's. Outside this McDonald's, a bubble protrudes from the ground upon which a map of the world is depicted. The map is replete with a little church, a replica of the one so marveled at in Red Square. In fact, the church replica is the only thing sticking up on this bubble. Everything else is just painted or stained glass.

The travel company I used gave me all my tickets in German. My new friend takes me to the train station to get mine. Apparently there are 2 stations in Mockba with the same name. He goes to catch his; by the way, we're staying in the same hostel together in St Petersburg.

I get on the train and the conductor comes up to me and tells me I'm in the wrong train. Apparently three different trains leave at midnight for St Petersburg. I go-to the next track and the conductor won't let me on the train. He can't read German or speak English. Great I'm stuck here.

A guy getting on the train right after me speaks German, Russian and English– reads all 3, too. He reads my ticket, talks to the conductor and I'm allowed on the train. He tells me,

"If you have any problems, I'm in this car, cabin number.... Just come get me. I will take care of any problems. Have a great time in St Petersburg."

In St. Petersburg, I get to my hostel and checked in. I want to walk around the park and city. To my surprise I'm lucky again. It's the 200th anniversary of the city! They have removed all the gypsies and street beggars for the summer putting them in a school. It was like walking around the empty streets of a combination of Venice and Boston. There will be too many foreign dignitaries in the city this year so they don't want the beggars messing up their image of this classic city. I'm hanging out with my mate and we're just walking around, looking at the Winter Palace, deciding we must go inside.

After spending a day in Versailles, being told it's the most beautiful palace in the world, I will tell you the Winter Palace is much more beautiful than that. The marble colors and styles are much more creative and free flowing than Versailles. The courtyard outside is breathtaking. I take a panoramic photo that requires almost a full roll of film. At the far end of the courtyard there is a cool archway; we walk over to see it. Another traveler joins our group–a French guy whose dad works in Baghdad. Some other tourists took our photo because as were talking in the center square, we realize we are a Jew, a Christian, and an Atheist. We talk about the hanging gardens of Babylon. It's 1 of 2 ancient wonder's of the world I haven't seen.

To our horror the local kids have a small black bear tied to a rope and when people walk by they kick him so he dances. I am thinking how long did it take for him to learn to dance. The three of us, quite pissed off at this, give the kids some shit and walk on by. We go see the grave stones of Dostoevsky and Tchaikovsky, both of which are in the same cemetery! My favorite author is Dostoevsky; *The Idiot* is amazing. A few days later I'm on a train for Estonia, stopping in Talinn. I was only in the city for a few hours. I had planned a full 2 days but my train was changed and I had to spend an extra day in St. Petersburg. Awe poor me.

I fly back to Germany. The trains from Frankfurt to Munich –or Munchen, as the natives know it– is a very beautiful ride through the country. Munich's cool beer gardens are fun. Yes, the Hofbrauhaus is all it's cracked up to be. The best thing I did was see Castle Neuschwanstein– it's where Disney stole his from. The interior of the castle is incomparable. The King's bed took 14 carpenters 4 years to make. It's the only castle I've seen that has all the original furnishings.

We hike the long way up along the waterfall line and overlook bridges of the Bavarian Alps. We take a bike tour around THE Swan Lake! Ultimately I walk away from my group and take a swim in the lake naked. It's kind of a requirement. Since I have piercings and I'm shaved I didn't really want to have to answer all those questions.

On the ride back, one of the girl's bike breaks. The chain popped off. Our guide informed us this would happen once in a while. The guide is far away from us; the girl is upset after she fell over in the gravel path. As per my m.o., I'm cruising along behind the group and espy the damsel in distress. I stop to fix her bike; check her scrapes on her knees. She isn't really hurt just shocked. She does not even say thank you. She takes off away from me as fast as she can! No thank you, nothing.... Have I ever mentioned how insane women are?

My first alpine slide ride ended up tearing skin off my elbows which should not, by the way be used for brakes on an Alpine ride. A genuine Bavarian apple strudel with ice cream, however, helps assuage the elbow burn nicely.

Back to Munchen I enjoy watching the people play bocce on the courts. Behind the marketplace under a gazebo, they were holding Lambada competitions. I rented a bike and went to my 2nd nude beach; (first one was in Greece). Most of the people you see on a nude beach you would never want to see again.

As I come back late at night through the shopping street in Munchen, I see an American girl who I noticed the first day. She is now completely naked with four dressed German guys laughing at her and playing with her under the water fountain. I'm thinking

"I hope you're so drunk you have no memory of what happens to you tonight."

I'm going to sleep in my 20 person dorm and a couple of girls walk in and ask me what I did that day. I told them how amazing my day was, going to the castle, lake, lunch and a bike tour. They ask me how much that cost me. I told them and their response is:

"If we do that, then we can't drink tonight."

They are from the east coast of the United States and I'm thinking

"They don't have bars where you are? You flew half way around the world and don't care about seeing any culture? You just want to drink? College kids. Does daddy know how you're spending his money?" Lol.

Must go to Check Point Charlie! I arrive at the hostel which happens to be in the red light district. I realized on this trip that most hostels seem to be in the red light district of these cities. I make a real effort to not subject myself to these areas again.

Inside the hostel for 10 minutes I relax and write a journal entry. A few girls walk in and start drinking. They admit they are not old enough to drink stateside. One girl falls face down in the lap of a local kid and says, "Let's go-to a strip club." Her friends look at her like she is crazy. I get up and walk away fully shocked there aren't more Nancy Holloway cases. I could fill up an entire book of stories just of the girls I have seen around the world putting themselves in very dangerous situations.

Time for bed. Wake up the next day and head off to the Berlin wall. Artists from all over the world have come in to paint a section showing their view of why walls are not healthy. Berlin center is awesome. I really enjoy how they are building modern attachments to old structures. They removed an old roof of one building just to put a see through glass dome with a spiral stainless steel walkway up to the top. I'm impressed with Berlin.

The Zoo was close to my hostel; I decided to walk around to see what a zoo looks like outside of the States. Watching a primate turn his head so he could hear the kids talking about him made me decide I must go to Africa and spend time with different primates in the wild.

Frankfurt, the Euro Capital, is not impressive to see. I use the last day of my train pass to take a full day's ride up the river and back. How beautiful. My room has 8 beds on the floor with no bunk beds. They put me in one bed that has a backpack chained to it.

"It already has an occupant."

"He is sleeping in the wrong number bed," she says. "This one is yours."

Ok. I'm tired. I just lied down and passed out. I wake up to some Midwestern kid yelling at me for taking his bed. Yeah ok. I tell him: "Check with the front desk. They put me here."

He keeps talking shit.

Fine. Upset, I stand up and tell him

"Shut the fuck up! Get your facts right then go fuck yourself! Any other problems! Feel free to let me know."

He quickly realizes I'm twice his size. I go back to bed!

The last leg of this trip leads me back to Iceland for my third visit there. Having friends in other countries allows you to visit unlike any tourist. I hang out with my friend and have some fun with the girls. I rented a car and drove around the whole island, which took me less than a day.

My friend was born in the Westman Islands; she has not been back in many years. I heard there is a famous volcano and the perimeter of the islands is jaw dropping beautiful. It takes 12 minutes to fly over. I want to see the buildings that are halfway covered in the cascading lava flow of the eruption in the early 70's. She tells me when the puffins are born the school closes for the next few days and all the parents and kids drive around the island and collect the ones that don't make it into the water. Then drive to the coast and put them into the ocean. Her rescue record is more than a hundred.

After the eruption the school would also sponsor days when the kids would hike up and place fresh young grass sprouts along the hillside to help the ground become fertile. We take this famous boat ride along the outside edges of the island, going into caves while the guide sang Icelandic songs so you could hear the acoustics. I was really enjoying being able to understand the language and the songs. There were so many birds flying along the coast and jagged peaks of the small island I was shocked they didn't fly into each other.

On my flight home I'm sitting next to this older couple from Sweden. We start talking; they are on their way to NYC for the first time. We're Christians and hit it off well. I decided to take the next day off from work to meet them in the city. I show them places off the tourist path that are cool. We have dinner in little Italy and head back to their hotel. As we separate, they tell me they really like me and want me to come spend time with them in Sweden. "Please don't say that unless you mean it." They assure me they are serious.

The following year I land in Stockholm. The airport has no customs –I just walk through but without a stamp in my passport.

The couple meets me and we spend the day walking around; we take a boat tour through the harbor. Stockholm is the most beautiful city I have ever seen and the cleanest major city I've seen, too. The man is a retired history professor from the university. As we're walking around he tells me the history of the city and of all the buildings. Stockholm consists of 15 different islands connected by 52 bridges.

At the end of the day we go to their town, Vasteras. They treat me better than my own family treats me. I'm there during some holiday. The woman loves to cook; the food was amazing. Walking through their town I learn an amazing local game called cub played in parks. They take me to this silver mine in Sala. It's many meters underground. I learn they had to pump water into the mine to build up the pressure to pump the water out of the mine. The main shaft leading down to the mine is about 10 meters wide. At least 100 meters down, the tour guide instructs us that the mine shaft is built before dynamite. Their technique was to burn wood to heat the rock then chip away at it. They could move just a few centimeters a day. I was thinking that must have been back breaking work, real man stuff. Any idea how many years of intense work it would take to make just the shaft to get down to the main room? That main room was bigger than the 3rd boarding school I went to times 2. With lots of tunnels breaking off in all directions!

I got to see a Viking burial ground and a marriage labyrinth. The burial site looks like an oval figure 8 of stones like Stonehenge. We hiked around the area with another friend of theirs who is also a retired professor of botany. He gave us the history and names of all the local plants and trees. I would not have been able to pay for that experience even if I scheduled it with tour companies. My hosts paid for everything, including my admission into the mine and the boat tour around the capital.

Before my trip to Russia, my wife and I bought a house that my parents bought as an investment. It's in a nice area of a town in which we enjoy living. Unfortunately, it's not the kind of town that accepts interracial marriages. The kind of sideways glances we got, the little disrespects we receive was frustrating.

Our neighbors didn't even talk to us. My wife went outside one Father's Day and waved to the neighbor: "Happy Father's Day." He didn't wave; just got up and went inside the house.

The house had many issues none of which were discussed when we bought the house. Plumbing in the upstairs bathroom didn't work at all. We had no access to the garage from the first floor; you had to go upstairs then back down a back staircase! The first floor was all made of concrete. I discovered this when I opened up the hole for the oven exhaust fan. My wife hated the house after just a year.

I cut down many trees to clear space, planned to build a retaining wall to get more yard. My wife started going on business trips and seeing her family. She went to see her family for 4 days and I decided to have my own episode of "While You Were Out."

I took out the upstairs staircase; put in a floor with supports; used my step-dad's street saw and cut a door into the garage and had the door in the wall resealed and framed up before she got home. I even put up more kitchen cabinets. When she came home I was so excited for her to say, "hey, nice job." Not one word! That was the last time I ever worked on the house. The other policy we set up was I'm not allowed to travel to any place alone that she would want to see. Cool!

Since I have no real relationship with my family I usually take the opportunity to leave the country during holidays. I'm always out of the country for 4th of July, Thanksgiving, even Christmas sometimes. Flights to Europe are cheap during major American holidays. The bed and breakfast trip to Ireland was during holidays. In fact we left for the trip the same day as the closing on the house; quite the stressful day.

I leave for London on Thanksgiving week. Get my flight, set up a guest house, it was a great time. I met a friend of mine there who I met in the Czech Republic. We have a whole day together walking through Hyde Park and Kensington Gardens. London is a cool city. The crown jewels at tower are beautiful. I'm a fan of medieval times so I enjoy the armory and stories of it all. I get lost on the underground– takes me a full circle to figure out directions of the trains. Too funny! Nothing like being lost on the U2 train!

I checked into my 4 bed room in London, dropped my bag and claimed a bed. There was a guy sitting in his bed from Finland. We started talking about traveling and the beauty of Scandinavia. Though I have never been to Finland it's a place I would love to see. He actually seemed like a really cool guy who had been on the road for a long time. He was eating food out of a can and carried a can opener on his backpack. We chatted for about an hour.

Down for the shower, come back up to discover the Finn is gone and some American guy is in the room already giving me the bad vibe feel. We chat for a minute. He tells me there is some kid in the room who doesn't talk to anybody. As he's telling me, the kid he has never talked to walks in and we exchange a pleasant hello. The American kid in shock walks out and changes his room that second.

We all have our unique physical attractions of the opposite sex we prefer. That special hair color, bone structures, body curves, and facial features etc, etc, etc. I met this 'perfect girl' during my time in London. She was staying in my room at my guest house. We hit it off well and agreed to hang out for a couple of days. Tower London, some scary indoor rides, Madame Tussaud's wax museum! Go out for live jazz and some pints. I am still married and although she does give me the green light to have sexual fun with her, I turn her down.

As I planned my trip to London I saw you can go to speaker's corner in Hyde Park, talk about anything except criticize the Queen. I wanted to stand there on a spot and preach open air true Christian stuff. I have some experience in this at my home city and on a short mission trip to another much larger city. I turned the girl down because if I fell to this lust, I would have no spiritual power to speak with truth the next day. Lying in my bed that night I have the incredible urge to masturbate while thinking of this sexually perfect girl who wants me just a few feet away. I suppress this urge with some prayer!

Headed to Hyde Park the next morning, I see a man who is standing on a large blue cooler–the kind Americans use when taking the whole family out for a Saturday BBQ in a park. He is completely twisting up verses of the Bible while looking for reactions. He has a fake hat on his head with 2 red horns sticking out of it. I feel like I should just stand here and listen to him.

Frustrated with what he is saying, I challenge a statement he made. He looks right at me and says:

"Who are you?"

After deliberating my response, I blurt out, *"I'm a servant of God!"*

"Are you an angel?"

"I'm just a man," I tell him.

For the next hour and a half we argue various parts of the Bible. I didn't appreciate him twisting the gospel for his own argumentative reasons. He asked me twice:"Why are you here torturing a lunatic?"

Every time I got sidetracked and talked about myself especially my lack of love for Western Civ, he just laughed and twisted me up. I wasn't that smart that day. I quickly recognized if we argued verses of the Bible, he had to speak the truth which he did not like. He claimed he chose to come down to earth rather than stay up in heaven and suck Jesus' dick. He professed that he and Mohamed met in the desert. His last comment enlightens me to my own personal beliefs; I said, "Thank you for this information."

Then he reminded me that I had spent time in prison, information I had not yet told him. He asked me if I had masturbated over my perfect girl I met the day before. It shook me, causing me to place my hands under my arm pits for the rest of the experience. They were shaking uncontrollably....

It dawns on me he might be a fallen angel, which he claimed. I decide to find out with the Bible. I recall the first few versus of Job which states even the fallen angels need God's permission to torment and kill us. He keeps asking me to leave his area and leave him alone, stop tormenting him.

"If you really want me to go away why don't you just kill me, or don't you have the authority to do that yet!" I said tauntingly.

He looks right at me and tells me that I am arrogant. Wow..... Shortly after I walk away and tell my Czech friend who was standing next to me the whole time:

"I have no idea what time it is and my equilibrium is so out of whack right now. I feel like the movie Ghostbusters, slimed…. Can we go somewhere? I don't care where you take us. My brain can't function on that level right now."

She says, "Sure, let's go to a park. That was amazing." I wish I could be strong enough to argue with people like that intelligently. This is an Elijah moment for me, from this day on my eyes are open!

One of my tactics to keep a happy wife was to take her on a holiday shortly after one of my trips. We are supposed to go to Roatan Honduras just a few days after I get back. After the mission trip we go-to Barbados with my parents and grandma. I was really surprised at this, getting my step dad on a plane is not easy. I just got my scuba diving certification and wanted to go diving in the islands. This gives my wife a day at the spa when I'm not nipping at her heels.

I'm not the kind of guy who wants to do separate things from his wife. I want to be around her all the time. Every single day when she would get home from work I would stop her and dance with her for a minute or two in the kitchen. I leave for work earlier than she does and thus getting home before her.

It was actually a cool trip, except that as I was waiting for my wife to come down for dinner after getting dressed, the girl running the resort is flirting with me. I'm waiting for my wife so I just stay there chatting with her. When my wife comes out, the girl turns and just walks away. A new argument with my wife ensues. To make matters worse, my parents walk in on her accusations. Now they think I was flirting.

Seriously, I was just sitting there waiting for them. I'm a guy; I get dressed faster. I learned that when she is getting dressed slower than me I get restless and can say sarcastic things to her. It's better if I walk away and give her space and time to get ready.

In anticipation of seeing my wife after my Russia trip, I bought her favorite perfume for her. My step brother picks me up at the airport instead of my wife. I go on for about an hour about how awesome the trip was. He lets me go on before he tells me my wife is in the hospital for Peracarditis. I'm in shock. I have no idea what this is except that it is heart related. Ok that's not good.

"Get me home so I can get the car and go see her."

It's pouring out and the windshield wiper breaks on the drive to the hospital, scratching the brand new windshield. I get to the hospital with awful jetlag; visiting hours are nearly over. The hospital is not in the best area of town and is all locked up. I try to get in through the parking garage but can't. I walk around the building but can't get in. I've never been to this hospital before, now I'm frustrated.

I force open the infrared doors by the garage and start my way down the stairs. Not a few minutes later I get cornered by cops. I'm not really in the mood. I try to explain about my wife being in the hospital, but they don't seem to be listening to me. I keep asking,

"Where is the front desk so I can find where she is being held?"

They just keep saying: "You broke in; what do you want"?

I'm really upset now. They aren't listening to me so I say again:

"If you were fucking listening to me, you would know why I'm here. If you saw me break in then you saw me walk all over the building looking for the entrance. Give me a break! Look up my wife, please."

More crap between us. I start insulting them. The chief comes in and I explain to him: *"I've only been in the country for a few hours after spending a month away. I find out my wife is lying in the hospital with heart problems. Can we please cut through this bullshit drama and let me see my wife? Seriously man, if your wife was in the hospital and you just found out, what would you do.....?"*

He looks at me then looks up my wife in the patient directory; he tells me where she is and how to get there. He asks me to consider their position.

Agreed. "Can I just go see my wife?"

I walk in, hand her the perfume and hug her. She cries and says, "I didn't want you to see me like this." To be honest I don't think I have ever seen such pure emotion from my wife before, or since. I was beginning to think she was just a very cold person.

I go back to work and wait for her next doctor's appointment. She was released in a few days on a regimen of steroids. I ask to go-to the doctors with her.

"It's ok. You don't have to go."

Are you fucking kidding me? You tell me you almost died because the first hospital misdiagnosed you while I was in RUSSIA, and I'm not allowed to go-to the doctor with you?

I went with her to the doctor. Walking in I realize the office belongs to the father of my first girlfriend out of school who owned the island! Thankfully he is not there. Too funny. My wife clearly expresses her unhappiness with my presence. We go in and because this is all new to me, I ask the doctor questions. My wife becomes agitated with my questions.

Seriously? I'm your fucking husband.

The doctor is trying to answer my questions but realizes she is not enjoying this so he focuses on her. As he should! We are supposed to leave for a Tropical Island in a few days. I ask him if she is going to be able to fly. My thinking is she will be able to relax on this quiet island, no stress and no worries. It's all inclusive! He says sure she should be ok but it's possible the altitude can react with her heart. My wife takes this chance to say nope she doesn't want to travel.

The travel agency says that if I go they will give us a credit for her for another trip. Fine! It's just for 5 days; I'm really upset at how this scenario went down. I go, spend the days scuba diving. Later that year we go to Dublin for St Patrick's Day. That was the last fun trip we went on together.

The next year we go on this same trip to the same island. Now there is a huge rift building between us. I ask her to play volleyball on the beach with me; she declines. She is not interested in spending any time with me. I quit smoking pot but my wife has not. I don't scuba dive as much this trip except for a dive with sharks nearby. As I'm leaving the dive place a guy comes up to me and asks,

"Want some pot?"

Sure. My wife still smokes. It's a holiday; I'm trying to do fun things with her to rebuild bonds and show her I support and love her by doing the things she does. I thought she might like to smoke some pot and watch the sunset at night.

Back at the room I present my token of island pot and propose a smoldering sunset viewing. "No. Let's not. I'm sorry you compromised yourself." She flushed it down the toilet. Another lesson in the insanity of girls.

I take the opportunity when traveling to exchange emails of people I meet. I exchange emails with a girl playing volleyball. First and foremost, I never cheated on my wife on any of my travels, even though I had plenty of offers and opportunities. My wife tends to doubt my assertions. We've been divorced for many years now; I've been brutally honest in this book even admitting things that don't paint a nice picture of me. The volleyball girl with whom I exchanged emails asked me, "Who is the girl on the trip with you? To me it seems like you guys are a blind date gone bad!"

This really struck me. I was truly devoted to her on that trip, trying to make up for the previous year's mishap and that's what a stranger thought of us. I tried to teach my wife how to swim so we could snorkel together on island trips. She told me how her dad threw her in the ocean and she almost drowned; so she was very scared of the water. I spent years trying to teach her, helping her overcome her fear. She never learned. In fact, she used this helpless girl technique to get guys to flirt with her while we are on islands. I got kind of sick of this and walked away as she used this tactic this time.

It's not but a few weeks after this that we start to talk about divorce. I plan to fly down south to meet the girl I met on the island. I tell my wife I'm going. We talk and she actually cried the day I left. I almost got off the bus and went back home because she showed me that moment of love. To be honest, it had been years since I felt real love from her. Heck, in our first year of marriage she had sex with me only one time. The 2nd year we had sex twice. I fought with her about this all the time. Now if any girl plays a sexual power struggle with me, I walk away the next day. I won't play this game again. I began to date this girl, flying down to see her every 3 weeks. My wife moved out within days of getting back from the trip.

I am enjoying my new job, with a new employer. No more feeling like I'm being slighted. Now I have new problems. It's been so long since I was allowed to fart at work without getting my step-dad's permission, I caused my new foreman some head-aches to get me to think for myself and work without being mon-itored. This is cool. I get prints and explained the entire scope of the job. I loved it.

My only issue is that I don't know as much of my trade as I should. My step-dad did give me a job and yes, I made some money; but it was just one aspect of the trade and a very small one at that. I'm getting to meet other people in the trade, and I began to learn some interesting stories.

I met people who had known my step-dad for years and had worked with him for years before he got his own company. They don't know who I am and, worse, they didn't even know he had 3 sons one of whom would be me. So I gave them this look and they gave me this look. I feel very hurt and frustrated by the knowledge that my step-dad never spoke about me.

When you work with someone side by side for some amount of time, you talk. I start by saying I grew up in boarding schools, and then they have follow up questions. I'm not shy: I have no problem telling people the whole story. This would happen all the time. I never asked my step father why he never spoke of me. I would just be told it didn't happen, I'm lying I made it up. This was always my parents excuse. So I learned to never confront them about anything. Just better to eat it and move on. It does hurt a lot to have to explain to people who have known my family for years who the fuck I am.

The very last time this happened was right in front of my step brother after he got the business from my step dad who retired. I'm working with someone who worked 25 years for my step dad's best friend. The guy comes back the next day and says, "Hey! I saw my old boss last night and told him I was working with his 3rd son, Shane."

The guy tells him, "I thought his son owned the business?"

He says "No his other son."

The guy responds: "The other son is an apprentice still."

He says, "No! There is a 3rd son."

The guy tells him, "I never knew that he had a 3rd son."

The guy and I just laugh. My step brother just looked at me. What am I supposed to say? Of course he now has all kinds of questions.

So as soon as my step brother walks away, he starts to drill me for the information. Again I am not ashamed to explain I've been through hell and back. Sure I'm not perfect but I'm not ashamed.

During my 4th year of apprentice school, I go out to lunch with my step dad. A slow day he asked me to meet him at a favorite lunch spot. Our trade has a small union; we often work for the same contractors again and again. We talk in what feels like a father son moment. I let my guard down and slip up.

"I'm excited that I get to leave school early this year. For the last 3 years, we have watched the fourth-year students get out of class early. We can't wait to get there ourselves, a rite of passage for making it this far."

I go on to tell him, *"I'm getting free cable in the new house I just bought from them."*

Apparently sharing with my step dad was a big mistake. The next night at school the director comes in and drops the bomb.

"Students are no longer allowed to leave class early. This requirement applies to fourth year as well. I am aware this practice was allowed in the past but as of this year, it's got to stop."

I look right at him and say in class, *"This is why I don't like my step dad. He's always fucking me at every step."*

The guy looks at me and gives me that look.

I tell him, *"I know you can't say where the complaint originated or why you changed the policy."*

"I understand exactly where you are coming from." His words!

Reading between the lines my own step father fucked my senior rite of passage and everyone else's in my class. Now my senior classmates are mad at me that we are kept in class 2 extra hours each night when they have waited 3 years to have this right. The same week my cable is cut off too. Since I live on the last house of a dead end street, the cable company would have to be looking for it to find it. Thanks dad. This would be the last time I ever tell him anything real. From this point on, all conversations are reduced to weather and sports. When I'm at the house, I talk to my mother only if he is not around. Once he enters the room, all real conversations stop. I told my mother privately that I had 2 abortions a few years later.

CHAPTER 14

My wife and I start attending a church every Sunday. After the debacle of the Mormon Church, I'm really looking for a trustworthy church that respects the text more than their man made traditions. I'm reading the bible every week on my own and listening to bible radio to learn as much as I can. Since I have had this special surrender moment to the Lord, I want to know who He is and what He really taught the world.

I encourage everyone to read the text on their own. Sure you can say the Bible is open for interpretation; but the book itself says a child can understand it. The problem when you don't understand something is adding your own narcissistic baggage into the equation. Plus no teaching of the bible is covered just once. There are other books in the bible that can help you get a better understanding of God's point, if you look deeper.

The trouble with this modern society is that we think we have arrived and thus we don't need to investigate anything anymore. We know it all, and worse we have become so lazy in our heads that we don't know the value of hard work. We want maximum input with minimal output from our end. This is not God's plan; He says,

"Study the word diligently so that you may be approved." Meaning, "people if you don't study my text which I have given you, then you will be misled by all kinds of shit and confusion out there."

For example, the largest religion on the planet has unmarried priests. First, they say Peter, the first pope, was not married. Really? There is a text in the bible where Jesus heals Peter's mother in law. Kind of hard to have a mother in law without being married!

Then there is an entire chapter stating how a leader of a church should act. Included in this chapter is a section devoted to being a married pastor, or bishop. Yes, people, God says in the bible you should be married. For how can you conduct yourself in a godly manner in my church as the leader and give advice, council on marriage, fatherhood, etc., if you don't know how to do this in your own house? I would like to know how the Catholic Church neglects and dismisses this section. Honestly, who gave them permission to ignore such a powerful and practical instruction? (Mathew chapter 8 verse 14 and 1st Timothy chapter 3). You can pick any bible up from any church in America no matter what the denomination and find these verses for yourself.

The idea that Mary is the 'Mother of God' is absurd since God created her. By the way, she did not die a virgin. Jesus had brothers. Mathew 4 verse 21. I could go on for hours about the lies and misrepresentations of God's word. I'm only giving a few examples to encourage all to read the Bible for themselves before they get misled. I think it's hysterical that we, the people are willing to follow the rules in every aspect of our lives: driving a car, buying a house, getting jobs, any sport on the planet. When it comes to life, which is the most important thing in the universe, we say those rules are just suggestions; we don't need to follow them anymore. They are antiquated! Yet we wonder why our lives are such a mess, stressful, and down right unfulfilling.

The church we attend is in an affluent area and most people dress up like they are going to a $200 dinner. I'm a simple man and I like to be who I am no matter what the situation. I'm an in your face kind of guy. OK, maybe too much. But hey, you just read my life story; you can see why I don't believe in bullshit facades, or sugar coating things. Life is short.

I wear my pajama pants to church because first, the service begins in the morning and I hate mornings. Secondly, I wear them everywhere else, too. Last time I checked God asked me to come as I am. I was a little nervous about how the pastor was going to take it. He is one of my closest friends to this day. My wife doesn't even give me any hassle over it either. We go-to a friend's house for bible study every Sunday night for a few years. I wear Christian t-shirts all day when I'm walking around. So at the gym I met this guy who invited me to a Bible study. I'm hungry for knowledge so we go for years. I do two missionary trips with the church – one abroad. It's a good feeling becoming closer to the Lord. I get baptized as an adult, and invite my parents to it. Though my step dad didn't come, my mother did. She ran out as soon as the service ended; I didn't even get to say thank you to her.

I help do work from my trade into the church during renovations, even doing work in the pastor's house and youth pastor's house. I'm not a money guy and God does say give tithing to the church. There is nothing in the Bible that says it has to be cash.

The pastor counsels me and my wife before our marriage to write our vows with him. Though I did memorize mine on the wedding day, my wife did not. We even lived apart for a few months before getting married. Since the first night we met, we've spent less than a month apart, other than my prison sentence. So we wanted to respect the marriage by not having sex before it and not living together. This was actually her idea.

We hadn't had the most Bible based relationship. The first month we met we drove down south for spring break and smoked and tripped on acid all weekend. This was not my first acid trip but it was hers. She did not have a good experience. I will not relate this to you for her own protection. In my trip I watched planes land on the beach and enjoyed watching a group of girls play volleyball on the beach backwards. Meaning, they stood backwards and the ball went backwards from the way it should play. Like watching a volleyball game in rewind! The experience was so bad we left the beach early and drove home.

As we went through the divorce I stayed friends with my pastor. He later resigns his position over church politics. He is the godliest man I know, never once passing judgment upon me for anything I did. Even when he found out I was buying pot from his son. Yup I'm an awful sinner and God has a lot of grace for us all. We are friends to this day. (What the hell? The pastor's kid is selling pot? Damnation. I guess that is another story).

CHAPTER 15

The volleyball girl down south is a model, so please excuse my reaction of going gaga when she flirted with me! My ex wife hadn't shown me that kind of look or attention in so long that I forgot what it felt like. In fairness to my wife, she never really got over the physical fights from the early years of our romance.

I fly down to see her all the time. She has a car and a place to stay. It's quite cheap to go see her, just the cost of the flight. I just got my trade license and I don't have to pay rent. My wife asked for the divorce and she didn't want counseling or anything; she just wanted out. Not necessarily to me, she just didn't want to be married anymore. She is making almost 6 figures and I tell her:

"If you want me to just let you go, then you pay the mortgage until the house gets sold."

Agreed!

So I'm saving my money to take this backpack trip across Africa. Working for my step dad again, I have a company car so it's easy to stay out of his way. I get to the shop every day about 30 minutes before the guys do. I get all the material needed for the day together even though I don't get paid for this!

We're working at a very intense pressure job that requires a lot of overtime work. So I'm trying to help out by getting the material early. Sure after working all night I'm tired in the a.m. I leave about 5 to 10 minutes early sometimes. I got screamed at one morning for doing this. So I stop going in early to get the material on my time. It's funny how people who are beaters forget exactly what you do for them.

Within a week I lose the company truck. I buy my own jeep. Now I go see the girl once a month. We have a great time for a while, free amusement park trips. She is a quite talented musician, and I enjoy watching her concerts. Things progress and we start falling in love. My mom gives me 2 weeks of her time share and I transfer one to a catamaran trip in the islands for a week. I take her with me. The girl doesn't have a lot of money; in fact, she has a lot of debt. I try to help her get things she needs. Brakes, tires, and a new battery for her car, etc, etc, etc!

It would be months before I find out she is a coke whore who enjoys fucking strange guys even 2 and 3 at a time. It's easy to hide things from someone that you only see once a month. I tried to get her to move north but I find out she gave me a *std* — a quite easily curable one, actually. This one has very little affects on men. I feel lucky actually. She is so insatiably horny that she sleeps with my step brother in my house in my bed. They both denied this.

One day when I got stoned with my other step brother, he slips up and says, "Hey, if that's what had to happen to get rid of that bitch, then so be it." I confront my other step brother with this new revelation and still get denial. The two full brothers had some blowout the next day and didn't speak for a few months. Lol. Their argument carries over to one of those rare Thanksgivings that I'm actually home!

When me and her get in an argument about the std, she attempts to get out of the car as we are driving down the highway. I grab her to keep her in the car and she starts slapping me. We get back to my house and the argument grows more intense. It starts to get physical; I've got scratches all over my neck and chest. I throw her across the room and she calls the cops.

"Help me! My boyfriend is beating me up." She tells them. "Bring lots of cops: he is a very big guy."

I look out my window and see cops sneaking up to my house like they are playing hide and seek. We both get arrested. They not only let her out but give her the keys to my house to get her stuff out of my house without an escort. No problems. I have to go-to domestic violence classes and charges will be wiped off my record since I got physical marks on me too. Shortly afterwards, she tries to get me to take her to Switzerland to go snowboarding with some mates of mine I met in Africa! LOL Did I mention the insanity of girls?

I did take her to Iceland to see the northern lights one year that I was going. I thought she might like to go. As we are having sex doggy style in the blue lagoon, I'm looking up at the northern lights enjoying the flowing colors. She says to me, "Could we please flip over so I can see the lights?" LOL

I save up the money to travel to Africa – 77 days of overland tours, an 18,000 kilometer trek. We landed in Cape Town two days after Katrina hit. Quite an interesting experience for me since the news in Africa was so different than the news I was reading on the net, and TV from the states. All guest houses, hostels have great internet service, even the ones in the middle of nowhere.

I send newspaper articles back home by snail mail to ask my friends if they are talking about these things. It would seem there are 2 girls from S.A. who are in New Orleans during this event and they are reporting back every day. They report stories of military trucks running kids over without stopping, shootings, and people who are running out of the stadium asking for help from the troops as their mother is getting raped inside. More stories of how they are using helicopters to pick up wealthy white people and their fucking luggage before they picked up the poor black people. I still have all these newspaper articles.

Starting out in South Africa and I met my first tour group: 14 people on the truck from all over the world. I'm the oldest person on the truck and thus the outcast! It didn't stop people from making slight comments to me when they get the chance.

"Hey, I could care less. It's not like I haven't heard it all before. I'm in Africa."

I'm taking an 11-week overland tour across the continent. I decided before I left that I would use two different companies just in case me and somebody didn't get along. I didn't want to be stuck in a truck with people that I don't like for more than 2 months.

We head up toward Namibia, stop by the river on the border of Botswana and Namibia and go canoeing down the river for a couple of days. Our guide knows so much about the bush and animal life that I decide to stick close by him for the entire trip. I'm last in the line of boats, padding along alone. None of my tour mates wanted to share a canoe with me so I got to ride with coolers of food none of which have learned to paddle.

I didn't appreciate the noise everybody was making so I stayed far behind. The guide joined me.

"Are we going to get in trouble for going slowly?"

"The guy who is running this tour doesn't like tourists," he says. "He thinks we owe him. But I say that this is your trip, and it's a long trip through Africa. Take your time; enjoy it. Ask me anything you want; I'm not like him."

The river trip is fun. I learn about the birds and how diamonds flow down this river. We get picked up by our truck up river and begin the trek again into the dessert of Namibia! As we cross the border our bush guide is denied a visa entrance. Because of some kind of political issue between the 2 countries, he got stuck in the middle! He picks up his bag, gets off the truck and has to walk for hours through the flat dessert to go back. Once his papers get sorted out, then he will meet us in a few days in Swakopmund.

I'm thinking that isn't happening. To my surprise he looks at us and smiles along as he starts walking and we begin driving. We stop in Etosha National Park on our way through. Not three minutes into the park, we see 3 young male lions hanging out together under a tree! It's quite bloody hot. Having to ration my water to 3 liters a day is starting to make my body very dehydrated. But we are responsible for our own water. We do stop every couple of days somewhere where we can buy water and fill our bottles up. Water is not cheap for tourists so I fill mine up and ration my consumption. I'm on a budget.

We play this game along the way with another overland tour company. As we pass each-other once in a while on the road, we all stick our asses out the window and moon each-other. Both guys and girls flash their asses.

Our ride stops at the tallest dessert dune in the world "crazy dune!" It's so breathtaking to walk around these dunes with the ocean just a few miles away! The guide tells us:

"If you want, you can hike up this large dune; but I have never seen anybody do that."

Challenge! I'm game. To my surprise, 3 Germans follow me: two girls, one guy. The girls are ballet dancers and they have no physical issues with the hike. As we embark on this hike I have no idea how difficult it's going to be. With every step we take, we sink about 8 inches into the sand; then pick up your foot out of the sand to take the next step. All along the knife's edge of the sand dune reminds me of hiking up the highest mountain in my area during winter season! Watching the spiders scurry out of the sand from the impact of our steps was cool. If it wasn't for the fact that the girls were kicking my ass, I would not have finished this hike. It was the toughest 200 plus meters of my life. The view at the top was worth every step. The German guy brought up a beer to the top. Popped it and drank it. Cool dude.

We pull into our campsite area to find lots of these types of trucks. How ironic to sleep in a tent in the heart of Africa and have a swimming pool and bars with any drink you could ever want! The site has a rep come by and give us the speech.

"There is a man made water hole on this place that is flood-lit for your observation. Please note the stone wall separating us from the animals; it even has proper stadium style bleachers for you to sit and watch. Please don't fall asleep on the bleachers. Last week a guy did and a lion jumped the wall and ate him."

He pauses as we all react with a gasp.

The stone wall is only 4 feet high. I'm not here in Africa to get involved with bars and sex like my other travel mates. I head out to the rock wall after dinner. Each meal is cooked by the guide. We have to help wash the dishes, set up and clean up, but this tour company did all the cooking. Some simple things we prepared on our own.

I head to view the animals, as my travelers head to the bar and pool. In the next 5 hours I watch 5 lions, 35 elephants, 13 hippos, 12 giraffes, 8 rhinos and hyena's all drink out of the water hole while jockeying for position during the course of the night. At a distance of 50 feet! When the elephants came to the water hole they chased everything away. The lions didn't stay away for long. They just hid off in the distance; I could see them with my binoculars.

The best part of the night was the little game between the elephants and the rhino. One rhino, upset at being kicked out of the water hole, waited for his chance to run into the middle. He then just hangs out and stands in the middle of the hole. Finally the bull elephant has had enough of his antics and goes in and chases him out. He then struts by the procession of people scattered along the bleachers and benches as if to say, "Did you see what I just did?" He is half covered in water and I get some great photos. I'm sure he was saying this because before he could get through his whole strut-procession, the bull elephant completely chased him away!

The behavior of the elephants was fascinating to watch. The adults set up a perimeter as the babies wrestled and played in the water, protecting them from the lions by standing in line. It was interesting watching them change positions so that each one could drink the water. When they ran as a herd, the entire ground shook from them rumbling in – such a large group. When the elephants were done, the giraffes came in for water. They were waiting their turn. No animal is more vulnerable than a giraffe when he drinks. Having to spread his legs and lower his head is so cute. A few of the elephants held guard on the side against the lions until all the giraffes had finished drinking. Then they tore ass out of there to catch up with the group. Cool!

The next day we head out into the main part of the park and drive around for a few hours. We see all the animals you can Imagine and head for Swakopmund. The day after we arrive our guide who had to walk all day through the dessert shows up again with a smile. We then head off to Botswana. Since I am going into the Serengeti later in my trek I want to experience as many diverse places of Africa as I can.

In Maun we separate on different tours. Most of my group goes to Moremi Game Park; I went into the Okavango delta for 3 days and 2 nights. During the drive out to drop me off, the owner of the tour company uses a very racist African term to tell a black guy to open the gate to the delta entrance. I looked right at him, told him if he ever uses that term in front of me again I will gladly teach him a lesson. He looks into my eyes and decides not to say a word. Smart guy!

Apparently it's where the bush guide grew up. He has been a guide in the delta for 15 years. I think he's like 22. We are preparing to go, getting our Mokoros, and coolers. Only one girl went with me to the Delta. Thank goodness because if not, I wasn't going to be able to go. In fact, I was only allowed to go because he was such a good guide and didn't need an extra man. The Delta was so beautiful. We rode along the delta from island to island getting out and walking amongst the animals. The baboons were quite upset that we were there. Wild elephants and packs of zebra's! We sat around during the first day trying to get relief from the heat. Jumping into the delta to cool off was risky because the specter of crocs put a damper on that idea. We were so hot; we had no choice but to jump in but only when one person played lookout.

I feel this thing crawling up my leg and look down to see a scorpion crawling quickly up my leg. I stomp my foot on the ground and it falls off my leg. My guide then leans down and picks him up and snaps his tail off before even 2 seconds go by. I look at him in shock.

Is it deadly?

"Yes, that one is deadly." He replies. "But he can't bother you anymore without a tail." On the second night we stopped at a small island. As we were falling asleep, a group of lions walked by so close to our tent I could see their exhaled shadow of breath. In fact, as they walked down to the river and purred before getting a drink, even the bugs didn't chirp for an hour. Creepy! The 'king of the jungle' indeed.

At the end of the Delta tour, I gave my guide some money for a tip. It was just for him.

"You don't have to share with the other guide or driver."

I'm in line the next day getting some cash from the exchange office when I see my guide hand the driver the money I gave him to get exchanged.

I asked him, "Why did you do that? I told you the money was for you."

"I don't have the proper paperwork to get it converted into the local currency". He explained. "I asked the other guy to exchange it for me."

Later that day I see my guide purchase a Discman and a CD of local music from his birth area. As I'm standing there, he puts the headphones on and listens to the music, saying it's the first time he has ever heard music in his ears before. The look on his face was very cool. He tells me:

"While I save money from this new job, the owner of the tour company lets me stay at his house. I never saw proper plumbing before either." Big smile.

Along the way out of Botswana we stop at the Orange River, a place to camp, get drinks and enjoy the locals. They actually invite the local kids who kick the shit out of us in futbol (soccer). The driver of our truck says, "Don't worry. I've seen pro teams come down here and still get their ass kicked. They were actually nice to you guys today; they only used the young kids."

At the bar there are a few photos of a tourist being eaten by a crocodile in stages. The sign reads:

"Please don't walk down to the river to piss. Use the loo."

One of my tour mates is an American girl from a state near mine who only wants to fuck fat hairy men. Another is from a country near mine who spent the first 5 days talking about how much she missed her fiancé and was going home to get married after this last trip of hers with her best girlfriend.

I go-to bed early each night and since I'm the oldest, no one shares a tent with me. I get woken up in the middle of the night by a tour mate. She tells me:"One of the girls got so drunk, she has alcohol poisoning and the guide doesn't want to deal with her. He said that it's her fault – deal with it. She was found face down in the sand puking into her own face." (It's the girl who likes hairy guys).

She and I have already exchanged unpleasant words. I called her a bitch to her face. At first I don't care.

"It's not my problem," I tell her. "This girl hates me. Why am I getting up to help her?"

"C'mon, Shane. She might die. You are sober."

Fine! I get up. We carry her to her tent and get a trash can for her to puke in. She fills it up a few times and puke is dripping all over the place. I have extras towels. I put one under her face so if she pukes, she won't have to smell it in her sleeping bag the rest of the trip.

I then search for food. I walk into the bar area to see if somebody left out some food. Each night our truck gets locked up; only the guide has the key. No luck there. So I head into the kitchen area of the campsite. We have only been at this site for 12 hours now. I walk into the kitchen and, low and behold, the girl talking about how much she loved her fiancé and couldn't wait to get married when she got back home is now on her knees giving the bartender she just met a blow job. Good luck to her fiancé!

I find some bread and walk out to feed the girl. The next morning she can't get out of her tent. I go ask her what she wants for breakfast, no reply. I get waffles, eggs, bread, some bacon and orange juice and bring it back to her tent. She offers no 'thank you' – no nothing. She gets sober later, walks out of her tent and drops the towel in my lap as I sit in a chair relaxing. Again no thank you! I give this look like *"Tell me why I lost a whole night sleep for this bitch?"* To the girl who woke me up.

Getting back to the truck, head off to Victoria Falls. During the dry season anyone can walk into the falls area and still have a view. I watch a monkey come down and steal the keys out of this guy's rental car. He left the window open! The monkey then teases him by showing him the keys. Too funny! They eventually trade keys for food. Those monkeys are quite brilliant.

On the last night with this group, I'm playing ping pong with the blowjob girl. She is starting to have fun and asks me why I didn't try to talk to her more. Really? I just look at her and let her beat me in ping pong, getting off the table as fast as I can.

I move to the bar where I sit alone waiting for my turn to play pool. I end up playing with a local prostitute. Though the flirting is fun, I don't pay for sex. Blowjob girl walks up to me and starts to tell me how much of an asshole I am for not talking to her the whole trip. Plus I laughed at her during a word game we played. (They all asked if you had to lose one sense of your body which one could you live without. I thought it was interesting and sad that she based her answer on her career). Yes, that's funny.

Live life, don't be a slave to your career. This world needs to stop defining itself by what it does for a living. I don't think the point of life is to be a slave to the grind. I'm thinking

"This is my holiday! I will talk to anybody I want to; and, if I don't want to talk to you, it's my choice."

I let her talk shit to my face and then tell her "Have a great holiday and marriage." Later as I walk to bed, I hear her say she just told Shane how much of an asshole he is. I didn't even let them know I heard that conversation. The next morning, I wake up and get a taxi to the place where tour number two begins.

CHAPTER 16

The next group was much more mature, friendly and interested in me! Though I'm caught in a fire already because a Swiss girl on tour has made it her mission to fuck every guy she comes in contact with. I join 21 days into their tour and learn she has already slept with every guy in the group. I switched groups. I've never had a one night stand and I don't sleep around. I just have to blow her off.

There are 3 people who are scuba diving instructors on tour as well. They immediately notice my dive computer watch and we talk about diving. They have been working in Indonesia for the last few months. One dive instructor's father actually owns the company with which we're traveling.

We exchange trucks for the Eastern African portion of the trip, getting us a different cook and driver than the ones that were part of the first 21 days. Another girl is typical white South Africa racist. Her grandfather owns a diamond company. She does not hide her displeasure that her driver and cook are black, both from Kenya. This really turns me off and I avoid her for the rest of the trip. Sure, we interact but only in perfunctory fashion and not as friends.

We go-to Zambia first where we are told that there is a driver strike. We might be stuck in this area longer than expected if we can't get diesel. The term 'TIA' is repeated over and over.

"What's TIA?" I inquire never having heard the expression.

THIS IS AFRICA! Relax, everything and anything can and will go wrong. TIA

We drive through this village–a complete shanty town. Kids have no shoes or shirts; they are all covered in dirt. The driver pokes his head out of the truck, asks if there is any diesel in the town. This town has no electricity or running water, but I will tell you the people themselves did not smell of bad hygiene. Wooden outhouses are used to keep their bathroom duties away from the markets and shacks. The kids must have told him they had diesel. He drops us off at our campsite – another beautiful spot overlooking another river with yet another pool to swim in. He comes back a few hours later and we find out the kids from this village bring 200 liters of diesel. He tells us they paid triple the price for it though. He had to make sure that they put it all in the truck. The kids tried to keep a liter per container of diesel.

We get to a camp site in Zambia and the elephants come through the camp twice a day. I learn they love melons. We left or truck door open and the elephant puts his trunk into the truck and takes out all our melons. We have a common fruit bowl on the ledge between the cab and our space. He throws out all the melons for his boys. We try everything we can to get him out of our truck: we throw dirt balls at him and even try to grab him. I slapped him a few times, but he just ignores me. Finally, we get him to move. He begins to walk away but right through a tent, completely destroying it! We find out there was somebody in it! Shockingly, the elephant didn't even touch the guy in the tent, just stepped around him. Wow! Good thing because I really didn't want to see a dead guy that day.

During breakfast the monkeys are raiding our food. While we're cooking, they have free roam in the fridge and food storage area. It was too funny to watch them take advantage of this situation. One monkey standing on the table next to the truck just throwing bags of bread and other foods to the ground while others come and pick it up and run off…

A sign inside the loo says: "Please don't leave rolls of toilet paper inside the bathroom." Apparently, the baboons take the rolls of TP and throw them around to each other from tree to tree.

Although this is quite funny, it creates a real mess. (Remember Mischief Night in the US)? It takes the rangers a long time to clean it up. They ask us not to go-to the bathroom at night alone! There are lots of predators here, and no fences to separate the animals from the people. We see leopard tracks in the sand around the campsite each morning!

I walk to the bathroom by myself one night thinking "I'm a bad ass with my K-bar." I hear noises off to my left and turn my flashlight to see what's there. To my horror I see about 20 different pairs of eyes looking back at me, from all kinds of distances and sizes and heights. It was the last time I ever did that.

During the day a hippo came up out of the river and jumped into our pool. We created a screaming scramble to get out of the pool before he got into it. Sporadically scattered around this campsite were wooden ladders nailed to the trees as escape routes. If we were chased by an animal, theoretically we could climb up these ladders and onto the platforms. I'm not sure how they would protect you from cat predators though.

A few stories about border crossings! We take a ferry across to see the island of Zanzibar, during the elections between Shiite and Sunni Muslims. We are informed that when the last tour company went to Zanzibar during elections a few western tourists were killed on the island. "So be prepared if they decide it's not safe for us there."

We ultimately go there and immediately are enjoined by hundreds of people attempting to get through customs. Our guide walks up to the window.

"I have some tourists."

The tour company has a great rapport with the locals and, as a result, they often get to cross the borders much more easily than 'normal' people. We get some preferential treatment. Some of my tour mates pass through quite easily. The border guard gets to my passport and sees that I'm an American.

"Are any other Americans on the tour?"

My guide says nope.

He then tells the guide: "I will take him last." He just looks at me and I look at him. Too funny! No reason except that I'm an

American. I have to wait at the corner of the building until everybody else passes through; I am last. I'm thinking

Maybe he has to do some special paperwork. I mean, some places do require special visas.

Nope. He just stamps my passport, smiles at me and sends me on my way. I didn't say a word; just went on by.

Zanzibar is an amazing island. The people are awesome. Being there during Ramadan was fun. We had to eat Indian food during the day and fish fry at night. I searched out the cheapest internet café. The owner of the Indian restaurant has family in my home state so he treats me like royalty. He takes me to the cheapest café, which is owned by a Muslim man. Since Ramadan is a highly religious time of year, I respect his call to prayer and leave the café when he went to pray. He would return and open back up again.

The day before we leave, we all come back from the beach side of the island. I bring my other tour mates to this café. They refused to leave during his prayer sessions even though I asked them to respect his religious duties before I took them to the café.

We cross into Kenya for the first time. All my tour mates get the student visa that allows them to stay for three weeks and costs 30 USD cheaper. I get in line and ask for the student visa.

He says, "No, that's not an option for you." He examines my US passport.

I explain: *"We're only going to be in this country for 2 weeks with no multiple entries. There is no need for the full 3 month visa."* (Besides it costs 50 USD)!

Looking at me he asks, "What countries have you been to in Africa?"

I begin to tell him.

He says, "No, that's not really Africa. You will need the full visa."

He puts the $50 in his pocket, looks at me, smiles and says, "Welcome to the real Africa! Enjoy your stay".

The real Africa, where at one country border crossing I witnessed girls being trafficked for sex slaves! Complete with a warning sign on the wall to inform the border agents of any human trafficking you see. As I look up at this sign and then back down to the girls in line being herded by a man who is trying to be inconspicuous. He realizes I notice him, and then shows me very slightly the gun he is hiding under his shirt. In that moment I wept for these girls, knowing there was nothing I could do. For the look in this man's eyes clearly said; you'll be dead before you finish saying anything..... It would not be the last country I witness this in!

At another border the local guards make all the trucks unload their bags of goods and check each one then reload them before they let them drive on. This process must take hours per truck. As they proceed through this, lots of beans and rice fall out of the bags to the ground. The ladies come up from the river banks and sweep up the lost beans and rice placing them in their baskets. There is an unwritten rule! I notice that the ladies all take turns, never taking too much from their sweeping. They leave some on the ground for the next person in line.

On the way into Botswana the guide tells us that we have to hide all leather products from the border crossing. Please hide your drums and anything you might have purchased that has leather as part of the product. The truck has a secret refrigerator behind all the other supplies buried behind things. There is another fridge closer to the front. He pulls off the road an hour before the border and takes out all the meat from the main fridge and puts it in the hidden fridge.

As we're waiting for the ferry to take us across a border, all these little kids dressed in blue clothes get in line. Apparently they have to cross the border by ferry every day for school. We are all bored and begin to play hacky sack to pass the time. I always carry one with me. The kids look and then begin to play.

"We have never seen this toy before," they tell me.

We form a circle to play. Each kid struggles to keep their balance but they are all quite good. I guess futbol is very popular here. The ferry pulls up after an hour and we get ready to cross. This little girl walks up to me with a translator and asks for my hacky sack.

"I'm sorry I can't give it to you." The look of sadness in her face sticks with me for the next few minutes. Waiting on the ferry to finish crossing, I walk up and hand her the hacky sack. The look on her face was priceless.

I was really looking forward to the Serengeti and Ngorongoro crater. We arrive in Arusha, and get organized for this excursion. I can't even begin to tell you what I'm feeling. It's just past peak migration season but not the end of it. I take a three day-two night tour: the first 2 days in the Serengeti and 1 full day in Ngorongoro crater.

The drive in these small trucks is fun. We drive through Masai villages and observe many nomadic people. Our first hour in the Serengeti we see 3 lions sitting on a small collection of rocks! The male is just chilling on the top. After spending a few minutes here, we drive off to see more of this great savanna. It's a massive place! We don't see much other than springbok and boars.

At the end of the day I get to see the prize– my first view of a leopard. He is actually very close to us. He briskly passed us as we tried to catch a glimpse of him. We attempted to guess his path to catch another glimpse of the sleek cat.

We get to our camping area and dinner is ready for us. They inform us not to leave the fire area because just 2 weeks ago a boy wondered away from the fire. By the time they found him, he had been eaten by a leopard. All that was left was his arm — his left arm. Get it? The arm that was left was his left arm. Tough way to teach a kid "Hey son, please don't wonder off."

My first experience with squatting toilets! Not really a problem; the key is to get used to the angle so you don't drop doo-doo on your pants as you bend lower. Hey I'm a tall guy. That night we heard a loud lion fight. It was incredible even louder than the hippo fight I witnessed in Zambia. We all talk about it that morning and hope we get to see the after affects.

The driver of the truck tells us we can remove the detachable sections of the roof and stand up on the seats allowing our whole upper body to be above the truck. "Please take off your shoes." We see a couple of trucks sitting in one spot for 5 minutes. I ask the driver to drive over there to see why they stopped. After a few minutes and a walkie-talkie conversation, we drive over there and quickly see 8 female lions just sleeping under the typical African tree. Amazing!

I open up my camera and put the right lens in. I take one deep breathe realizing that, if these lionesses wanted, they could jump on our truck and tear us to pieces. We are no more than 5 feet away! Fortunately, they could care less about us. Instead they paw at each-other and scratch the tree, moving very little. They do not really acknowledge our presence.

After 30 minutes of watching and chilling, we head off to more parts of the savanna to see many wildebeests and zebras. The very last thing we saw before leaving the Serengeti was a leopard chilling out in a tree, with his tail hanging down. How incredibly beautiful to witness! Of all my photos from my travels, this is one of my favorite prizes.

I spent the night on the rim of Ngorongoro crater. When I was in Cape Town, everyone who worked at my lodge was more excited about this segment of my trip than anything else on my entire itinerary – except the gorilla trek in Uganda. The crater is 10 square miles of a volcano that blew its top. The walls are very steep and jagged. 30,000 different animals live in this space. Flamingos, hippos, crocs, elephants, lions, zebras, cheetahs, everything you can dream of. The walls of this crater are very steep and jagged. It takes the truck more than 1 hour to drive zig-zag down the embankment to the floor. This causes an effect for this well balanced ecosystem. No animals can get in and no animals can get out. A modern day EDEN! How did they get there?

It was amazing to know you can drive around this place in 7 hours and see all the animals of your dreams. We even got the pleasure of seeing a lion kill. We did not watch the ladies take down the wildebeest; we just saw the male sitting over it with his mouth covered in blood and the ribs of the kill fully exposed. Sure, this sounds spectacular. But I'd like to focus on the fact that along the road there were 10 trucks parked in a line looking at him. It was very anticlimactic. We drive along the crater head over to the hippo pool and see many of them. Along the way we catch a glimpse of a cheetah and her cub, just 100 feet away! I got a great photo of a blue balled monkey and his exposed parts as we were exiting the crater! As we turn to leave I notice these 2 elephants eating this tree called devils thorns. It has this title due to the 2 inch long thorns that grow in bunches on a branch. These elephants were eating them up in bunches, I was shocked, first that they could eat such trees then at the fact that their mouths were not bleeding profusely.

In Nairobi we pick up a couple of new passengers and drop off several more. We're on our way up north to visit gorillas. I've been worried about this for a month now because I've developed a cough. If you have a cold, you are not allowed to trek them. Just 2 days before we got there the cough goes away!

We stopped at the equator line along the way. A guy standing at the line informs us that if we give him a nominal fee, he will show us that at opposite sides of the line you will see the water flow in opposite directions. Really? *I thought it was a rumor.* Nope. It's true; witnessed with my own eyes.

His demonstration went like this. Twenty feet apart on opposite lines of the equator, the water did flow in different directions. He held an old steel milk jug upside down with the bottom cut out. As he poured water into one jug until it was full, he put his hand on the mouth of the jug not allowing the water to spill out. He placed a blade of grass into the still water in the open ended jug. When he removed his hand from the mouth of the jug, the water would spin in one direction. On the other side of the equator, he repeated the same process, only the grass would spin in the other direction. We were told that if you place a scale on the center of the line, your weight would be less.

We get up to the campsite that marks the start of the gorilla trek. The guide reviews the guidelines and rules of the trek the night before. We are separated into groups of nine people; our whole group is 8. We have 4 guides who carry AK 47's and inform us

"We are not here to protect us but to protect the animals from poachers."

My fee is 350 USD for the trek. I've heard it's up above $500 now. There were only about 800 gorillas left in the world at the time of the trek. Post my trip the population increased by 100. In Bwindi Impenetrable Forest in Uganda, on the border of Congo and Rwanda, poachers patrol the jungle all the time. Gorillas are hunted in order to sell the hands, feet, and head to the Chinese people for ashtrays and mantle pieces. Seriously! What's wrong with the Chinese?

We hiked and hacked for 6 hours through dense virgin jungle. Very little sunlight reached the jungle floor due to abundant flora. We arrive at a point when our bush walking guide says,

"We've found them! You can now drop your packs and walk toward them on the right. You can spend one hour with them."

My heart is racing. It's beautiful out. I slowly walk toward our spot behind my other tour-mates. We watch 2 brothers act in the typical gorilla manner. Play-fighting they punch each other and roll down the little hill. They get back up pounding their chests and repeat! They aren't even 3 feet tall. We take a few photos. They look at us for a few seconds and get back to their battle, rolling down the hill and finally disappearing!

We're told we can walk down the hill toward the group. It's a group of 9 complete with a very young baby. The male is sitting there and grooming one of his girls. He pops his head up, looks at us and then goes back to what he is doing. Before we started they asked us not to touch them; if they touch us, it's ok. One female walks toward us and out of respect we all take 2 steps back. We can see the silverback is watching us casually. The young ones are now climbing trees and swinging from branches. One even falls out of the tree on his mothers head. She picks him up looks at him and puts him back down. The hour goes by way too fast. I got the feeling that we were the ones on display and not them.

As we're hiking back down, I slip on the angled and mud surface, putting my hand out to brace myself for my fall. Great! The first tree I get to has spikes all over it; it's too late to change trees. It stops my descent and causes my hand to bleed a little. Who puts spikes on tree trunks?

The hour I spent with the gorillas is the most amazing experience I have ever had! I don't think anything will ever come close to this again! The sheer majesty of the experience, being around such an intelligent creature that has no ulterior motives was a great lesson in what really matters in this world. Nothing did compare to this moment until I was in Tahiti snorkeling with humpback whales at less than 5 feet distance.

One of the people we picked up for this 2 week extension is a guy from Switzerland. He has a heavy accent and most of the group doesn't want to talk with him due to the fact that it takes time. I think this is quite rude. The poor guy is in the middle of nowhere and nobody wants to talk to him. I make it my mission to befriend him and chat. I haven't been to Switzerland yet and I'm starting to get around the little blue ball we call earth. We became friends and still are to this day. In fact, later the next year I go-to Switzerland to hang out with him. While there I get my crevasse rescue training skills for high altitude climbing.

When I arrive back in Cape Town, I check my emails. My volleyball girlfriend and model tells me she has cheated on me and doesn't want anything to do with me anymore. An email *Dear John* while I'm out of the country! This upsets my whole experience for the last few days.

Nonetheless, on the Robben Island tour/experience seeing the penguins from a nude beach. Nowhere else in the world can you sit on a beach, see penguins and beautiful naked girls, while smoking joints and playing Frisbee. I hadn't shaved or cut my hair for the entire trip. I have been bald since I was 20 shaving my head every few days. I wanted to see what my hair looked like. LOL!

In Zanzibar I tell my tour mates I wanted to spend the first night in the city enjoying the local fish fry. My tour mates get into a large taxi and head to the resort part of this island. As they drive away, I see my reflection in the glass of the taxi. WOW! All my hair is grey, even my beard. Shocking!

At the airport in London on my flight back to NYC, the customs guy tells me the photo in my passport isn't me.

"I just spent 3 months across Africa mostly in the middle of nowhere," I inform him, *"I chose to not shave or cut my hair. If they really want, I can go get a razor and shave my face for you, if I do, I will miss my flight. Are you gonna pay for my flight?"*

They decide to let me go telling me I should really update my passport photo. When I was going through customs in Tahiti, they said the same thing to me. I let my hair grow out just a little, but I was shaven that time. I guess I should be a spy because my look changes so drastically. Lol.

CHAPTER 17

Arriving home, I head back to work, wait for my house to get sold, finalize my divorce and get my life started again. Despite the trip across Africa, getting divorced really shook me up. I didn't cook myself any food for 6 months. The house was sold but my ex-wife didn't tell me about the closing; suddenly I had only 5 days to get out and find another place to live. Meanwhile I'm working 7 days a week.

Good luck! It wasn't easy getting all my stuff into a storage container and finding an apartment so quickly. I moved into the back area of an older British lady's house near the beach. I would walk there when I felt strong enough to get myself out of bed. It's very hard to figure out who you are after you lose everything that makes up what you are.

You go-to a movie and think "what does my wife like to watch?" Or, going grocery shopping, I'd think: "what does my wife like to eat?" Holidays alone take a lot of getting used to. I even found myself considering. "what do I wear?" With her in mind.

In fact, the first 6 months as a divorced man I lived in the apartment but didn't sleep in a bed – I slept on the floor. I just didn't have any energy except to go-to work and come home.

I ate very little and did not work out either. My climbing mate finally tells me,

"It's time to come out and start to do living things."

I begin climbing again, of the sports I do, ice climbing is my real passion. In the order of effect all my sports have on my adrenaline addiction! It goes as follows, ice climbing, surfing, skydiving, scuba diving, snowboarding, and lastly rock climbing. My climbing mate and I train very hard this season and head up north, I am leading the 3rd and final pitch of this 550 foot high ice flow. As I get to the top, finish setting up the belay station, and begin the work to get my mate to the top. He comes up a few feet to my right at which point I inform him to look down and enjoy the view. He tells me he will accommodate my request once he gets safely clipped in. Telling him to grow a pair, stick a bomber axe in and look down, since at my belay station our view is obstructed by the trees I used for safety. Watching my best climbing mate of 5 years I see him set his axe then take a 2 second look down. Laughing at him it dawns on me he is afraid of heights. Amazing I find this out at 550 feet on almost vertical ice. It would be 4 more years before I broke him of his fear by allowing him to use my go-pro camera while making his climbs.

I start sleeping on a bed, begin cooking small meals and it's time to start planning a holiday. I always wanted to go see Istanbul and the Blue Mosque. I've heard so much about it. I book a week in Istanbul. I also start planning my 2nd large backpacking trip –54 days in Australia. My ex-wife comes over with my half of the proceeds from the sale of the house. This small windfall pays for the airfare to and from Australia and all the internal flights during those 54 days. My aunt –my step Dad's sister –lives in Tasmania. We used to get along so well, talking about books and such. She is the only one in the family I got along with on an intrinsic level.

As I'm in the climbing gym working and getting my persona back from my divorce, I meet another girl. She is much younger than I and we decide to give this relationship a shot. All I asked was that she be honest with me and tell me when she doesn't want me anymore. No need to cheat and then lie about it all.

Just talk to me like an adult. We have some fun: I begin to teach her how to play pool. (She is from a strict religious family. In the interest of her well being, I will leave out quite a bit of her life. I will include our interactions). Shortly after we met, I leave for Australia.

Arriving in Sydney I'm not jetlagged just really excited to be on the road again. I plan on staying in Sydney for 4 days before heading off on a bus tour through other parts of the continent. Love the harbor and the bridge; even walk across it to see the city from the other side. The Opera house is majestic. The coolest thing about Sydney to me is the way the monorail goes through the hotels in the city. Being just an exposed steel rail lends a very unique visual in the city.

Australia has incredible surfing which is a big part of the draw for me. I schedule my first lesson and immediately get hooked! Learning to surf became my mission for the next several trips of mine. I fly to Alice Springs, get on my bus tour and by sunset I'm drinking wine at Uluru. Actually I think that Fish River Canyon is more breathtaking than Uluru. The surrounding rocks near there are just as sweet. I hike and play climb, and take time to look at aboriginal artwork. The people on the bus are much younger than me, so I'm on the outside again.

My experience has trained me to be incredibly fluent at the lost art of reading body language. 80% of all communication between people is non verbal. With my wealth of experience with the human psyche I am quite literate.

I'm very concerned for the human race. We have become so internet dependant that we've lost this ability to understand or perceive meaning through body language or 80% of human communication! I'm convinced this explains in part why we hate and misunderstand each-other so much. We have so much anxiety and fear of contact and being around each-other. We're only using 20% of communication– SMS, texting, emails – and we think we're in complete understanding of humanity. This modern culture is so lost and backwards; we're all going to be shut-ins if we don't start getting out there and learning, focusing and interacting in the 80%. Plus we will not be able to actually communicate with each-other face to face in a very short period of time. Wondering why we won't be able to get along on the simplest of levels and interactions.

While surfing I quickly realize the girls on this excursion are not interested in me. Must be an age gap thing. I'm afraid to ask any of them to put suntan lotion on my back. I was not fully prepared for surfing: the thought never crossed my mind to bring a rash guard. I spent the whole day in the water, even during lunch while the other sensible people took a break. (I just presumed they got tired out much earlier than me. Can you guess I am a type-A personality)?

I got the worst sunburn you could ever imagine on my back. It was peeling off in sheets. Blisters the size of a chess board! The woman who ran the tour was married to the driver. Awe they were so cute together– just full of life. She looked at my back as I was coming out of the pool the second day and said come here.

"I really get my jollies off of popping blisters!"

Awesome because I can't get at these things!

She pops them each day, even peels the skin off my back and applies Aloe Vera twice a day. Thank God for her. When I tell you sheets, the peels were bigger than the size of notebook paper. They came off for a few days in a row. Gross, I know but it is what it is…

We head up to Darwin and I have my best day of my life. I've always wanted to climb up behind a waterfall and sit there behind the thundering water as it cascades upon the rocks. We had played all these ice breaker games on the bus. Making knots with gummy worms, for example and asking each-other what our dreams and fears were. I wish the tours in Africa would have done such a thing. I tell them that I've always wanted to climb up behind a waterfall and sit there, or even jump through it. The driver tells me I might get to have that chance later in the tour.

I got to spend my birthday, my actual birthday at the oldest bar in the outback. I put my favorite pair of boxers on the wall; mine is one of hundreds of pairs of underwear on the walls. That day we got to swim in hot springs, which were more like a hot river that is bubbling up out of the ground. They tell us

"Be careful because the hot pools run along another river that has crocodiles in it. Sometimes the crocs come into the pools."

I tell them of my experience with crocs in Africa. "My bush guide told me a way to protect oneself from them. When you see one pop his head up, you move left or right from your location. They have this film to protect and cover their eyes once they drop down into the water. The film prevents them from seeing very well when underwater. So if you keep moving left or right you're ok, because he will pop right up where you just were! Creepy but hey you can protect yourself." The other alternative, of course, is to get the hell out of the water as soon as you see one.

The last day of the tour was amazing. We saw these termite mounds that are even higher than the ones I saw in Botswana that are 5 to 10 feet taller than me! I stood next to them to get a perspective. From there we head off to the spot where, "If the water is flowing," the guide says, "You will get your waterfall moment. Please be careful because 2 tourists drowned at this spot two weeks ago."

As we're hiking in I see it. My eyes light up as I see another guy doing exactly what I want to do. I'm gone- down the path, ahead of the group. I jump in and hug the wall of the plunge pool to make sure I can grab the sides if the current is too strong and save myself. It's not long before I realize the current isn't strong enough to hurt me. Sure I have to work for it but I'm not really working very hard.

I dive under the point of the impact of the falls and pop up behind it. I inspect to see if I can climb up! Hey I'm a climber; I can figure it out. I soon find a spot that I can grip and get some leverage. I get up about 10 feet and find there is a 4 foot section of rock sticking out just far enough for a person to sit on. You can't see anything because the water is spraying all over your face. You could jump through this waterfall and then climb back up and do it again.

I share the spot with a girl on tour who is also a Christian. We have many talks about faith and life, about places we've stopped in Australia that had swimming pools like Africa. I know we could have snogged (snogging is when you tongue kiss. REAL

FRENCH kissing is when you kiss cheek to cheek saying hello or goodbye) behind that waterfall; I know she wanted me to kiss her, but I didn't want to spoil this experience by tainting it with such childish things. I really was just thankful to the Lord for this experience and that I could share it with somebody who understood and appreciated the moment.

My time with the group ends and I'm off to Cairns. I booked a week long scuba diving excursion off the Great Barrier Reef on a live aboard boat! One hundred miles off shore with no pollution and incredible beauty along the reef! The reef closer to shore is dead due to our human traffic. With 26 dives I had the most amazing experiences under water. The shark feed at North Horn was truly fun. Having 20 plus sharks all competing for the tuna heads stuck to the chain takes your breath away, or at the least causes you to breathe a little quicker through your regulator. They were only 15 feet away from me.

I dove with millions of glass fish that were being balled up by a school of barracuda. We dove each site twice so I asked the videographer to take a video of me inside those glass fish. If it came out nice, I would buy the video. You can see for yourself at my website!

It's a small world. My dive master checked all our certifications the first night. Asks us how many dives we have, and our deepest depth. I'm one of 2 people who are single traveling alone on this trip. Most are married couples. Finally, he looks at my dive card, sees who trained me and at what dive shop I learned. He looks at me and asks me if so and so still owns the shop.

Sure. I say, "He's an awesome guy."

He tells me he was on their Papa New Guinea dive expedition. He tells me, "Have a great week!"

The second day we experienced severe waves. I got so seasick I can't sleep in my bed. I sleep on the back of the boat just puking over the side every few minutes. That continued the first dive morning: I had to lean my head over the boat and puked every few minutes. As the dive master was going over the dive flow and site, I'm lying on the deck. I could not stand up. I had to wait until everybody else was in the water before I ran over got my gear on and jumped in the water.

It's hard to communicate with your buddy how the 2 of you are going to interact underwater when you are puking every moment. I did not miss one dive during the day however. My masters were so impressed, telling me they had not seen anyone so green in the face before. They loved my passion for diving despite my condition.

"The world stopped bobbing while under water. It was the best place to be for my seasickness."

After the 3ʳᵈ day, the waves calmed down and my sea sickness ebbs. Yea! I can sleep in bed again. At the end of the week we all chat on the back of the boat exchanging stories and SD cards. One couple tells me:

"You are an adrenaline junky! If you want to see and do something cool, you would love this place in Laos called, the Gibbons Experience. It's a Zip-line park where you live in tree houses and zip around 500 feet above the ground on 1 kilometer long Zip-lines."

I'm thinking: Laos? I'm never going to get there.

Back in Cairns, I notice in the guest house that skydiving is offered nearby. (I have one drop in the city just a few days before 9/11. I even have the Twin Towers in the video. My next drop is in the Swiss Alps above Interlaken. I spent a week there after a week on the banks of Lake Geneva in a time-share my parents gave me. Then I went snowboarding at Matterhorn, actually it was my 3ʳᵈ day on a snowboard. Talk about biting off more than you can chew. I digress).

The drop in Cairns was beautiful, so beautiful that I decide to get my skydiving certification. I now have 3 tandem drops. I do love adrenaline.

The next leg of my journey takes me to Tasmania to spend a week with my aunt. She told me that the son of her neighbor is a climber. Before I left home I increased my workout regimen in the gym to be prepared for climbing. To be honest, all these great plans for my time there went unfulfilled. I can't do anything because I am just plain exhausted. On a side note Whitehaven beach in Whitsundays is the most beautiful beach I have seen in the world.

We managed one climb up the cliffs at Coles Bay. We climbed as the tide came in and washed over the belay station on which we were just standing. We heard the wave's crash beneath us which played games with our head. The guy tells me to be careful when reaching up for holds because sometimes the blue jelly fish get wind blown into the cracks of the wall. It may still kill you even though it's been stuck there for some time. My aunt took me into Hobart to meet this guy and go climbing. She has a friend who holds a stall at the market. After my climbing experience I meet them in the market and help them set up and take down their stall. He gives me a ride back to my aunts, they are close neighbors.

Melbourne is a nice city! I'm still quite exhausted. I decided that on the next backpacking trip I will take more trains and buses than flights. Flying home all I can think about is getting back to my Noogy. (On a side note, ladies, if a man calls you baby, honey, darling, etc, he's not really in love with you. Those are thoughtless names. When he invents a private name that only applies to you, then you have his heart. Same with roses: red roses are thoughtless. Every gas station in the country has red roses at the counter. If he gives you some colored roses he spent some time and depth of thought into your flowers. The rules of love according to Shane)!

My jeep toy seems to behave like a woman! Every time I go away for a long period of time, it breaks the week I leave. Seriously it's kind of comical. For this trip I lost my transfer case. I get back home and my jeep is my first priority. I get to my mates house and pick up the toy. The drive home is a struggle; we go straight to my mechanic.

I head back to work and lots of it. During off hours I get reacquainted with my new girlfriend. Within a couple of months we start planning our first holiday together. She has never been on vacation; her parents are so strict I don't think they would ever let her. We plan to go down to Atlantis for 5 days.

The day before departure, I visited her on her college campus. She dropped her phone in my jeep. Five minutes later she gets messages from a boy she just met on a conference in the capital.

"I love you! I'm excited to come see you."

Seriously? I blew up. I bring her phone back and we fight. The trip is already paid for so I decide to take her anyway. It was a trip to show her that the world is beautiful and you can play even if you are working hard. Great trip, the water park at Atlantis is fun. Love the lazy rivers. The dig is worth every penny. I want to spoil her but not in some sugar daddy sense. She is awesome and intelligent; she will get her Masters and PHD with no student loans only scholarships. It's clear to me she has greatness in her future. I want her to have as many experiences as she can, learn as much as she can.

We go out to expensive dinners, $200 plus each night. At the Martinique, I decide it's time to taste caviar but I don't see it on the menu. I ask the Maitre De

Can we have some caviar when he comes back?

"Let me go talk to the chef." He comes back and tells me, "Beluga is 225 dollars an ounce."

I don't want an ounce. Is there anything he can do for me?

It's not really about the money; an ounce is a little too much caviar for two people.

"The chef can make this pouched egg topped with caviar and cream."

Sure I've had this before.

He tells me, "It's about $90 in New York; we'll do it for $60."

What a trip to order something that isn't on the menu! The dish is served with pumpernickel bread and it's amazing.

I really enjoy catamarans as well. After spending a week living on one, hopping around the islands near St Marten, I can't go-to the islands and not spend at least a day going snorkeling and such. We go on the cat to snorkel and I find out she can't really swim.

"The life vest will help you," I tell her. "Just try."

She does and I'm impressed. After dealing for years with my ex-wife not even trying, I'm excited with this girl. She climbs. She is adventurous – a little bit of a rebel like me. As soon as we get away from the cat she becomes afraid. I can see it in her eyes. I take her right back. It takes me the better part of the next year and a half to teach her how to swim.

I do have a hard time when we get back from the trip. The boy comes to see her. Lots of drama. It affects my job performance while I'm working for my step dad. I get over it and begin to come out of it. I get this amazing apartment right near the beach all by myself. After work every day, I ride my bike down there and just relax. I could never live too far from the ocean; the world just doesn't smell right away from it.

I have chosen to live debt free. No credit card debt, no car payment, no mortgage. When my ex-wife and I got together she had $10,000 in cc debt. When I started to make money we set up a structured settlement plan. I saved all my money even though I was an apprentice not making very much. She often fought with me about this. I told her it's all ours. Stop this silly bickering!

I pay for the trips, repairs on the car, and furniture purchases etc, etc, she never sees it this way, and it becomes a daily battle. Even though right before we went to Paris for the week I asked her how much she had left on the structure debt payment plan. She tells me it's just over $4,000. I'm making about $400 a week. So you can imagine how long it takes to save up that kind of money, plus traveling all over the place. I tell her just take the money out of my account and pay off the balance. She gives me a big hug that day.

I decided to put everything in her name, her credit was better than mine since I've never had any. It doesn't bother me I never thought we would get divorced. So when we got divorced I had no credit history. I got my trade license that year and began to make $70,000 even going over $90,000 for 2 years straight. The banks would not give me a credit card. I try to get a secured credit card. That turns out to be a nightmare. They asked for a company letterhead plus my pay stubs plus my bank statements, before they would give me a pre paid card. Seriously, I guess when you live debt free you're a threat to society.

I ask my parents for the company letterhead and they even wanted a copy of my social security card. I already mailed them 400 USD. The mailing process took more than 2 months; they sent me 3 letters requesting more information. Eventually I asked for my money back. Too funny!

So I turn to my parents and ask them if they would cosign a credit card for me so I can start my credit history. Sure I live debt free but I do need to book holidays, get rental cars. Someday I may want to buy a house or condo. They tell me they can't; it's too risky for them. Yet they did this for both of my step brothers. Once again the rules for Shane are very different than the rules for my brothers.

It's all good. My pastor tells me I can use his Amex card but it has to be paid off immediately at the end of the month. Many years later I'm still tethered to his account. I make all big purchases on it which produces points; he can get the miles and fly to see his brother once a year. Yea for family... In all the limited time I've spent in my family's presence, I've never stolen anything from them. When I'm around, they often lock up the jewelry. Lol.

My coworkers and I have become quite friendly. I do some side work with one of them. Now if I were so irresponsible, trust me, he wouldn't have me working for him at all. I give him a break on the pay scale; he has kids and a wife. I have nothing but passport stamps. He often walks in and says to me,

"Your father is an asshole! Why do you put up with him?"

What did he say?

He never once tells me; just says, "He is an asshole to you."

It's normal, I really don't care. The only thing I'm interested in is a relationship with my mother. So I never bitch to her about all the sideways things he does and says. When I got back from Africa, for example, he came to the jobsite every day at coffee break and lunch break telling my friend not to let me talk about my trip. I mean really? You're working with a guy who just went across Africa for three months and you are told not to ask him anything? Even during break times? Asshole!

He is finally forced to let me talk when the guy we're working for says, "Hey! I want to hear about the trip. I'm buying lunch today."

Must have broken his heart to sit there and hear about it. Another funny tactic of his happens the day before I leave for my trips. Be they short or big trips, he always gave me the worst jobs you could imagine. I just laughed after the 5th time this happened. C'mon seriously! It even becomes a joke among the coworkers. Before I went to Africa, I asked him if I was going to get 5 weeks of consistent work. I needed that extra money for the trip. He assured me he would get me that work. I book the flight and after 3 weeks I have no work. In fact, I'm the only employee not working those 2 weeks. I had to budget myself tighter because of that lost money.

My friend is not the only coworker who comes up to me and asks, "Why is he such an asshole to you? The things he says behind your back are amazing."

I tell this other guy: *I really don't want to hear it. I'm here to make money and have fun. Fuck him.*

When I left for Atlantis I did not yet own a digital camera. The company has 5 of them. I saw no point in buying one yet. I asked my step dad if I could borrow a camera. He tells me that he can't find any of them that I should buy my own. Leaving for work that day his partner says, "You can borrow the one that's in my truck. I'm not going to need it for this week. Please don't break it."

The company got turned over to my step brother who is just like him. He has a bad habit of talking a lot of shit behind your back; turn around and you have to pick the knives out of your back daily. His brother is much the same way. In the end I'm very happy that I didn't grow up in his house. I don't treat people this way. I couldn't imagine being this way.

So we all have no idea that the company is being turned over to my step brother. We have pizza at the shop with a few beers maybe once or twice a year; we do have a company Christmas party each year, too. We get told its pizza day at the shop after work. We all get there and my step dad pulls me around the corner 2 minutes before everybody else to tell me my brother is getting the company. He didn't want me to be upset that I found out the same time as everybody else, but it was a last minute decision. Too late I'm really upset at this. I could care less about the company. I don't want that kind of responsibility. I love traveling for months every year. I'm very upset at finding out the same day as everybody else when the other brother knew about it weeks in advance. I found this out later drinking with him.

I ask for my slip the very next day. There isn't much work. I always tolerated his abuse to me by thinking at least my mother is being taken care of. I'm certainly not going to put up with it from a kid –my step-brother– who is such an asshole to his employees. Having witnessed his style of management first hand, I'm not interested. I go work for another company. Those 2 years I made over $90,000 per year and only took short trips: a waterpark in Orlando the month it opened; went to an all inclusive resort in the islands. I even booked one of my dream vacations: hiking the Inka trail to Machu Picchu!

It's another 13-day backpacking excursion. I arrive in Lima and head off to the beach. To my surprise there is surf. I rent a board and continue my education at this sport. My dream is to ride inside a pipe someday. Catch the plane to Cusco. As I'm getting off the plane, I see a sign being held up for a baseball player who did an incredible choke job at the end of the season – an historic kind of choke job. Since he's on a team I can't stand, it took all my energy not to tell him he should learn how to hit a curve ball for next year! I wear my favorite team's hat. In my travels I meet many Americans who put Canadian flags on their luggage and backpacks. Since I've been all through Canada I ask them where they are from. Within a few seconds they tell me the story or they just lie and make up stuff. I'm an asshole but not that bad. I just let them be.

I wear a New York Yankees cap on my head when I travel, I'm proud to be from this country. I am not afraid to tell my fellow earthlings that our country is fucked up and we have problems. I even point out our arrogance and lack of real culture. This is a very superficial country that defines itself by our material possessions. We define our self worth by our occupation. This is insane to me. You get one chance at life and you spend it working to keep up and ahead of the Joneses. So in a very quick period of time I'm respected among the global citizens. They often tell me it's nice to hear an American who understands the real world, who respects other cultures and can talk in such a manner. This always makes me feel good. Especially when I'm in 3ʳᵈ world countries, for we all know western civilization is only about 20 % of the world's population.

Macchu Picchu. I bring my boots that have seen about 30 countries now. I check them before I leave the States. In my hotel in Cusco I'm debating whether to bring my blue kayak sandles. I read that at the end of the hike you can take a shower. After 80 kilometers through the Andes at a peak altitude of 14,000 feet you might need one. Ok I bring them, cutting down weight from my backpack to my hiking pack. I leave the extra stuff behind in the guest house! First they give you leaves from the plant that makes cocaine to chew on if you get altitude sickness. They even make a caramel candy out of it. I get some cool walking sticks with rubber tips to do my part in protecting the trail.

The check point to register is the first stop. Our group is 10. I get to the check point and I'm greeted with a guard saying:

"Oh, you're an American. We need the extra paperwork for you."

I ask my guide, "Is there going to be a problem?"

"This trail requires a limited number of tourists all of whom must book months in advance. It's ok." He says, "No worries; he has it, just has to get it."

Only Americans are required this extra paper work. Our hike begins along a narrow path. After about 1 kilometer, the soles of my boots have disintegrated off. At first I tried to walk with them missing, but the rocks were hurting my unprotected soles. Boots have a tongue, of course, that cannot relate the adventures of the feet that employ them. My pen tells only a fraction of what they have seen. After taking a few photos of them, I discard my worn and faithful boots.

I pull my Meno's out from my bag and put them on my feet. The porters who carry our tents and food wear a similar shoe so I'm unconcerned about my new footwear. My tour mates are a little shocked.

I'm not missing this hike even if I had to hike it barefoot.

The shoes work just fine. They even provided a lot more grip on the stair cases than expected, never giving out under me even on the 3rd day when we traversed those 5,000 steps down! The little ruins along the way are just as beautiful as the end game. On the second day you make the highest elevation and then begin the down climb to your night's stay. Just before you make this pass you stop for lunch. It's the last time you can get western stuff like Gatorade and batteries and such. The locals are drinking this maze beer. So I go over to get a glass; I enjoy sampling the local culture when I travel. I don't eat western food when I'm traveling unless I'm in a western country, and then I don't eat American western food. The beer is quite good for being crudely made at 12,000 feet. A girl from the Swedish group makes a stupid comment about how I'm going to drink while hiking.

"I'm just tasting the culture. No point hiking up here and drinking Gatorade; try to enjoy the culture that is around you."

She then asks for a sip. I am reminded again of the insanity of girls.

Before I left for Australia my girl gave me this stuffed bear to take with me. There is not another trip I take where he isn't hanging off my backpack. He is named after the falls in Australia that I got to climb up behind and jump through.

At this point I'm giving myself a shameless plug. I have a webpage:

www.shaneoffthegrid.com

The webpage has photos and a blog of all my travels. The bear has his own blog. I got tired of taking photos of myself everywhere so I started taking photos of him all over the place. That bear has been to over 35 countries now. I even record all the sports I do. With my go pro camera since most guys are full of shit... In the toolbar under videos are all my sports in each of their own categories....

I've even learned a little about protecting yourself while traveling. First walk casually through the country. Find the natural speed of the culture. Every culture has its own operating speed. Now walk either faster or slower than the natural pace. You will feel when someone matches your speed. Since it's an unnatural speed you know that feeling is not good. You just stop and do some window shopping and mark the person tailing you.

Second I have my bear clipped with a baby carabineer to the top of my day pack making it impossible to open my bag or even bump it without moving the bear. He hangs in a mesh bag. So I can now go casually about my time, not worrying about my safety. Some side notes about places. In Cape Town they have a law called, 'crimes against poverty'. Meaning if you're mugged by someone under 18, you cannot defend yourself; if you hurt the robber while being mugged, you will spend the night in jail. Kind of strange, isn't it? But hey everybody knows this, so no one carries much Rand (the local currency) in this area of Cape Town.

Back to Peru, the view from Manchu Picchu is amazing. I leave my group so that I can hike up Wyana, (Wyanapicchu) and get a great view. I read they closed that hike after 12 PM and only let 200 people go up there a day. You have to sign a ledger on the way in and out. I see the girl in front of me on the list is from the Czech Republic. I race up the path so I can practice my Czech. We have a great day talking and hiking.

On arrival the place is surrounded by mist clouds and rain. When I get halfway up Wyana the fog lifts and it's crystal clear and sunny the rest of the day! I even pause to take a nap on a grass patch of M.P. soaking in the ambience. I get my bus down the hill and then get my train. I'm told in the main area when we get off the train there will be a guy holding a sign with my name on it waiting for me. I get off the train among the mass of people and see no sign. It's about 2 hours back to Cusco. I try to catch one of the buses but they are all booked for tours. I end up sharing a taxi with a few local guides and we drink beer and eat local snacks all the way back to Cusco.

CHAPTER 18

Back home and back to work and back to the jeep which broke again the day I left. Too funny. Go see the girl and have some fun dates. By this time the American economy is collapsing. Work is drying up and it's getting tough. I decide it's cheaper to backpack through Asia for 6 months than it is to stay in America.

I put all my stuff in storage and furnish my girl's apartment. She is getting her Master's degree near me and I want her place to be nice. Big flat screen TV! All the couches and cooking things she needs dressers and my bed. She already used it for many times anyway. Even staying with me one summer while she did some work for a lab! We rode bikes to the beach every day. When I was married I bought 2 of everything. Including full suspension mountain bikes! We took them to Nova Scotia to bike along the coast, taking the ferry from Bar Harbor.

I start my planning with India. My girl took two trips there in college to work on projects but never made it to the Taj Mahal, though being just a couple of hours away. I've heard that India is a very tough country to backpack through. I have now been to every country in Europe except Spain, and Scotland, 18,000 kilometers across Africa, 20,000 kilometers across Australia, 17 different

Caribbean islands, and some parts of South America and Eastern Europe! The last place is Asia.

Gleaning information from my fellow travelers I hear all kinds of horror stories about the food, water, and culture! So I decide to make India my first stop; that way if I hate it, I can tough it out for 28 days before moving on. I wanted to go to Bhutan and Nepal after India. In my investigation it would be too much to go from one to the other then back, so I skip Bhutan.

I'm determined to go-to Tibet! I have found that when you investigate tour companies if you are willing to search the local ones you can save so much money. Instead of using some British or American tour company where the proceeds go back to some rich guy in Greenwich in either country, I prefer my tourist dollars to stay with the locals. I generally don't use tour companies, but the PRC won't allow you to enter Tibet without a tour company. So I have a hard date for this portion of the trip.

I also realize that I'm doing something most people don't do: enter Tibet from Nepal. It's much easier to get your visa for China then enter Tibet then head out through Nepal. In fact, all my correspondence emails from many tour companies tell me they have never heard of someone making the trek in reverse. I'm told I can get it done though with a certain company. So I wire the money to the Tibetan company, and the Chinese tour company. My plan to travel to Beijing from Lhasa via the world's highest train, requires a tour guide as well. (PRC will not allow me to travel through China alone either. I must have a tour company or they might not allow me into the country).

After that I plan to fly to Thailand. Head up north to Laos for the Gibbons experience zip-line jungle tour! This gibbons experience also requires a set time and date since its booked solid for months in advance. So I have some flexibility but not fully free. I decide I want to head into Vietnam then Cambodia then back into Thailand again. Go-to the islands. Then to Indonesia to surf in Bali and head over to these Gili islands I've heard so much about. There you have it folks: The Plan.

I attend a U2 concert with my girl the day before I leave. I wanted to show her what a real concert is like. We get general admission, wait in line and get inside the circle. It's now my 5th time seeing U2, and they are amazing as usual.

Next day I leave for India. Arriving at night I pay for a taxi to take me to my first guest house in Delhi. It's like landing on the moon; everybody working security or customs is wearing space suits, masks and checking us for health. This is quite strange to me later on, as I reflect on that first day.

A short drive from the airport and we're inside the bazaar district. All cheap guest houses are in dodgy areas. He stops the taxi. As we get out I pick up my backpack that weighs 22 pounds. It holds all I need for the climates I will be experiencing.

I learned how to wash my clothes by hand in Malawi Africa. I tried to wash them in Victoria Falls but they didn't come out that clean. After I got mine back from the ladies in Malawi I asked them to take me the next day so I could watch and learn. I went with the ladies for the day so they could teach me how to wash my own clothes. Cool day with them.

I got to play with their kids. One told me he didn't want to run up my front and do flips while I hold his hands because he was afraid of getting my clothes dirty. Wow!

So I only have 5 pairs of boxers. A few shirts and some cloth-ing I use for ice climbing. I plan on hiking through the Annapurna region. We turn the corner to head deeper into this bazaar area. As we do I get hit with the stench of human excrement; it engulfs my entire body. Within seconds I throw up. Lean right over and puke. Wow, my body screams at me,

"Please don't take another breath."

Too late! I gag but no vomit. My driver just laughs at me. We get to the guest house and I book a room with an AC unit. I didn't plan on AC originally but I figured some flow of air would be good for me. I have iodine tablets for drinking water and a bag of jolly ranchers. I usually drop one in the Nalgene bottle after I put tablets in it. It helps with the taste.

Wake up the next day and head to the train station to get a ticket to Rajasthan. I want to take a camel trek through the des-sert and see the Pink Fort. Some guy walks up to me and says he works for the tourist information and foreign travel office. Yeah ok, the way he targeted me it gave me the creeps. So I blew him off and went and stood in line.

It takes an hour in this long line which barely moves and is replete with the same smell that made me vomit a few hours earlier. It runs through my mind,

"These people wanted to check me for a disease on my way into the country, wearing space suits. There is nothing unhealthy I could bring into this country that is anything worse than the bacteria and diseases that already exist here." Lmfao.

A man walks up to me with a good feeling around him, and informs me they won't give you a ticket here even if you wait all day. Please come with me, I will get you a taxi for a good price that will take you to a place that will help you. I have been told that 90% of the people in India are trying to rip you off in any and every way imaginable. He kept his word the taxi was a fair price and I do get to a tourist transit office.

To my surprise the first guy that approached me who I read as creepy is in the office. We give each-other this look of recognition.

"I respect you for your carefulness." He says. I sit down and explain to the guy my plan for 28 days in India. He says you have a lot of places here to visit in short time. I have kept my schedule to just northern India. It's a massive subcontinent and I've learned in my travels that less is more sometimes.

Delhi is a city of 15 million people with an average temperature of almost 100 degrees. There is no public toilets; people just piss and shit wherever they want, even if it's right next to a market. By no stretch of the imagination can you draw a picture of this market unless you have seen it.

The food is displayed on the ground. Veggies, fish, meat or dry goods; no matter –all food is displayed on the ground. People do piss and shit right next to it. Drop and squat, Wow! When I take my rickshaw ride through the market I gag from the smell of human waste a few times.

It's quite the city! More people all over the place with the most unnatural body parts you can imagine! Breaking your heart every couple of seconds! People walking with their legs bent completely sideways or walking on their calf bones. Faces so restructured you can hardly look at them. Children barely old enough to feed themselves running around wearing nothing! Two of them even walk up and beg for my bear.

For this trip since I'm heading off to China I decided to bring 2 bears. The black one and a panda are both gifts from my girl. I planned to take photos of them on the Great Wall. The way people smell in this place is horrifying. I couldn't stand near anybody without wanting to turn away and vomit. Having spent time in Africa with very poor people and villages, this lack of personal care far exceeds the African continent. At least the people in Africa keep their human waste away from their daily life. The Indian subcontinent could stand to learn a little about this.

As a compliment to this culture, however they recycle everything. Every day the ladies walk up and down the district and sweep the streets clean, and then pile the waste nearby in these wooden carts. The people scour these piles and take everything. When I was looking for tinfoil to cap off my gravity bong, I couldn't even find a small piece. They package this tobacco in it that actually turns all their teeth purple and black! Even the pretty girls use it. Hard to keep looking at them when their teeth are such colors!

On the flip side they have this tree called Neem. If you brush your teeth with a twig it turns your teeth whiter than expensive procedures in the western world. As long as you are not using those tobacco products! The tree is quite bitter though. I hear that if you eat a fresh leaf from this tree everyday day for 3 days it cures asthma for life. I really love how they recycle everything. We could all stand to learn a little of this. Sure I don't want to scour garbage piles; but watching them I learned to reuse many products in my own consumption.

There is a temple in Delhi that has been renovated in homage to a great Yogi with an amazing life story. Its design is the most impressive temple I see in India, especially for Hindu temples. Most just have paintings inside and some incense burning. This one is massive with amazing frescoes and architecture; the sculptures are as beautiful as you can imagine. At night they have a water and light show while the monks come out and pray.

My 14 days through Rajasthan including the camel trek is a logistical nightmare to transfer all these trains and buses to see this vast area. I hire a driver for this portion. He takes me around Delhi and then through Rajasthan and my camel trek. He doesn't come with me on the trek but he will wait for me. He informs me he has girls all over the country. I find out that he makes triple what most people make in India for this job. He also works 16 hours a day sometimes. I refuse to sit in the back seat, choosing to sit in the front with him.

My new guide and I head off to Rajasthan stopping in towns along the way and the James Bond palace, etc, etc. I do enjoy some pot once in a while. Maybe 30 days a year I get high. I want to smoke some hash; I hear it's pure in India and Nepal. This guy walks up to me while I'm waiting for the temple to open –I got there 1 hour too early. He asks me about my bear. I give him the story.

"Do you smoke?" He asks me.

Sure. I would love some good hash.

He walks me around the corner and into his house. We smoke a little hash in his hookah right in front of a baby which bothers me a little bit. I never smoke in front of kids. In his house there are now two other males. I shut my mouth and play the exit game in my head. I become uncomfortable. These people are half my size and since they don't eat meat they have no muscle mass. I'm a big guy. He offers me a couple of grams at a price of about 10 dollars. I buy it because I don't want to upset him and put myself in a bad situation. It's not a good quality hash. I leave and go-to the temple for the day. Head back to my guest house with the rooftop view of the Bond Palace.

My guide asks me how my day went. I tell him about the hash incident.

"I told you: if you need anything, please ask." He says, "You are lucky we are only here for one more day. Usually these people sell you hash, and then go to the cops to report what you are wearing and what color your backpack is. You then get arrested and have to pay fines, which they pocket."

Great, they play a similar game in a part of Sydney, too.

OK. I want some hashish 100% pure.

"Give me a few days and you will have it," he replies.

This changes our friendship. He is no longer so rigid and pro-fessional. The next day he has a bag of milk – that's black liquid opium for the uneducated. We dip our fingers into it a couple times a day; it has the consistency of honey. We then wash it down with a soda! Nice effect.

We have some long drives together. He apologizes that the drives are so long between cities and confides that he has had some problems with American tourists complaining about the long rides.

The long rides are fine, I say. *Americans can be assholes when they travel; they think the world is made up of all 7/11's. Since more than half of them never even leave their home state, they don't know the reality of the world.* Easily I lapse into rant mode and continue. *Only 13 % of Americans even have a passport ,*I blurt out incredulously. *This I feel is the main reason why Americans are so arrogant: they don't know that the western world is only a small fraction of the rest of the world, and it functions just fine without us. Houses, apartments, kids, jobs, social structures, and a quality of life America seems to have forgotten!*

It so happens that a full moon tomorrow will escort me for every night of my trek. Very cool. I tell the guide who is 16 that I want to sleep on the dunes each night to see the moon. He gets his baby brother to be our cook for the 4 days. They share a camel; I get my own. The camel, named Shiva, never once spits on me.

A short 1 hour ride inaugurates our trek – just long enough to watch the setting sun beautify the horizon over the dunes. In love once again, I'm having the time of my life, speechless by my surroundings. After stepping off the camel, I tell my guide I don't like to be around a lot of tourists making a shit ton of noise disrupting my brain. We stop away from the other tourists. It's quiet and peaceful. He walks over to his friends and I can see him chatting and laughing in the distance. Within a minute I get my first taste of India.

A boy who has no arms walks up to me. He draws in the sand with his stubs just below where the elbow should be the amount of rupees he's asking for. I notice immediately that he has severe scars around his stubs, indicating a violent loss of limbs. I made a decision before I left not to give to every person asking for money even if it's just pennies. I keep a stern face and tell him no.

He walks away and within seconds I'm in full blown tears wondering why God allows this to happen to people. It would not be the first time I cry over this reality of India. I look down the dune to my left a few minutes later and see him dancing with friends. I tell my guide:

Do not take me to places where little beggars try to get me to buy stuff. I really hate this experience.

We have to stop at the waterholes every once in a while to let the camels drink and get cooking water. I learn that my guide has the hots for the daughter of a farmer; we stop by their farm to get watermelon and veggies and use their well. Watching him fumble through flirting with her, while the dad watches carefully was very funny! Awe so cute! I didn't know watermelon grew in the dessert.

We are only allowed to ride the camels from 7 am until 11 am then from 3 pm until 7 pm. It's 115 degrees by 11 am! It's not fair to the camels to ride them during this oppressive heat time of day. We attempt to find shade; inevitably limited shade can be found near some bush that is covered in falling balls of spikes. The second day I develop saddle sores; by that afternoon they are bleeding. It's still quite beautiful and I still love it but I am counting the number of times I have to mount and dismount this animal.

At night they tie the front feet of these animals together so they can't run away. There is no place to tie them too. The last day we go by a farmer who is raising female camels, and Shiva begins to get unruly. I laugh knowing the cause: he is young and he wants pussy.

I tell the kids he will run away that night. They tell me no way. Tie his feet together and we go-to sleep. Amazing to watch the sunset each night on a dune, and then watch the full moon rise up a few minutes later. Waking up we only have one camel. I laugh, knowing exactly where he is. The young boy goes off looking for him. One hour later he comes back with Shiva and yup he was with the girls.

We get back to base camp and I take a proper shower and clean myself up. In the heat I remove my shirt. As we get closer to people, I'm asked to put my shirt back on. He tells me, "It's not fair for the men here to have my body exposed for the women to look at." My driver tells me the same thing in Agra.

The second day in Delhi I got sick from something. For the next 28 days I'm in various forms of this dysentery, ultimately costing me 32 pounds of weight and many days of diarrhea and vomiting. In fact I ate very little during the camel trek to keep from having to go-to the bathroom in the dessert. I also got sick while in Namibia Africa, we had to walk into the dessert and dig a hole, squat, take a shit and then bring our toilet paper back to the fire to burn. I was so sick I slept away from the group near my hole. I learned that Cipro does not work on all diarrheas but Imodium seems to work best. That's an FYI for the readers since Cipro is prescription and Imodium isn't.

Keeping with this medical theme, Malaria is prevalent among these parts of the world. I used Mefloquine in Africa and it caused adverse hallucinations. Not as bad as Lariam. Some of the girls in Africa used Lariam and they had screaming horrible nightmares while sleeping. Even wicked hallucinations during the day, the day or 2 after taking it! Since LSD is my favorite drug I'm ok with hallucinations. Malarone is the safest anti malaria drug, but it is expensive and a daily pill. You can get this medication in Victoria Falls and Cape Town at any Green Plus store for a fraction of the cost stateside. For this trip I did not take any malaria medication with me. I learned that malaria is only active among females. The bacterium that causes it is mostly active at night –nocturnal bacteria, and it's mostly active above 3,500 feet. So you can cut your risk way down, if you are careful.

Working our way back east to Pushkar, my guide says to me, "Today I can get your request. Would you like some girls with that hash?"

Not a chance; that's not the kind of traveler I am.

I do not refer to myself as a tourist. In fact, I like breaking tourist's balls. For example, I notice a tourist couple come into India the same day as me, then head over to the only McDonald's in Delhi. I'm playing with the undesirable children waiting for my driver to come around. I just look at them and say:

You flew all the way to India to eat at McDonald's?

The reason I chose to use a driver for this portion of the trip is because it would be easier considering the vast distance I'm covering and the transfers I avoid. It only cost me 100 USD more for this service.

He tells me, "In Pushkar there will be monks walking up to you with flowers in their hands offering them to you. They will not tell you they cost money. Once they put whatever item they have in your hand, they will not let you walk away without paying for it."

He continues his educational orientation to Indian tourist culture. "Never walk around with your palms up. Please don't tell anyone I told you this. You're here for a month but I have to come back here all the time."

No problem. I like him. He's honest and helpful. He helped me get some curd and special salt to help settle my stomach. I was eating cucumbers and sprinkling this pink salt on it each morning with curd to help my stomach settle for the day. He tells me to get ready for girls to chase me here. There is a lot of human sex trafficking in this city as well as a lot of Jewish guys who smuggle drugs through this city.

Many men have nice houses here and they spend months away from them smuggling drugs and sex. I will experience being asked up for lunch by some woman whose husband is away. Since I'm a very strong physically fit man, it won't be long before they come after me. I'm thinking yeah ok.

Off to the market and the famous temple. First the temple lake is bone dry. The hike up to over look the temple is beautiful. Coming back down I get a few compliments from men who say, "Wow! You have a great body."

Actually I get this a lot across Asia. Even some Chinese guys buy me a drink on a 5 star Yangtze River cruise, saying, "We're not gay; just saying you have a perfect body." I don't even know how to respond to these moments. Thank you! Make it a tall beer.

Within an hour a group of women walk by me all dressed in saris, only seeing their eyes. They are Hindu not Muslim. My guide explained to me how to recognize the difference since they both wear saris and burkhas. The difference is in the color style! They walk by me and check me out; one of them is over 6 feet tall. I think she can't have many matching men. These people are so small.

The last girl says hello. I smile. She comes back a minute later and asks, "Are you hungry?"

Damn straight. I am starving.

We go up the hill to an amazing house. They tell me I'm unclean and ask me to bathe. It's like Eddie Murphy's 'Coming to America'; I'm getting a bath by 2 women without the underwater blowjob. Hee-hee. It's a great lunch and a great afternoon.

Back to my guest house, it's during Diwali! The colors the music the celebration, from city to city was breathtakingly amazing. I learn this cool board game where you flick pieces similar to chess pieces into corner pockets. I love it. I play it every-time I see it while I'm in India.

My guide comes up to me and says, "I have your request, sir, but it's a little expensive."

That's ok. I can't get 100% hash in USA anyway.

"I have 10 grams and its 13 USD."

I retell this story to someone in Nepal later on my trip, and they tell me he overcharged me. I reply: *Seriously? In USA, hash costs 30 USD a gram. I just got 10 grams for 13 USD. He can overcharge me all he wants.*

We get to Agra where we are parting ways; I get trains for the rest of my trip through India. He tells me he hasn't seen his wife and kids in a while and they live near here. I tell him our term is supposed to be for another day, but I want him to leave a day early and spend the night and next day with his family on me. He takes me to a tea shop and lunch after the Red Fort day. We say our goodbyes and remain internet friends.

The first night in Agra, we go to the back side of the Taj to see the sunset and my first look at the palace wonder. Very shocking afternoon; a gypsy village is on the back side. Most people are running around naked. Though I will give them credit for having an outhouse! The river is very dry and there is razor fencing between us and the river bed.

Waking early the next day, I look at the map to find my walking path to the Taj. I'm very upset they won't let my bear on the premises, forcing me to rent a locker and put my day pack inside. Removing my ID and currencies, I give up the bag and the bear. It's further away from the entrances than I expect. Beautiful garden.

Glad I'm not in a tour, those buses drop off people and they get 30 minutes in the Taj. It takes 10 minutes to walk to it. They ask that you either remove your shoes or cover them before they let you walk in the actual structure. Only tourists cover them; I actually wanted to walk around it barefoot.

I try to imagine a softer time in history of the days when princes rode camels through the dessert to see this palace. I spend a few hours here, finally leaving to head out back to my hotel.

The train station in Agra is tough to stomach. I learn that they worship rats in this country, so rats are allowed to run free. There are people rolling themselves along in carts with incredible deformities, even 2 dead bodies lying in the platform of the station. Nobody even bats an eye or comes to get them. I sit on my backpack against a wall of the stairs to protect myself while waiting for my train! Actually nobody bothers me, just the fucking rats.

I pull out my K-bar and decapitate one of them as it gets way too close for my taste. I get yelled at in Urdu for this behavior. I just look at them like

Shut the fuck up! Mind your own business.

More rats come around me, and flashes of Ben play through my mind. I decide I can't handle this. I can't even close my eyes and relax because the fucking rats are everywhere. If I look right to chase one away, there is one on my left getting even closer. There are empty bags of snacks on the ground that rats go into for the crumbs. Each time a rat walks into these bags, I stand up and kick the bag as far as I can. They bounce off the wall and don't move. I killed 4 of them before my train came.

I'm heading out to Varanasi, excited to see this Ganges river city and the burning Ghats. The trip takes all night to get there. I don't eat the day I travel because I hate trying to find bathrooms.

In this case the toilets on the trains in India are just feet indentations and a hole in the floor. You can see the train tracks under them. Sure I could take the 1st class trains, but that doesn't let me experience the people. So I take 2nd class.

I love how they serve Chai all night as you're trying to sleep on the train. It's good Chai tea. Outside the train station in Varanasi is a zoo; any white person just gets mobbed. I separate myself finding the area least busy to get a rickshaw and give my guest house address.

These guest houses are not as bad as you may think. I have a king size bed, a private shower and bathroom, a roof top restaurant and I'm paying 12 dollars a night. After getting settled in I head off to the river.

My first glimpse of the river is mesmerizing. The Ghats, people praying, bathing, etc. After the first few minutes the beauty wears off as you look more deeply into the scenery. There is no plumbing: the sewage runs down the natural grade of the city toward the river. It leaves a strange colored slime on the stones making up the flood wall of the banks. The people praying in the water are also bathing and using the river as the toilet. It is no surprise that the Ganges River is muddy and brown.

There are dead bodies floating along the river. Dead bodies often get chewed up by the power boats so various body parts float along as well. I even saw a decapitated head float by with an unnatural color. Birds would peck at these pieces as they float by. Some people burn bodies along the banks. I did take a photo of that and got yelled at by a guy in the prayer session. If I had known what they were doing I wouldn't have taken it. All I saw was a mass of smoke coming up out of a fire; from my position I couldn't tell it was a body.

The kids play the kite game from the roof tops. I take video of this at the request of my girl, whose family is from a Muslim country which has banned this game. The man who runs the guest house tells me he used to write 'I love you' on his kite and let it get cut so it would fall near the girl he was interested in. *Very slick, my man.*

We smoke my hash together each night. There is no way I can smoke 10 grams in a month by myself. He has a friend who he is teaching English and training him to run a guest house. They have been friends for a long time; he is attempting to give him a better way of making honest money. We all sit around and smoke. The kid can't speak English very well yet. I am using my 80% of communication to talk to him. I understood everything he was saying by watching the 80%. The guy who runs the guest house just watches this experience and tells the kid in Urdu that he can learn a lot from me. I have just had a full conversation with a man I can't understand a word of what he says audibly but because I am so smart I can understand what he saying. *Man, this hash is amazing.*

I met a Swedish couple who is planning on spending 6 months in India; the girl is doing some correspondence classes for university. We sit on the top of the guest house watching the monkeys steal food or clothing, and the kites while we smoke hash together. I take a sunrise and sunset Ghat ride the next day and walk a little further up and down the river.

I discover a man who is making hamburger patties out of human shit and drying them on the banks of the river! He sells those dried patties back to people to burn for heat or to cook their food. Yet the government dresses in space suits and checks me for bringing in some disease upon entrance into the country! Complete with doctors! Really! I mused later that I should have offered the shit patty man an American donation. It would have been a great feeling to know that my shit was helping to cook someone's *roti*, not to mention putting a little change in the man's pocket. *Would that make me a shitty hamburger helper?*

The monks pray each night at the same spot, burning incense and drawing a crowd. It's beautiful to watch from the river and from the land. The next night I get a front row seat and attempt to get good video of it all. Unfortunately I have severe diarrhea that day and I can only get a few seconds of it before I must find a toilet by walking all the way back to my room!

There is a monkey temple in this town as well with a sweets store inside the Temple that makes and sells Indian style pastries. The trouble with this is the monkeys are all over the place. In fact, they steal the sweets from the people as they walk out, taking the bags right out of their hands. The people consider it a great honor of god that the monkeys chose to steal their sweets. Strange place!

While in Pushkar I met a family who was there to celebrate Diwali; they were very curious about me during the dinner in the restaurant. We talked and had 2 meals together. They invited me to spend some time with them when I got to Calcutta; they live outside the main city in Barasatt.

Calcutta is as bad as they say it is. Wanting to experience this I get a hostel for 2 dollars a night. No toilet; no sheets; just a common bathroom and a shower that I can't even stand up in. I head out into the city to explore. Arriving at the market I see the different stalls of meats, poultry, veggies, beans and rice. As I explore this open market I notice the chicken market booth. It's walls are made of canvas and the ceiling is made of blue tarps. There are milk crates on the ground, dirt blood and feathers are everywhere. He has a female helper who is removing feathers from the fowl, and helping boil them. He slits the throats of the animals and turns them upside down in the dividers inside the crates on the floor! Letting the blood drain out on the floor! I ask him if I can take video of his stall and killing sequence. He smiles and nods his head. To my right is a fish market stall, with dead rotting fish laying on a blue tarp in the street. The smell from these 2 markets being so close was intense to handle and the video does no justice to the experience. I spend 3 days here, and then call my friends and get a taxi to them. I meet his family again in his home which has been in his family for generations. They have a pond in the back. They make me a dinner and pack me a good meal to take on the train ride to Darjeerling. They gave me my first taste of fresh honeycomb.

Since I don't eat the day I travel, I take the food and give it to some deformed person I see at the train station in Calcutta. I have this special train ride from the point up to the hilltop city. The toy train, as it is known, is a 7 hour cog train ride with switch backs the whole way that skirts up the Himalayas to Darjeerling. The people have built their villages so close to the train along the path that if you stuck your hand outside the train window you would lose it.

We get up in the dark; the place is full. It takes me 4 hostel attempts to get a room. Actually, I take some person's reserved room; but because it is 9 pm, the guy rents it to me. The next night the guest comes in and is told because he was 1 day late he rented the room to make the money.

I need to wash some clothes. It is cold up here! After being in such intense heat, my body is in shock. I wash my clothes then realize they won't dry. So I sleep in my wet clothes bundled up in the fleece blankets. I know from climbing that my body heat and the fleece will dry out my clothes by morning. Success, clean dry clothes! It's also my first experience with prayer flags, around the Temple. This area is a mixture of both cultures, Indian and Asian. As a man I will tell you, the most beautiful women on earth live here.

CHAPTER 19

The taxi takes me to Kharkavita where I see the customs office of Nepal. I discard the last of my hash on the ground including my bowl, and walk in.

I present my visa, my photo and passport and put my bag on the counter to be searched. The customs agent looks at me and says, "No need. Have a great time in Nepal."

Night and day! That's the difference from India to Nepal. Not 20 feet into Nepal you will find proper public toilets, proper plumbing, filtered water and a bustling city!

I get approached by a guy who asks? "Do you need bus tickets?" *Yup*. We head over to his office to purchase an overnight bus ticket to Kathmandu. They tell me the roads are a mess during the day so we make the long trips at night. Twelve hours later I arrive in Kathmandu. As a climber I'm very excited about Nepal where climbing stories are legendary.

Upon check in I call my girl to say, 'hello' and ask how the Yankees are doing in the playoffs. Remember! Her entire apartment is furnished with my stuff including TV. She asks her roommate's boyfriend to switch over to the game and check the score. He is a Red Sox fan, and while sitting on my couch, watching my TV, he tells my girl, 'no'. She goes online to give me the score.

A concierge in the hotel offers assistance with my itinerary of what I want to do while in Nepal. He calls a local associate over and we go to his office to talk business! I give him my schedule and my budget.

"Sure. I can do that no problem." He constantly increases the price with additions; tells me he can't use my card– wants cash only. I get up and walk away. This city is the ultimate tourist trap! There are dozens of guide shops here, so I just keep walking into them until somebody treats me with respect.

After the 5th store, I get a great feel from the guy behind the counter. He apologizes for being busy, offers me tea and says, "Relax for a minute please". We go over my desires and my budget.

"The budget is non-negotiable". I tell him, *"I'm willing to give up amenities to keep the budget."*

The final bill is 50 USD over my budget but comprises an optimum trip itinerary. Nine days of hiking through the Annapurna region, 3 days white water rafting in class 3 and 4 whitewater, and the world's highest suspension bridge bungee jump will cost 550 USD including visa, food, guide and lodging. I'm good with this. The first guy I told my non-negotiable budget was $500. Before I walked away from him, he was up to $650 and still climbing. (Those legendary hiking stories are not about prices)!

Back at my hotel, the upset travel organizer walks up to me. "Where did you go?"

I went and got my schedule sorted out.

"How much did you pay?"

I tell him.

"I could have done that."

I say sarcastically, *"You had your chance; you tried to get more. This isn't my first trip around the world. Have a nice day."*

My room is furnished with a bed, TV and a private shower. After a shower I walk into the city to explore. So far nobody has tried to pickpocket me, even while in India. Walking through the streets I head toward the visa office to discuss my connection for Tibet. All the correspondence with tour guides pre-trip has warned me about entering China from Nepal so I have some anxiety!

As I walk through the street, this guy walks up behind me which is odd since I'm going faster than the culture. He then bumps into me very hard almost knocks me over.

"Excuse me," he says and attempts to put his hand in my pockets. I am wearing these very oversized cargo shorts with very deep pockets –almost down to my calves. I leave papers and stuff in there giving the impression my important stuff is there. In reality, my important papers hang around my neck in a bag. Because I wear baggy clothes that conceal the neck satchel, most people would not realize it's there. I figure if you get that from me I am not going to need it anymore, Lol.

I walk back toward the guy and he speeds up trying to avoid me; he changes directions. We're in the middle of the intersection of the main market of Kathmandu! Five rickshaws are queued up waiting for clients. I pin the pickpocket there, grab him and throw him into the rickshaws. He gets tangled up in the rickshaws as they all fall over. I look at him straight in the eyes and tell him.

"Next time I see you even close to me, I'm going to assume you are trying to rob me and I will put you in the hospital for months."

He looks toward the police standing on the corner who just saw the whole thing. I look over and see them, thinking, 'ok, Arrest me.' But my safety comes first. They take one step toward me; I head down the street in my original direction. They see the ruckus is over and say nothing to me.

Getting to the office for my Tibet visa, I express my concerns over being denied entrance. They assure me it will be ok; they can and will take care for it. I leave my passport with them with a plan to pick it up with my visa to Tibet when I return from my wilderness trek.

Now that that's all sorted out, it's time to get settled into some sleep. I'm exhausted. Tomorrow will require a well rested traveler.

Morning dawns and holds the promise of an adrenaline rush. No need for coffee. A long 3 hour bus ride through gorgeous mountains brings us to the Last Resort and the world's highest suspension bridge bungee jump. Wow! Breathtakingly scary is the walk over a suspension bridge that long and that high–one hundred and sixty meters above the river. The bridge is bouncy underfoot.

A jumper's weight determines which rope thickness and corresponding strength will be used to 'hang' the jumper. We all weigh in and get oriented to the jump experience in about two hours. The scale shocks me to realize I lost 32 pound in India.

Number one on the jump list, I decide to take my bear for the ride. Whooosh! What a feeling to free fall through the air! I bounce a few times and decide I MUST get certified to skydive. (The jump and view are on my blog. The bear's entry for the day is rather amusing as well. www.shaneoffthegrid.com).

After lunch we head back to Kathmandu. We ride upon the top of the bus on the way home. We're told that no locals can ride on the top of the bus: just us tourists! This would be a theme of my experience in Nepal. My shorts ripped for the second time. I had them sewn in India once. I'm walking around the city to find a local seamstress. Success, except that she can't speak English! I show her the tears and she looks at the stitch work of the India job. In hand signals I explain I'll be back on x date to pick them up.

The next day another bus ride takes me to Pohkara, the town where all treks through Annapurna begin. Traffic is hell, some bus flipped over and we get backed up for 7 hours. On the return trip it only took a few hours to get back.

I stop along the way at a special temple where the Swiss built a cable car system that goes up into the mountains to the temple. I get off the bus at my stop, walk to the cable car and head up to my first active Temple in Asia. The temple is beautiful; my first view of the higher mountains, equally majestic. It's a holy day so monks or priests are slaughtering animals in sacrificial offerings. Blood pours all over the altar. Out of respect I choose not to take photos, though my fellow travelers didn't feel the same respect.

The line for the return car down the hill is very busy and has many switch back turns. Some teenage kids take offense to me being there. They throw rocks and spit at me. Not interested in getting in trouble, I just avoid the rocks. Bob and weave, baby;

bob and weave. They are frustrated at my lack of reaction to them, so they attempt to cut the line and surround me.

I'm now quickly considering my options while planning my defense strategy. Suddenly, the security cops who maintain order in the line throw them out and to the back of the line. Not for harassing me but because they tried to cut the line.

I nestle down for the night in a guest house nestled at the bottom of the hill in town and get some daal for dinner. While waiting for my bus the next morning, a car comes by and stops in front of me.

The driver leans over and in heavily accented English says, "There has been another accident; where are you going?"

Pohkara.

"Me, too. Jump in. We'll take you; just split the petro with us."

It's a 3 hour taxi ride from Manakamana to Pohkara. In the first 30 minutes he starts to tell me he is part of the communist resistance force that is sick of the government of Nepal. Since I am a socialist at heart, we had a great conversation. Though it did give me the creeps to be in his car, knowing he is the real deal: a Chinese militant. I couldn't get out of his taxi fast enough.

Pohkara is beautiful, replete with lakes with boats in which you can paddle out, and, of course, the World Peace Pagoda. At the guest house, a message left for me lets me know what time the guide will pick me up tomorrow for the hike. I shrink down my backpack and make the hike to the Peace Pagoda. Heading up the final leg I see some kids playing on a huge bamboo swing with an intriguing construction. I demonstrated how to do back-flips off the swing, and showed them how to hold the camera to video record me doing one. They are amazed and want to try the flips as well. They got it on the first try! When I was a kid it took me a few tries to get it. My afternoon at the pagoda offers great pleasure and fantastic views of the Himalayas!

The next morning a bus takes us to the starting point for trek-king! I don't have enough time to hike the whole thing so I choose a 9 day hike over 120 kilometers. First few hours are quite casual, I'm wondering how long before we go up. We stop for lunch; relax in some lodge as the lull before the storm. Then it begins.

Welcome to Nepali staircases. Up, up, up, up. No switch backs. For the next 4 hours our hike is completely vertical. Each step differs in height and length; your legs scream after the first hour and you are not even half way up. At last, we arrive at our first night's lodging. My legs are so tired I can barely get my pack off.

Wake up and we start all over again. The next night we relax before our sunrise on Poon Hill. I ask my guide, *"Can I get some yak cheese? I would like to try it."*

He then sends a boy down the hill, in the dark! One hour later I get a pound of yak cheese. It tastes like Swiss with a twang of sharp but very dry and crumbly. I share it with a bunch of kids in the lodge.

We meet up with a Dutch girl who is retracing her brother's steps from a few years earlier. She is completely unprepared for the temperature drop. Since all rooms are doubles, I tell her she can share my room and save herself some money. My guide and I pay for her tea each stop we take. We're only on the same path for 3 days, and then we separate because her path is touristy.

After Poon Hill I tell my guide, "I don't want to take this beaten path; get me out of here." I also ask, "I hear there is amazing hash and pot buds on this trek, is that true?" I could actually smell it all day long. The stalks are so high with huge buds all over them.

I find them easily once he shows me. He admits, "The quality isn't very good; that's why they make hash." The most amazing thing about this hike is the change in ecological environments. You find every type the planet has to offer. The view at Poon hill was anticlimactic, packed full of tourists. I had to give the Dutch girl a fleece, hat and my extra gloves, even my extra shell to keep her warm that morning. Boy, I'm glad I packed all that stuff.

The 6th day I'm told of a hot-spring pool nearby that is close enough to walk down to. "Not to worry! The bill for your trip is all inclusive". It is a cool pool made of slate stones, right next to this river. A small runoff waterfall and springs flow out of the walls.

"Can I jump in the main river to get the change in temperature and get my legs to relax?"

"It's very cold and the current very fast."

Ok I'm good with that. Before I walk over and jump in the river, two guys go 50 feet downstream to catch me if I start to flow away in the current. This would be the only time anybody actually cared about my well being on this trip. Safely out of the cold, quick current, I hustle back into the hot spring! Walking back up those stairs to the lodge again afterwards is arduous labor.

Last day I'm so tired and cranky. My guide walks quite a few feet in front of me as he knows I'm beat. By the way, he is 63 years old. He has reached the summit of Everest twice as a *sherpa*. We talk about Everest because I'm going to base camp in a week from the Tibetan side.

He gets me some dried out pot and shows me how to roll a local style joint. I smoke all day long the last few days. At the last guest house on the last night, I ask the owner if it's ok if I smoke outside or does he want me to go-to my room? I see the police station close by.

He tells me, "It's ok. They won't arrest you, just us." Funny!

As I am sitting there in Dhampus looking at the Himalayas, a woman comes by to talk to me about where I am from, what I thought of Nepal. We have a few laughs and she tells me my laugh is refreshing and enjoyable. This strikes me because nobody likes how hearty my laugh is. My own mother hates it so much she gives me sarcasm about it every-time! I've given up laughing around my family, choking the feeling down when it comes up.

Back at Pohkara, walking to my guest house, I'm stopped by somebody screaming my name from across the street. I look and see the guy who was in Varanasi with me.

I thought you were staying in India for 4 more months, I say surprised to see him.

They tell me it was horrible! Right after I left they watched a gun fight in the street below from the roof top restaurant. Some gang war had just broke out; people were getting killed every day. They couldn't handle India anymore– too dirty, too crazy. They were running out of hash.

"*Funny. I just bought some local sandwich at a rolling cart and the guy offered me hash. I told him I would be back in a few. Let me drop off my bag and I can come back and meet you.*"

"How's your girlfriend doing?"

Great.

"We talked about you yesterday and about your favorite story about Sweden. We met another girl from there in our guest house."

Cool. See you in a few.

He decides to walk with me to my room. I get settled in my room; drop my gear before heading out to buy hash from the man with the rolling cart. The guy tells me its good stuff. I tell him,

"*Listen, I know you have good and bad stuff. I want 10 grams of good stuff. My friend is going to be here a month. If you give me bad shit, he won't come back and buy more from you in the future. Your choice, you can get 2 sales or one.*"

He puts away the first bundle then hands me a second bundle from a different stash. As he's cooking our food, I take it from him and open up the plastic. It's thick sticky tar. I give him the money, buy our food and head to their room. The man with the rolling cart is amazed at my skill level.

Hey, I've been doing this along time in many countries now.

I meet their other friend and tell them how in Stockholm they regulate the water levels in the lakes to make it optimal depth for this famous breed of swans. It was a very expensive project. I thought that was cool: no benefit of the project for mankind except for his eyes to ogle at the swans. You won't see that in Central Park.

We smoke hash all night. Since I'm off to another country in a few days, I leave him most of the hash. I board the next bus to Kathmandu in order to catch a flight to Lhasa Tibet in 3 days. I go-to the office to pick up my visa and passport. It's a group visa for one person! At least I can enter Tibet, right?

CHAPTER 20

In Lhasa, Tibet, travelers are met with the same procedure as India's: get heat detected and have my health screened. Though here, they weren't wearing space suits! They x-ray my bag and hold up paper that has about 6 sheets attached together and is twice as long as notebook paper.

The customs agent calls over the guide who will be with me for the next 14 days. Tearing off a couple of sheets, he gets the guide to sign a few of them and files the rest in his book. I shake his hand.

"I'm very excited to be in Tibet."

He tells me he isn't going to talk to me until we leave the airport area.

We walk outside through a crowded lobby. Within a couple of seconds, I'm breathing with great difficulty. The air is thinner than on Kilimanjaro and the section of the Himalayas I hiked in Nepal, even though I was at almost 16,000 feet in Nepal and 20,000 feet in killimanjaro! (They have a beer called *Kili* whose slogan is, "If you can't climb it, then drink it").

It's a short ride to my lodging. There is no way to describe how excited I am at being here. We drive through the city by the Potala Palace. The mere sight of it will make you cry. A massive

Palace on the top of the highest peak in the area strikes a sharp contrast with the brown mountains surrounding it. The pristine colors of it are just magnificent.

I'm told I have 2 days to wander around the city before the tour starts which allows me to get acclimated to the altitude. I have read that tourists are not allowed to walk around Lhasa without an escort. I am a little nervous about the Chinese troops that are quite visible. It's the 2 year anniversary of the last protest and crackdown. I've not planned this date. It happens to fit in my schedule and give me plenty of time here and in China before my next fixed date in Laos; The Gibbons Experience.

I settle into my hotel itching to head out into the city! My step brother asked me to get him some prayer beads from Tibet. I know it's illegal to bring them into China, but –I'm told– they will search your bags but they don't search you. Not YET, anyway. I plan on wearing them when I leave the PRC (People's Republic of China). I plan on taking the world's highest train from Lhasa to Beijing; my next flight isn't for more than a month, or so I think....

I head over to the courtyard across from the Potala Palace to soak in the view! The air is thin, but if I walk slowly, I can keep my breath. I make my walk around the outside of the palace, see the rows of sutra's and do my next Eddie Murphy impersonation:

"I, I, I, I, I want the knife, please."

I crack myself up laughing. When you travel alone, you become your own best audience. I walk on toward the center city. It's beautiful: a full square with huge chimnea burners at either end, each at one side of the temple.

The euphoria begins to wear off as the 'troops' ubiquitous presence is inescapable. They are everywhere! The soldiers wear full body armor replete with blast shields over their faces. They carry automatic weapons. A platoon marches around in a preset circle through this square over and over and over. There is a technical team walking around and making sure nobody kneels in the square past the chimneys.

Apparently worshipers can kneel and pray in the small area between the front steps of the temple and the chimineas.

Anyone caught kneeling past that line is confronted, digitally fingerprinted and told to stand up. If they give any retort they are immediately smacked in the head with the butt of their automatic weapon. I personally witnessed a child getting this treatment, even taking a photo of it at my own risk.

Troops stand outside every grocery store in the same intense gear. Also, a group of 8 troops with no guns or body armor, just batons march up and down the market section of the city. They pass my hotel entrance many times a day. Anyone who has ever been to Asia knows the culture does not pick its head up or face their fellow citizens when they walk. They just come and go. When they get close to people, they just side step out of the way. This is also the practice for entering and leaving a store.

This group of baton wielding soldiers will and does strike anybody who walks out of the shops getting too close to them. It's quite brutal to watch. I wanted to take video of it, but I didn't have the balls to do it. It was like watching a black and white movie on the History Channel from the 1930's in Germany, except it was in amazing 3d and Technicolor!

Pissed now, I head over to the internet café to send an email to my girl. I attempt to attach a photo of this and the PRC blocker comes up and tells me I'm no longer allowed to use this website anymore while inside the PRC.

I then go-to a messenger account and connect with my girl, typing a message to her not even pressing send. Yet again, the PRC blocker shows up and closes my account. At this point I'm nervous. I don't want any trouble; I want to see the Temples, mountains, lakes and then get to China proper. I learn the definition of freedom in that moment.

My fellow Americans, freedom has nothing to do with materialism or being able to buy Reeboks or Nike's or going to eat at Burger King or McDonald's. Freedom is speech. Being able to say 'fuck you' to my government with a reason why without being silenced. We need to keep this in mind as we begin to create laws to limit the things we can say. If you do not make a real effort to exercise your freedom of speech, you will lose it entirely. The right does not mean 'freedom of speech if you don't offend anybody'. It means freedom of speech! Common knowledge recognizes you will not please everybody all the time. We must not silence our opinions and freedoms in the interest of not hurting somebody's feelings. Feelings are just as subjective as my speech! It hurts my feelings and offends me that my freedom of speech is being silenced because I might hurt somebody's feelings or offend them!

I meet the guy who will be on tour with me the next day. We're just hanging out together in the city for the day, walk around take a nap near the palace! Get food and play hacky sack with some locals. My friend is from the Czech Republic. Yeah, I get to practice Czech again. By day 2 our conversation is laced with many words in Czesky.

We go through the market area and scope out the things we'll buy on the way back. I see the movie 2012 is opening in a week on the same date all around the world. I play this game with my girl: when we are apart, we select a specific date to see a movie. We each go-to the predetermined movie at the same time but in different locations sometimes — like now– halfway across the globe. We rent movies sometimes too and do the same thing. We make a date to see this movie; I go buy my ticket in advance. I am also in the market for a protective cover for my camera. Trying to communicate through the language gap is boat loads of fun. I finally find a technology store; 10 minutes later after a lot of hand signals, we get it accomplished.

Our guide meets us the next morning and we are escorted to the Potala Palace. No cameras are allowed inside. It's the most incredible palace I've ever seen. No nails were used in its construction. The stupa's inside have more gold and jewels than Versailles can even imagine. The king and queen apartments are coated gold. The stupa's of the bodies of the Dalai Lama's and their vice president, so to speak are solid gold with jewels bigger than my fist on the outsides!

We slowly walked through for a few hours. We are told the local people donate the materials to paint and maintain the palace every year. The PRC gives nothing to maintain these palaces and temples. The pilgrims who came through the palace give money at every entrance and stupa. Their donation is a lot since these people have nothing. I began to really appreciate using a local tour company. At the hotel that evening I begin to get sick. I pick up altitude sickness pills at the nearest Green Plus store and spend most of the night sick in the bathroom. I try to stay warm and healthy. I can't find any gingerale anywhere, just ginger teas. I feel a little bit better when I wake up, although I'm still sick.

In the car to start our tour, the guide asks me if I'm ok.

"I'm not feeling good but it's better than yesterday, so I will be ok. I got altitude sickness stuff in case I get sicker. We just have to keep me hydrated and full of Gatorade."

He tells me, "A doctor from Indiana died in his arms last month from altitude sickness. Another girl recently had to be flown to Thailand to the nearest hyperbaric chamber."

I will be honest with him about how I feel, Ok!

The first temple is the private palace of Dalai Lama's. I stop along the way up to play a game of pool on one of these outdoor pool tables. Inside the temple is amazing: the hanging flags, the spinning sutra's ornamentation. (Pix are available at the website). The smell of the butter candles is tough to handle at first which doesn't help my upset stomach. The butter tea is even worse.

We drive out to other cities with more temples through some amazing countryside along the way. Reminds me of the great plains of the western US! The way the nomadic people lived is similar to these people. Getting better but I'm still sick. We head over to Everest base camp. It's completely empty. We can't see the mountain because it is covered in clouds!

We head out to our night's lodging and I finally begin to feel great. During this day we saw some spectacular blue lakes of glacier runoff, with a perfect mirror reflection of some 7,000 meter peaks on the blue lake. In some of these lakes, I espy Everest in the background. At 6,200 meters I get to take some photos. In the photo section of the toolbar on my webpage it will drop down a list. Click on countries and it drops down another list. I encourage everyone to go look at the blue lake photos in Tibet.

Last day on the road and I send out some emails to the Chinese tour company setting up my meeting point and pick up spot. They send me back an email telling me my group visa will cost me a lot of money and lost time to get changed and extended. I look up the Chinese policy for group visas into Tibet. Yup it's true. I go ballistic! The local tour company in Tibet was responsible for coordinating my transfer in and out of Tibet and entrance into China. I go to my guide and we have a very heated discussion. He calls his boss and I began swearing at them over the phone. Hang up and walk away. I apologize to my guide who is a great guy. I'm just pissed because I'm getting kicked out of China when I get to Beijing. We all go out for beers the last night and low and behold were listening to a live band play hotel California in Tibetan language. They also drink beer from shot glasses.

My tour mate tells me that his first day in Lhasa before we met he saw the troops perform brutal tactics as well. He then calls his wife on his personal blackberry from Czech and begins to talk to her. The PRC comes over his conversation and informs him that he will no longer be allowed to use this mobile while inside the PRC. We went out to eat in Lhasa to get local food. As we head up to the rooftop section of the restaurant, we see snipers on all the rooftops of every building in town. I didn't even see so much as a stick in any local's hands in Tibet. As I get back to Lhasa prior to my trip to Beijing, I go see 2012. The movie is dubbed in Chinese and subtitled in Tibetan, which does surprise me a little bit since the language is no longer allowed to be taught in schools. Written or spoken. Only English and Chinese are taught!

My train ride to Beijing is amazing; the view among the mountains is very beautiful. For 24 hours it's all Himalayas. Then I enter China proper. For the next 24 hours I can't see anything, just smog and pollution!

Arriving in Beijing I immediately head to the US consulate office. I am told there is nothing they can do for me since my president just arrived 15 minutes ago. The security guard writes on a note in Chinese the address of the visa office. I get there and I'm told they don't issue visa extensions for group visas from Tibet. I have to fly to another country and apply for another visa.

"Where is the nearest country so I can save on flight costs?" I ask her.

She tells me, "Hong Kong is the closest country."

I look at this woman wearing full military uniform, carrying a gun and inform her that H.K. is part of China. Not arguing with her just trying to make sure I don't fly somewhere that is not able to issue me a visa.

She tells me, "It's another country."

I laugh and walk away. Now I have to find an internet café to investigate where the visa office is in H.K. and check on flights. I call my girl from a pay phone and start her on the search for flights in and out of H.K. It's Wednesday. My first thought is to find an expensive hotel that has a business center. They will have an internet office. It does cost me some money to get to use it but I need it. Who cares? On a second phone call to my girl, she gets me a flight reserved but I can't pay for it over the net! I have to pay at the airport. We get a flight in today and a flight back into China on Saturday morning. The hotel takes me to the airport and I get my flight paid for.

Arriving in Hong Kong I find long term lockers and drop my bag off go-to sleep in the airport. The tram tickets run in 24 and 48 hour passes. If I wait until 6 am, I won't have to buy a second pass. I catch my tram into the city and drop my visa application off. It does cost me about 100 USD to get an emergency visa application processed. I'm then free to head out into the city; up to the peak tram I go and then on to the city's sights.

Hotels are very expensive in H.K. I know the bars are open all night long. I meet a guy who is also getting his 24 hour visa. It's a fun day: Big Buddha then bars. I am not prepared for the night life of this city. Apparently everything is for sale. There are so many professional girls all over the two of us; it's difficult to keep them away.

I walk away leaving him with the girls and head to the back. I fall asleep in a dark corner on a chair. I got quite drunk during my 6 hours in this bar while fighting girls off all night. I have only paid for sex once in my life in the Swiss Alps. When I didn't get the experience I wanted, I made a decision it's not worth the money.

It's now 6 am. I'm incredibly drunk and head over to the visa line throwing up a few times along the way! I get to my line and lie on the ground, waiting. Some girls come up also waiting for their visa and start giving me sarcasm. I laugh.

"I've been to 60 plus different countries; go bother somebody else."

They laugh and call me a liar. Who cares? We get in line, go up and wait for our number to get called. I walk up and low and behold I get my visa. I was worried that I wouldn't get it. As I'm standing there, the bitch who was laughing at me was denied her visa and was now swearing at the visa officer. I just looked at her and smiled.

Walked out, found an internet café and emailed my girl: *I'm good to go.* She is awesome. I drop an email to my tour company telling them I have my visa and my flight number for landing in Beijing. Not wanting to deal with prostitutes all over me again, I head to Disney, then the tram back to the airport. Sleep seduces me in the airport and I later catch my flight to China.

CHAPTER 21

Because of the change in schedule I lost some experiences in China but gained a day by myself. Mao's tomb is a must see. After getting picked up and delivered to my hotel, I just want to pass out and get some sleep. My room has heat and I'm grateful. I turn it up and pass out. Sleep forever. I do my laundry because they have proper machines.

I get picked up the next day for a tour with a few people, and we're off to the Summer Palace. I'm still fuming over my experience in Tibet. I want nothing to do with buying anything in this country. I am not going to spend any more money here than I have to. I'm forced to use a tour company, getting brought to all these tourist traps, pearl shops, silk shops, herbal doctors, tea shops, jade shops, etc, etc. Everything I hate about using tours. I'd rather have the extra 2 hours in the Palace, Great Wall, Forbidden City, or Tiananmen Square.

A few days later I'm on a train to the Terracotta warriors. I get picked up and taken to a shop that sells little replica statues of the warriors. *Nope. I'm not giving this fucking country a penny.* It's so foggy here you can't see a thing.

The irony cannot be ignored. The last thing I did in Lhasa was go-to a bar, drink some beers. I met a photographer from National

Geographic who by the way was Chinese! He has the expensive camera, ID badge and begins to tell us: "Tibet is pretty but it only has high mountains; it's really shit compared to China," his home country.

The bartender just looks at me and my mate with this 'fuck the Chinese occupation' look. I'm thinking, *Geesh! We are in the capital of Tibet. National Geographic should teach their employees some sensitivity and respect for the area in which they are shooting.'* This is the second Nat Geo photographer that has been an asshole to me while I'm traveling. I never buy or accept anything from Nat Geo again. Don't even watch their TV programs! I just have this vision of this asshole in Tibet in my head the whole time. I've been to most of the places they film. I have my own memory; I don't need to watch some aristocratic, disrespectful, elitist photographer's action and views.

In fact, for my entire time in China I couldn't see anything further than 100 feet in front of me. The water cube wasn't even worth taking photos due to being covered in smog. The Olympic village that we the people spent millions to build is protected by high fences and razor wire. Apparently they are equipped with flat screen TV's and microwaves, dish washers and all the amenities of western civilization which nobody in China is allowed to live like! So I say *the next time we spend billions on an Olympic site in this global economy, we had better make sure that our investment doesn't get buried in mothballs and dust. But, hey, let's kiss China's ass.*

In fact, they control the weather. We talked about this during the trip. Apparently they seed the clouds with sulfite and then it rains this nasty, smelly rain. Afterwards, it is clear for a few days. They did this during the Olympics. We only find this out because the government is upset that during Obama's visit which I happen to overlap, they did it again. Instead of getting rain, however, they got 50 cm of snow. Funny to watch humans shovel highways instead of snow plows! This angered the government enough, to let this info get leaked!

China will only let 3 western movies into their market each month, unless the movie displays some Chinese place in it. Since China's a growing market, movie makers are putting Chinese cities in too many movies lately, just so they can make money. We're selling our souls. The last time I checked, you can buy human Tibetan skulls on the internet in China!

The Terracotta Warriors were amazing. Though I didn't realize they were in domes and very close to the surface. I expected more mystery and rock coverings. Doesn't take away from the beauty– just a little disappointing as usual! The city is cool, too, with a Temple where some monks still live.

Again without seeing very far in front of me due to the smog, I head by train to the Yangtze River cruise! I am happy to see the gorges and get to live like a human – it's a 5 star cruise. I find every 5 weeks or so you have to step into comfort to feel human again.

I'm very lucky on that cruise. It's booked solid with only 3 extra beds on board. Since I'm in a double room, I was worried I would be with someone with whom I didn't get along. To my pleasant surprise I was all alone. Meals are standard cruise style, table of 8 to 10. I'm at a table with all English speaking guests. A full family from the Bahamas: mother, son and spouses that are all lawyers. They are Christians, too. We have some great talks.

I have to wash some clothes again and turn on the AC in the room to get them dry. This gives me a cold on the last day. When I skip a meal, I'm called up by the captain in my room to find out why. I tell him *I'm not feeling very well*. When I come out again, I'm watched very closely. I get some juice and load up on vitamin c. In just a couple of hours I'm fine. I loved the smaller boats we took around the gorges one morning, and the Temples we stopped to see along the way. They even made a museum in another town devoted to this gorge culture, because when they made the damn, they buried the valley in 200 feet of water losing many artifacts! They transferred some of these to this museum, and they paid the people to relocate.

Getting off the boat I'm picked up by a guide who first says to me, "How did you like Tibet?" Looking at her oddly I tell her *"It wasn't a very pretty place."*

She takes me to the train station, with metal detectors at the doors. I do have a large K-bar in my bag. As the security guard tells me to walk through I say "I have a knife in my bag." He doesn't speak English and my guide tells him in Chinese that I have a Tibetan knife in my bag, which is illegal in China. She tells me to take out the Tibetan knife and then I can walk through the gate.

I look right at her and pull my K-bar out of my bag and ask, "Is this a Tibetan knife?"

She just looks at me. My bag goes through security and there is no other knife. I give my guide the finger as I walk away. Catch my train into Shanghai!

Not much to see except the Bund and the center square, some historic areas. I do my thing and walk around at night after getting dropped off from my daily tours. I constantly get accosted by Chinese pimps along the way every few feet, like the way they do in Vegas while walking and holding your wife's hand. Sick of this attack for prostitutes, I look at this guy and say,

"Let's be real. I'm from the western world, where women have bodies, asses and tits. Not flat little girls built like 12 year old boys. I'm surprised you people even procreate. You find this look attractive?"

He looks at me in shock. A girl who clearly understands English and is sitting near this encounter is horrified at my comment. I walk away, but it doesn't change the assault of pimps. On my flight to Bangkok the next day, I feel so much weight off my shoulders. I can email my girl and talk to my friends about the atrocities I just witnessed in Tibet. My email comes back online and I get an email from my Czech friend. He tells me as soon as he crossed the border in Nepal, his phone came back online....

CHAPTER 22

I arrive in Bangkok, happy to be free from the oppression of the PRC. From a tourist information station, I get a bus ticket to the city center near Khoasan Road, where all the guest houses are. I make sure the name and address of my lodging are written down in Thai on a disposable piece of paper for the taxi cab driver.

I always take a taxi to my sleeping arrangement the first time entering a new city. I've tried to find these places on my own; it's never very successful. First, I'm usually tired and or jetlagged so it's best to not stress in the dark late at night. So I get off the bus, get the closest taxi and show him the paper. He assures me he can find the place. We drive around for a few minutes and, nope, he can't find it.

I'm upset. *"I'm not paying you because you didn't find it."* I get out of the taxi and wander around the city on my own. I hate being lost in a city this large and this confusing. I meander my way back to the rotary and by now my orientation to the city improves. I get back in a taxi and, low and behold, it's the same driver. *"Find me a cheap guest house to stay in."* This week happens to fall during the Thai King's 82nd birthday celebration, so thousands of extra people descend on Bangkok. We do find a guest house off the path a little, but not too far away. Ok all checked in. It's 4 am.

I have some time in the morning to explore Thailand before heading north to Laos for the Gibbons Experience. Exploring around the city, I find the Wat, various temples and river. To spend my first day just walking around a city, even getting lost while walking around is usually much more rewarding than going to a fro with precision. I always do this in all cities.

The Wat is packed full of people. The birthday party has brought millions of people to this city. The Wat is free today but it's a crazy line to get in. I'm asked to wear coverings over my legs which is a challenge because the pants they give me don't really fit. The mass of people shoving to get in is insane. In fact, it's an uncontrollable mass of people. They just move and the whole world moves, too. I stepped into this mass and got moved just like everybody else. The force was so strong that I had to brace my arms against the wall as I was pushed along to keep from crushing the people next to me and myself. Never experienced the power of so many people pushing! I can see why soccer riots get people crushed to death. It was scary.

Inside it was much calmer! The space is more open so we're not being forced through a narrow passage. I am impressed with the amazing architecture; the colors are vibrant. Many people asked to take photos of me with them, mainly I think because I'm so tall; they have not seen many people twice their height.

At a local tourist place I schedule tours of the city's unique areas like the floating market; I try to accomplish all my local travel needs in one stop, i.e., bus tickets, passes, etc. The tourist attendants always have recommendations for travelers; in this case they suggest some islands to stop by on my way back through Thailand after Cambodia.

Major rivers flow through most cities. The river banks of Bangkok are thriving and bustling with merchants, people. In contrast to China, I enjoy the friendliness of the locals who exude a festive mood because of the birthday celebration. People are even giving out free food and water.

A local internet café provides service to send my mates and my girl some information about me. Remember I lost my internet sites while in the PRC. I send my girl some photos of kids from all over as well as photos from Tibet. It feels nice to be able to send emails again.

This is my free day to walk the streets. I anticipate some authentic Pad Thai. The night comes and the world is just waking up. There is nothing in your life to prepare you for the nightlife of Khoasan Road! Not even the blow job competitions with strangers on Cyprus Island, inside and sanctioned by the clubs can compare. The girls are everywhere, and everything is for sale. The most fun is watching the lady boys attempt to pick up straight guys. After one night in this place you figure out this game.

To cut down on the temptation to bring girls home with me, I always book a guest house that doesn't allow local girls inside. It is hard to say 'no' after a few cheap drinks and a girl's aggressive persistence. So this is my trick to keep from being entrapped. They ask you, "Where are you staying?" As soon as you tell them, they walk away.

Most men talk a lot of shit about how they would love for girls to be all over them, grabbing them and groping them. I find that most guys who have had this experience don't appreciate it. I can honestly say I understand why women get upset for being treated this way. It's creepy and makes you feel creepy.

On the flip side, ladies, you can't have it both ways. You can't go out dressed sexy, looking for the right guy to treat you sexy, and then get mad at every guy for treating you this way. If you're going to dress sexy and show it, then you can't get upset for being noticed as a sex object. That being said, after having my crotch grabbed for the 30th time that night and asked if "You want to have some fun?" I retire to my guest room, tired of the scene. *I'm going to bed.* Some hours later I am awakened by the sound of a party. I go out to town and see the huge party now and the best fireworks display I have ever seen.

The next day brings an early start to the floating market which is the most unique thing to see in Bangkok for me! The merchant boats ride up and down the area. The women can even make you the best Thai food you'll ever have as they float by you. The market is completely on water. Tea, fruits veggies, even trinkets can all be acquired as you float along this market area. The colors are quite captivating. We go by this boat full of fruits, since I love to try things from all over the world. I see this red spiked fruit in her basket.

How much to try one? I ask.

She says, "Take it, it's free."

How do I open it?

After a quick lesson on unlocking the fruit while avoiding the spikes, I taste the best fruit on earth. Rambutan immediately becomes my favorite fruit on earth. For the rest of my time in Asia, I buy lots of them.

Departure time draws near. I ride on the back of a Moto-scooter with my backpack zipping in and out of traffic to the bus depot. Again all long bus rides run at night to avoid daytime traffic. The bus travels north toward the border of Laos.

The Gibbons Experience wants me there the day before to fill out forms and get sorted. I gave myself an extra day to get there just in case of any delays. I get the last seat for the northerly ride and the last seat on the smaller bus to the border. Just before the border, we stop at a market to get some drinks and food. For more than 20 hours of travel I have had no food or drink.

The market has everything you need as well as things you would never buy. They sell rat, dog, and every kind of meat you can imagine. Most of the meats were skinned, except for the rats and bats. We get there only one hour before the border closes; I plan to cross it tonight. I jump in a tuk-tuk and head to the border.

Once all the paperwork is sorted, I cross the river. On the other side, after a brief 5 minute wait, my passport and visa are stamped: good to go. No real problems! I heard this border can be very slow.

The next day I met some of the people on the bus with me. They ask me how long it took to get through this border. I tell them.

They say, "Wow! It took us two hours the next morning."

Yeah, that's why I cross borders late in the day when I can. I find a guest house and split the room cost with a guy who is heading the same way. We hit it off immediately! He is a captain of luxury catamarans that cruise all over the world. This can be useful information for future reference.

I find the office for the tour, fill out my forms and ask what time they want me there the next morning. The rest of the day is spent chilling on the Mekong.I walked up to witness a fully operational Monk Temple; took some video of them praying at sunset.

All set, I'm excited to ride zip-lines. I'm told these zip-lines are 1 kilometer long and they run 160 meters above the canopy floor. Plus, we get to sleep in the tree houses each night, too. Sounds like a shit ton of fun.

A couple of hours of a tuk-tuk ride and we're at the beginning of the tour. My tour-mates are 6 kids from Australia, new very loud and noisy travelers who complain about everything. We hike through the jungle for a few hours. I choose the tour option that has the most diversity; again, my goal is to see as much of the culture, people and geography as possible when I travel. I want to walk through these jungles, experience the local life.

My particular goal provides 3 additional hours of hiking before we get to the first stop! The extra effort is totally worth it. We arrive at a beautiful lake that has to be crossed by a bamboo raft! The water is very cold but since we have been hiking in the jungle, it's very refreshing. A small waterfall adorns the northern edge at the end. We all cross; some of the kids jump in naked. I try to stay out of their way.

They complain about the food, and ask for a vegetarian lunch. Apparently vegan was an option. I didn't care to attempt to get special food in this kind environment. After playing and cooling off in the water, we get to our first zip-line.

The zip-line crosses the entire valley; the cable runs from one end to the other. Amazing! The cable is a kilometer long and takes 40 seconds to ride across. The guide shows us how to clip in and how to stop! We then just jump on and ride around.

On the next one, the guide explains, "The red cables go one way; the green marked cables go the other way. Use it this way so nobody hits each other on the line."

Then we're on our own. He encourages us not to spend the whole time on the zip-lines; walk around the jungle floor as well. We go zipping around some of the other lines near us until it starts to get dark. It's not safe to zip around at night, because the animals may be hanging on the lines. We might hurt them or get hurt by them.

The only way in and out of the tree houses is by zip-line. Even our dinner is brought to us from a zip-line. Dinner is rice, and some boiled stew-type meat. It was ok. Later that night all the kids in the tree house threw up at one time or another. In fact, everybody eventually threw up except me. I was thinking, *"Maybe this is because I just had a full month of being sick in India that maybe my stomach is getting used to the water and food bacteria."*

The violent nature in which each person threw up that night concerned me. Each person would run over to the house walls and slam against it before violently throwing up. It shook the house each time. I was starting to get concerned for their safety that one of them would fall over the side. But I was too tired to get up and look.

A beautiful jungle morning, we hike to the next tree house. Each morning the guide came in and would ask if anybody wanted to go for a walk. My tour-mates didn't want to go. They were all sick from the night before.

The kids had played a game with the driver on the way to the park. I thought the scheme was very clever myself. One kid climbed up on the roof. When the other guide went up to tell him to get down, he created this sort of 'us against them' attitude. In fact, the girls started to talk with the driver about how upset they were that the boy should not be allowed to go on the roof. It was all just a ploy!

What really happened was the other guide sold the kids a bag of pot while on the roof; because the other guide and driver didn't smoke! Good scheme boys; they were not older than 19. Then they spent all day trying to figure out if I smoked or not. On the down side, these youngsters were so fucking loud. I mean, c'mon! If there was a wild animal within 2 kilometers, they could hear us coming. I wanted to see a Gibbons monkey. So I made a great deal of distance between them and me when hiking. I think the guide understood why I did this. He just smiled when I asked him to give me a marker ahead on the path to stop and wait for them.

The next day was awesome: a short walk through the jungle and, oh yeah, baby, 5 more zip-lines along the way. The tree houses are visible from some of them as we go by. The jungle is very close as you zip through.

The morning rides were amazing. A thick blanket of fog accompanied the noises of the animals waking up across this jungle basin! One zip-line ride scared the shit out of me! After 10 seconds, I hit a wall of fog as thick as pea soup. I was unable to see more than a foot ahead of me for 30 seconds! Finally, the jungle comes back into view. I didn't make it all the way across (because I braked in the blinding fog), so I had to pull myself along the cable to the end to unclip.

The breaking system is made up of cut motor scooter tires. They chop them up into 1 foot sections then bolt them to the pulley. When you pull back, the tire rubs against the cable causing you to slow down. If you don't, you will hit a tree or the houses very hard!

In the bush of Africa, deeper into the continent, the people use these same tires for shoes. They cut them up and sew a string to make a top like sandal-shoes. The last day one of the girls doesn't want to hike anymore. She lies on the ground and just whines, "Somebody has to carry me." The boys fawn over her. She gets up to start again then shortly just sits down crying.

I'm off! Tell me where the next marker is… Eventually the kids work things out. The whole second night we're smoking pot; they got quite high. I thought it was incredibly weak because it yielded a very poor high. No wonder Asia has so much hash – the pot sucks. I tell the kids it's just ok!

We start talking about traveling. They are amazed at how much I have traveled. For the first time in my travel life, I am the person with the most experience. The ride back to the city was full of beautiful vistas of the peaks and valleys of this jungle country!

I try to get a taxi that day to get out of the city, heading up north to a border city to cross into Vietnam. Long bus rides up here on roads that are tough and underdeveloped. Along the way I meet a British guy who seems to be in love with Laos. He's trying to open a business there, working on networking to create the clout it takes to accomplish this. A great guy, he teaches us the sensory plant. That's wicked. He takes us to a guest house because it's 9 pm! They have very little power at night in this village. We get settled and get some sleep.

Next day we're chilling in this village. He takes me and another girl across the river for breakfast. We had the same attitude: let's hang out with this guy for the day get an insider's perspective of the village. He owns an apartment here. We cross the river attempting to see a beautiful beach but a tree had fallen across the path. We had to turn around.

On our way back, a giant millipede crosses the path on a step we were just on 3 minutes ago. The guy says, "Hey stop. If that bites you, you're dead. If it even crosses over your foot, it leaves a nasty rash for a month."

We go-to 'Whiskey Village' they make this green 62% alcohol in huge stills. Very cool to go inside and look. We go our separate ways for a few hours, enjoying the various areas of this village.

We meet up later with these local ladies who are having a snack. They start teasing my new mate about another woman in the village. Apparently he and this woman spend time together and the village is starting to notice. He doesn't know these girls; has never seen them before. They were snacking along the upper river bank interestingly enough, on the same thing the local women in Nepal snack on. They peel grapefruits and tear the pulp off in chunks. They dip the pulp in a mixture of sugar and chili powder.

I tell the guy," *It's amazing. Please try it.*"

We sit and try it. We talk about his girlfriend playing with the ladies' kids. He thought it was very funny that the local ladies have gotten the gossip about this interracial relationship that is developing.

We head out for lunch now. He said if we just hang out with him, we'll have a great lunch in his favorite restaurant in this village.

Sure.

He begins to tell me about his plan and why he's spending so much time in Laos. During lunch time, we're met by a few businessmen from the village. The girl in question is a banker from this area; the other guys are also important business people in the area. Lunch is amazing! They order four dishes of different foods and we all share everything. They offer us a beer. My new friend gives them a bottle of the 'lau lau' that he just purchased from Whiskey Village across the river. Apparently, it's a very famous alcohol in Laos. Since it's only made here, it's not easy to get. A hawk is tethered to a post just a few feet away from where I'm sitting at the lunch table. Yes, it's real! The view of the upper Mekong is beautiful.

I meet up with my other friends who took the bus with me to this border city; we continue walking along the river and decide to go to the market together. It's just like any other market – tables displaying foods of all types, including bats. I've already tasted bat here. Tough taste, bitter and tangy!

Since I'm describing eating bats, let me admit that I have already eaten some very interesting and exotic foods on this journey through foreign countries. Sheep's balls in Iceland are tender and delicious by the way. Raw shark I found distasteful; the curdled sour meat is horrible. I'll take a few shots of the whiskey after every bite just to wash it down.

I've eaten everything you can think of in Africa and probably many things you would never think of eating. They make many different types of jerky. Kangaroo meat is really tasty. The green ant in Australia does taste like sour patch kids on steroids. Termites taste like chunks of pineapple Wow!

Back at my hostel, a couple of new guys are making plans to catch the boat down to Ventiene to some tubing place. I see the girl who hung out with me earlier in the day sitting at a table with other people. The older couple to my right is from Iran. They don't speak much English. We're trying to get the couple some food other than rice and eggs! With their religious related diet we're trying to see what they can eat. The woman made a comment to my friend that she wanted more than that for dinner.

So here we go. The other girl sitting across from us is French. I ask one guy for his Farsi to French dictionary and get the French to English dictionary from the girl. We begin to have a 3 way conversation about what to eat for dinner. The dictionaries were very abridged so it was not easy finding common words to translate. It took us about an hour to figure out what everybody wanted to eat, as we sit in this open walled restaurant overlooking the river. Now it's time to get drinks.

I was shocked at first to see an older couple traveling this way. I have not previously met a Muslim couple traveling in this style. I've only met one Muslim person traveling. My first thoughts were: *"I'm glad the world travels this way, too."* I have seen very few Americans traveling this way, and fewer the older you get.

My second surprise was that she still wears her head piece while traveling. During dinner she took it off. So we order a local beer and tell stories about going to whiskey village across the river. We finish our first beer and begin to order another round. He looks at his wife and she gives him 'the look.' We all just laugh and translate that the woman is the boss.

She said, "He had one too many the night before!"

This argument is not over! He says, "We're with friends tonight. I'm not drinking alone. It's ok! This is a good night." All this through our 2 dictionaries! These moments of connecting as human beings across boundaries of nationality, language, age and gender are treasures of traveling. It is a great night.

As I go up to sort the bill, the girl comes up and says she will pay for the couple's dinner. We decide to split the cost of their meal. We even make sure they get the breakfast they want included on the bill we're splitting. The waitress comes out and serves us another round of beers on the house.

So we sit and talk about traveling. We have all seen some of the same things and some not. Voicing my desire to go see Mecca someday impels the couple from Iran to talk about Tehran. I decide my next backpacking trip will be 6 months through the Middle East. I'm studying Arabic now.

I don't have a visa to enter Vietnam, but the guide books say the border is now open as a test run; visa' scan be processed the same day. So I am going to try. Scheduling a visa ahead of time in such a fluid part of the world is impossible. The couple from Iran goes off to bed. My guide for the day shows up; it's time to move on. The girl seems to connect with my guide. I head over to three guys in the corner to have another couple of beers and just hang out.

The weather is so beautiful and it's such an amazing place; I'm just not ready to go-to bed. We chat about surfing and traveling. They give me this cool book about surfing in Indonesia in the early years to read. I already read Vanity Fair while on the train from Lhasa to Beijing. We talked about me wanting to go to Bali to surf. After spending some time in Australia trying to surf, then Peru, I've decided to spend 2 weeks just surfing in Indonesia.

In the morning, we all gather around the river side and wait for the ferry as the sun comes up. The ferry arrives and we cross, starting our journey into Vietnam. We stop along the way to buy fresh chickens and other edible goods! I love the way they make bamboo baskets to hold live chickens.

We drive along this cut out dirt road which is still under construction. We are forced to stop for an hour while the earthmovers are working! Finally, we arrive at the border crossing. Each side's border is 2 kilometers apart.

We get to the Vietnamese side, get off the bus and pile in. I'm told to wait. Everybody else gets processed.

"Can I get my visa processed?"

"Do you have a letter?"

Nope. I'm told this office is now capable of processing same day visas.

He looks at me and says, "Yes, for everybody except Americans. You will not be allowed to enter."

The walk back to the village is 30 kilometers! The Iranian guy comes walking through the guards as they are yelling at him. He gives me a French kiss on both cheeks and says, "It was a pleasure to meet you."

Time to walk back — 30 kilometers is about 18.5 miles. Heading out, the guard says something sarcastic to me; I return the favor. I walk away toward the Laos border. I'm told, "The next bus comes in two days; there is a hotel over there."

Forget that! I'm walking. After a few hours I get to the construction spot. A truck there carrying fertilizer bags is stalled due to the construction. They offer me a ride. I climb back up into the back and lay on the bags. We get to a smaller village where we stopped on the way up. They let me out saying this is as far as they go.

I just use my flashlight and continue walking down the path/ road. It's just one road with no turns. I walk about 30 more minutes before I get passed by a truck. The driver stops to tell me, "It's not safe for you to walk this road. Get in."

He takes me to a guest house and tells me there is a party up on the hill for the SEA games. "A big futbol match is going on tonight. Come on up." The party hosts a full spread of food! I share my bottle of lau lau with the driver. All kinds of food! Shortly after I find out my host is the manager of the 'highway' construction. Tonight's party is to make the workers happy since they have been away from home for so long. His truck pulls back up and 6 girls get out of it–all paid for the night. I'm told one girl likes me. I'm not the kind of guy who enjoys sex with professionals. I flirt with her to not be rude but then head off to find a bathroom and walk down to my room for the night.

The next day I catch a ride with the guy in his truck since the bus didn't come by. He drives me to the next little town. Then I pay to sit in the back of another truck and enjoy my ride back to the main village. Success! I only lost one day. My clothes are covered in dirt from my foot excursion and dusty rides. I'm going to spend the day in the early morning sun and wash my clothes by the river. It takes me 4 hours to wash and dry my stuff.

As I walk back up to my guest house to see if they have a vacancy, I see my mate and we just laugh. He says, "I thought that was you washing your clothes on the river. I've never seen anybody come back from that border crossing before. I've seen 3 people walk up there without a preset visa."

Yup, I say *"The border is fully operational except for Americans. Lol. I'm going to take the river boats down tomorrow and enjoy the view."*

"I'm going into Luang Prabang tomorrow by bus," he says. "Come and join me. We'll have lots of fun for Christmas! I'm meeting more people there."

Thanks.

Getting up early I want to see the market place where the monks walk before sunrise. Their path takes them by the local ladies each morning where they collect the food they will eat for the day, picking from the baskets the ladies have brought to the market to sell that day. The locals all kneel down in a line as the monks proceed by them. It's very beautiful. No communication is exchanged between the monks and the women.

I head out to the bus stop and wait there by myself. I set my bag down and begin to look at a small local pond which is used as a fish farm. It's funny how they make these little fish farms growing fish to sell. Looking back up to my bus stop to check on my bag, I notice a woman who is playing with the bear's bag. I assess that she is harmless. She isn't going through my bag, just the sack that holds the bears. I walk up toward her just as a precautionary measure. She begins to yell at me in a high angry voice and gestures as if choking the black bear. She put him in the bag without leaving his head out. I bow my head apologetically and leave him in the bag.

The buses are so much fun themselves. They sell every seat they can at the stations and then open up these plastic seats to fill the center aisle. Then the driver will pocket anybody's fee that he picks up along the way. They fill these buses in tight.

My mate tells me at the transfer station after the first bus, "The monk sitting next to him took up 2 seats on the bus and wouldn't move. He kept his stick and bag in the seat next to him"!

I thought that wasn't very monkish of him. Seeing monks with cell phones was odd.

I need some food so I head over to the bbq stands just away from the station. Looking for something safe to eat, I decide on chicken. They cook them without removing their heads. OK a little gross; but not as bad as barbequed scorpion on a stick for Thanksgiving dinner just a month ago in China.

I break it apart and start to eat. A dog is begging me for food and since I don't want to pick apart the whole animal, I throw a leg piece down for him to eat. He starts tearing that up. I then break off the head and throw that on the ground. The dog immediately stops eating the leg and attacks the head part. Apparently he prefers the head. That is gross.

Arriving in Luang Prabang my mate calls up his friend and gets us a ride to a hotel. He is upset the hotel is farther away than normal, but it's a nice place. A private bed, hot water, private shower with TV and ceiling fans on the upper level with a balcony too! All for 12 dollars a night!

Wake up and my mate is gone. I'm off to the city center and find another seamstress to fix my shorts. When I find one, they offer some food for me while I wait. Apparently I stopped by during lunch time. I head out to the temples and marketplace. Walk out toward the river and I'm met by my mate. We hang out along the river and talk about the market and such.

We head over to get some food and play some pool with a local who has never been in a tourist bar before. In fact, he has never played pool in a bar before. He kicks our ass. Then Christmas dinner, though it's a little over a week before Christmas. A full spread includes anything you want, Laos style. Again the local businessmen accompany my mate.

After a few drinks we head to the bowling alley –a four lane proper alley.

I ask my mate, *"Am I supposed to lose this game for business sake with your friend?"* The head banker is playing pretty well and it would not be a stretch to be beat by him.

"Nope. You're an American. It would not be right, if you didn't win."

Ok. Game; set; match. We are taken to a local dance club and party all night long. I'm heading into Cambodia the next day and then Thailand. We discuss meeting at a local island near Cambodia in the next few weeks. He likes to go there all the time. We set a possible date and exchange emails.

Catch a bus to the airport the next day and board my flight into Cambodia. My visa processes and I walk out the door. I'm in Siem Reap to see Angkor Wat. I've heard so much about this temple complex; I must see it. A taxi takes me to a cheap guest house nearby. Siem Reap is a huge tourist city, so it's organized well. The guards outside of the airport ask you your needs first, then get you the taxi to the type of guest house you request.

My driver and I talk about getting a motor hire for 3 days to drive around the temple complex. He will pick me up every day at 5 am to 2 pm for 10 dollars. Plus I pay for my own visa to the temples. I get a room at the guest house with my own bathroom and bedroom –no sharing.

I head down to get some food and meet up with another smoker. Off to his room we smoke up for the afternoon. Then down to this guest house for food, drinks and we play pool without fee on a public table. I need the internet to tell my girl about my last week's adventures. In the city market first I get a shave then go shopping. I like to collect t-shirts from all over the world at places where I've had a great time. The t-shirt I buy for Angkor Wat cost me 2 dollars and was made by old navy. The tag is still in the shirt. Early to bed knowing I have to get up at 5AM to get picked up.

My motor driver is waiting for me first thing in the morning. I pay my driver for the 3 days and get my visa at the check point. *"I hear the sunrise is beautiful but that everybody goes there. Take me to the Temples so I can have some time alone each morning to relax and walk around."*

He understands. The first Temple I see is 'faces.' They have names to describe them a little. It's beautiful – most amazing thing I've ever seen. In all my travels, I have seen many sights and buildings all over. Most are very disappointing in person, especially the ones that have many photographs published about them. They are nothing like you had imagined and often nothing very magical about them.

The Mona Lisa in Paris is so small I was wondering what the hub-hub is all about. Dark and not clean brush strokes for a piece marveled at by so many. Monet's place in Giverny is more breathtaking than his work.

The 2 boys sucking off the nipples of a dog inside the Vatican is creepy and confusing. The garbage pile near the pyramids is sad. The law even protects the unfinished buildings dirtying up the eyes as you look around. Really have to love the hard rock café store and Pizza Hut not far in front of the Sphinx. The Blue Mosque is beautiful but it's very dark and always packed with people.

Anaiya Sophia is much more surprising. Though my favorite place on earth is the cistern under the city in Istanbul across from Anaiya! The next favorite thing is the salt mine in Poland. It's in my top 3 things to see in the world. Angkor Wat is the only place to truly take my breath away all day long. Each Temple is more beautiful than the next. The existentialism of the trees growing among the stones and Temples, often the only reason why some Temples don't fall! Some doorways that have the root growth along them transport you far away from planet earth. The ones that are not in the pages of National Geographic I find more amazing.

I caught a bus out to Thai Islands along the border of Cambodia! Another long bus ride to a ferry, and then a tuk-tuk takes me to my guest house in Kho Chang Island. After experiencing the more touristy islands, I wanted to stay away from them and from the prostitutes that hang out at these party islands. A full lunar eclipse happened to occur at midnight New Year's Eve. Won't be another one for thousands of years! I don't enjoy being around thousands of drunken people and thousands of prostitutes. I prefer a quieter environment.

The beach in the morning offers a magnificent view of the northern islands of Thailand. Yup, very beautiful! Still too touristy for my taste! I notice an ad on the wall of a guest house offering a more reclusive resort on the other side of the island. "No electricity; no fresh water. Just a restaurant, and some bungalows."

I plan on leaving 2 days after Christmas. Christmas Eve I go out to the beach fish fry and partake in the festivities. I imbibe a Mai Thai and some fresh food from the beach! I get barracuda for the first time and some vegetables and rice with a mojito. Got some deserts after, along the beach.

I want to work on my tan now, since I'll be going to Bali soon to surf all day. I wake up and head to the beach for a day of being a bum. Within an hour I'm sick to my stomach; hits me like a brick from a cannon – hard and quickly. I'm throwing up everything in my body. A local 7/11 provides Gatorade. It doesn't last in my stomach more than a second. I stumble to my room, and for the next 32 hours I'm violently ill, even throwing up in my sleep. I fall asleep and wake up in a pile of vomit and diarrhea. I decide to sleep in the shower area so I can get hot water poured on me. I'm so cold. I can sleep naked and not ruin anymore clothes or sheets. I have severe hallucinations and even feel like the next time I fall asleep will be the last time.

I say a few prayers and resign myself to the idea that I am not going to wake up. To my surprise and relief I do. I even feel a little better for the first time. I head to the store to get some Gatorade and head back to my room. Still quite sick, a few hours later I head out get some rice and eggs, and pay for my ticket the next day to the other side of the island.

On a tuk-tuk ride to the other side, I sit in the back because I'm still very sick and weak. I dismount the tuk-tuk to check in and have to wait there for a minute. I couldn't even stand up I'm so tired and sick; had to sit and wait my turn. They hand me my room key and say, "We'll see you in a day or two."

Later they told me they took straws as to who was heading to my room; they did not think I would be alive the next day. I woke up the next afternoon and walked down to the beach. The lagoon has a normal sandbar and not too deep to lie in. I would just go lay in the 85 degree water with the sun beaming on me. Took an entire day of this before I got any strength! Opening up a fresh coconut I was able to hold down some nutritious milk.

I met an Italian family who was smoking joints. I thought maybe it would help settle my stomach, recalling my childhood moment with it. I ask them for some and they teach me how to roll joints with cigarettes. Since rolling papers are not common and cigarettes are very cheap, they simply use this technique. Cool, I'm feeling much better.

The third day I decide to try some eggs and rice, figuring it's the safest thing to eat. "The first meal is free, because you are still alive," the staff says!

Back to my sandbar, the casual way the coconut trees hang over the lagoon with swings on them is picturesque. Wild puppies playing with half coconut husks like balls can help you forget all the concrete jungles of the world. The family asked me to come with them; they would take me to where they got their smoke. We lunch at a place nearby and complete our transactions. I'm nearly back to normal, and feel my strength start to come back. Ten days later, I head back to the other side.

How loud and obnoxious the world can be, especially after ten days in such a tranquil spot with very little noise and lights! That and a near death experience change one's taste for tourism's delights and superficiality. I found the touristy side of the island mildly horrifying. No matter. I'm out of here the next day. My bus barrels back to Bangkok, where I catch my flight to Jakarta.

CHAPTER 23

I want to see Borobudor but missed the first train! The next train out leaves at night; I am stuck in the station for an all day wait. Again I don't eat the day I travel. The overnight train arrives in Yogyakarta the next morning.

Once I find a guest house, I then try to get on a tour to see Borobudor. Success! The tour leaves in an hour. I have enough time for breakfast at the market before heading out. I've seen plenty of temples at this point in my trip, so it's getting harder to focus on their uniqueness. The stupa's adorning the top are very unique. My time there closes as I head down to the market place in search of a t-shirt of the temple that will fit a man my size. Success! Now we go look at some other temples and a jade factory. Up the road I take some photos of the rice fields. My guest house room and dinner await my day's end. I am getting comfy with the spices of Asia now, a fact that upon reflection will cause some pleasure back home.

(When I got back home there was a farewell party for my parents who were moving out west. Some-one came up to me and said, "Hey! Did you try such and such appetizer? It's very spicy but good." I walk over and take a bite. It was very sweet.

Smiling to myself, I eat a few of them all the while missing my spicy Asian flavors).

The Indonesian government does not give a very long tourist visa. Since this is a large archipelago, it takes time to get down the islands. So it's a mad rush to get there and see a few things along the way. It's a 5 day journey to Bali, not including stops at Borobudor and Bromo. I've seen 2 volcanoes already; I'm getting quite familiar with the smell and burnt eyes from sulfur. Learning along the way it doesn't take millions of years to build a mountain.

In the Westman Islands off the coast of Iceland, a volcano gave no warning and erupted. The lava and molten rock hardened to form a 'hill' 900 feet high in 10 short days. They made an amazing IMAX movie of it.

Arriving into my lodge late at night, we get sorted and told pick up is 6 am. A local band is playing, *Hotel California* in an Indonesian dialect. LOL!

My new surroundings are nothing like anyplace I have seen. The grounds are black and dusty –a vision of the apocalypse. The jagged peaks along the distance are black and razor sharp. It's creepy. Climbing up to the summit is tough because your eyes burn from the sulfur. Breathing is difficult except through your shirt. The cone is warm and foggy, revealing a glimpse of the center every once in a while when the wind blows away the plume.

Walking back down, the sun has finally come up. The wind slows down and we see the surrounding mountains. While waiting for my ride to the city to be on my way to Bali, I learn how easy it is to get to Borneo! Next time I must see Borneo.

Travel and transportation often involve waiting. Two hours pass before my bus takes me to the ferry; 16 hours later I'm on the ferry to Bali. My plans include hiking in Bud, then off to Kuta to surf. Having heard so much about Bali, I'm very excited. Arriving I find a very different story.

The Australian men here are assholes. They drink and love to fight; they enjoy pushing Americans around. I watch a few guys get harassed from my 'back of the bus' vantage point. As always I place myself in the back and out of the way when first arriving anywhere. I even witness some guy pull out his dick in public on the street telling a strange girl he was going to fuck her with it that night. The girl giggles, walks toward him and says hello. I'm out of here. The surfers throw their boards at the snorkelers in the area simply because they feel they own this place. Apparently they do.

I take the next ferry to Lombok Island and seek a more peaceful place to surf. I've heard a lot about the Gili Islands nearby. So I rent a moto scooter in Lombok and take a drive along the coastline to see what these Gili Islands look like. A day of riding along the coast yields beautiful photos of islands off in the distance. I espy some kids who use cows and goats to keep the grass short on futbol fields.

With no real fresh water or electricity, the Gili's offer limited lodging. At a dock in Lombok, one can find smaller boats that transport to the Gili's. I'm staying at Trawangan which is a mere 45 minute boat ride away. There is Meno and Air, but I've heard both can be very nasty and rip off tourists. From all the intel I can gather, Gili T is the best for service, respect and surf. Maybe I can get a chance to scuba dive with giant manta rays.

Immediately upon exiting the boat, we are accosted by a sales force for lodging. I'm used to this so I just walk along the beach. I talk to the dive shop operators and arrange to drop off my big bag while I search for suitable lodging. It only takes 2 hours to walk all the way around this island.

Walking up the beach I notice store upon store with signs advertizing mushroom shakes. The stories I have heard about the magic mushroom shakes are real! Almost every place I see sells magic mushroom shakes each having little pithy signs on the entrance about how their shakes are the best.

I walk down the beach and see a guy who has surf boards for rent. He offers me a room that's clean and has its own bathroom and shower. I tell him, *"Let me look around and then I will be back."* I can't find anything close to the rate he quoted me. Additionally, he is the only one on the island that rents surf boards. I'm back there in 10 minutes.

My private room has a large bed, my own shower and a small foyer / lounge area by my entrance door. Nice. My new host escorts me to the back of his place and confides, "I have all kinds of drugs."

"I'm only interested in mushrooms and pot."

How much do you want?

A little nervous about carrying drugs all day long, I reply, *"I tell you what. I will pay you something extra each day. Since you smoke a lot, I will just hang out with you and smoke when you smoke. This way I don't have any drugs on me."*

He is amenable to that arrangement, so we consummate the agreement over a few joints. Now to partake of the legendary island mushroom shakes.

As I mentioned, the shake shops are as common as a t-shirt store on Ocean City's boardwalk. For my first taste of this hyped product the closest shop will do. Within moments a healthy sized helping is plunked down in front of me.

Those with experience recommend drinking the shake slowly. I find myself following their instructions. Yes, it does have a dirty gritty texture and a just plain horrible taste. They usually add a mango juice box (or any other flavor you want) with a shot of red bull and vodka. Wow! Rough start.

I'll be skipping the red bull and the vodka from here on out, but insist on the juice to kill the taste. An hour later I'm walking along the beach, tripping my balls off. The island sunset is enjoyable on this trip.

All the stores serve the shakes in these polka dotted cups. So when you walk around with a polka dotted cup in your hand, all the locals know this person is tripping. Plenty of other people on the beach sport the specialty cup which makes it easy to meet and greet with a knowing smile.

Walking along I see the locals play ping pong outdoors. I jump on a table and start to beat a few people. Next thing I'm playing a local who is paid to get me off the table. After 20 minutes we realize that we're evenly matched. Only the wind adversely affects my game a little, and he beats me. We play for money in a contest that takes 30 minutes; it's fun. I'm still tripping on my inaugural mushroom shake.

The lounge area of my room provides the perfect setting to smoke some pot which helps navigate the landing from the 'shrooms'. Coming down takes a few hours and a few joints.

In the morning I negotiate a surf board rental with my host. *"I want to surf for the next 10 days,"* I explain. He throws in a bike with the board that makes transportation to the surf spot easier.

The surf is a little shallow; I'm worried about my feet and legs getting cut up in the coral and craggy ocean floor, *hey, I'm here! Got to give it a go.*

I have no problems the first day except for getting thrown off the board in 5 foot curls. Trying to gain my balance is obviously the primary challenge of surfing. I spend the next 10 days surfing from 11 am until sundown which is only about 5 hours a day!

I really loved watching the turtles spin inside the pipes of the waves as I was surfing. I got the impression they were doing it for fun. These islands are known as the turtle capital of the world. Turtles are always popping up around us while we wait for the sets to roll in. With the backdrop of Bali and Lombok Island off in the distance, the beautiful view makes waiting for sets satisfying.

Then what I feared most came upon me. I get severely cut up on the reef, causing significant injuries to my ankles and shins. The reef tore the flesh off the bone of my ankles and shins. It will be impossible to stitch the injuries as chunks of flesh are torn off.

It's two days transport to the nearest hospital. I decide to stick it out. I'll wear a sock and my keens to protect my feet and keep surfing. My thinking is that the best place for my wounds is in the salt water. At least they are cleaned every day. I keep surfing, starting to get up on the board now and turn a little.

Each day I wake up, my legs hurt so much from the wounds that it feels like my insides will pop through the skin. I have to take baby steps until my wounds stretched out and can flex without pain. Takes about 40 minutes before my fresh tissue can begin to stretch.

I make my way to the beach each morning and find a place to get my tan on for the next few hours. I begin playing basketball in a court each day before I head off to surf. My basketball skills have brought me a lot of attention. Each day I either play alone or with others before I wait for the swell to come in and go surf.

In the evenings I go down to this little restaurant that has private booths to view DVD movies. Occasionally they offer new releases in an open viewing area that they cover in black blankets. They ask that you spend 5 dollars on food and drinks per person to view the movie. I get a banana split and a beer each night to meet their requirement.

Seeing Avatar for the first time while on mushrooms was a lot of fun. Even watched Surrogates as well as Up in one of the private rooms. It helps pass the evenings by. Wake up, repeat the same thing all day long for 10 days.

Each morning I stop by the dive shop to see if they spotted manta rays. (After watching them at Atlantis, I want to see them in the wild open water). It would not be for another 2 years until I get to scuba dive with manta rays in Bora Bora. I snorkeled with humpback whales at a distance of 5 feet as well on that trip off Moorea Island. But that is another story. If you don't want to wait for that book, watch the video on my blog: shaneoffthegrid.com in the snorkel section of the tool bar you can see the whales, and hear them sing.

Night times are fun. I'm doubling up on mushroom shakes now and enjoying my nighttime walks along the beaches. After such a walk on this particular night, I want to sit at a bar and watch sports to occupy my twisted mind. I sit down with a drink in front of the Australian Tennis Open; I figure the bouncing ball will help with my trip.

This blonde next to me starts chatting me up. I don't like blondes; they do nothing for me. I could care less. She has this inserted piercing in her arm with a stud that looks like a drop of mercury. I ask about the drop just trying to ascertain if it's real or not.

She tells me, "It's a body piercing. Have you ever heard of them?" (Did I mention she was blonde)?

Yes. I just wanted to make sure it was real.

We talk for a few more minutes and she is telling me about her tattoos. Strike 2. I don't have any tattoos and I don't like tattoos on girls anyway. We're still talking about piercings it becomes clear to me that she is trying to impress me.

I look at her and say, *"I know all about body piercings. I have 2 of them myself. I have 2 inverted Prince Albert's."*

My attention turns to the right of my seat. I'm still tripping hard. After sitting there for 20 minutes now, I notice a spoon next to me all bent up like the matrix. I almost freak out. I know I'm on mushrooms and I know my surroundings are not all real. The matrix is one of my favorite movies. The bend in the spoon is a perfect match to the movie. I pick up the spoon and ask the girl next to me:

"Hey, is this real? I'm on double mushroom shakes and the matrix is one of my favorite movies; I just want to know if this is real."

She says, "Yes, it is" She just laughs at me and gets up and walks away. Thank God! I can't stand blondes. I see her the next day and she says hello. I said hi but kept on walking toward the basketball court.

Playing basketball on a dirt court, barefoot on a small island in Indonesia, I am getting physically beaten up because I am bigger and stronger than my local opponents. This goes on for 10 minutes before I finally let them know that they do not want me to get physical with them. *I am trying to play a clean game; please don't force me to get physical.*

Their style of play against me does not change. Finally, after being punched in the groin for the 3rd time, I reach my limit. Upset, I decide to play chippy with them as well. A very heated argument about their behavior and mine ensues. I slap a guy in the face letting him know *"if you really want to get physical, then we certainly can go there."*

Obviously, I am quite the hot headed sports player and always have been. I think it has a lot to do with growing up in 5 different foster homes and 4 different institutional boarding schools where I always had to fight for all I have. Before we played a real game, I spent the afternoon trying to teach them the subtle things about playing basketball, like how to make passes to a shooter in rhythm.

Although I am ultimately a guest, they decide to throw me off the court, telling me they don't want me to play anymore.

I'm done with this! I decide if I can't play, then nobody will play. I run, jump up and tear the rim and parts of the backboard off the pole where it was perched. As I land on the ground, I see 20 people suddenly charging toward me. As I back away from this angry mob – most of whom were not part of the game– it dawns on me that I'm in real trouble now…..

I tell myself, *"Standup, Shane, before you get trampled on."*

I lose my girlfriend's NYY hat when I trip walking backwards on something. I stand up and see people rushing at me. I run down the alleyway to try to close off as many angles for them to come at me as I can. They are trying to get in close, but I just keep pushing them away, walking backwards. It's a little late, but I try to get everybody to calm down.

Holding the broken piece of the rim, I realize I need to get rid of it! The piece has nails sticking out of it. I really don't want it to accidentally puncture somebody. I dodge rocks coming at me from above while one man punches on me for all he is worth. Lefts, rights, etc. I protect my upper body and allow him to pound on my mid-section. It becomes quite clear he does not have the strength to hurt me. So I don't pay him any attention anymore even though he is standing in front of me punching on me.

My concern is the rocks coming down out of the sky on me. Next I see a man walk up to me with half of his face sliced off from a rock that hit him in the face. I tell him, *"I have not thrown anything; your friends did that to you."*

I choose not to throw a punch in retaliation, figuring it will only escalate the violence to a point beyond control. My safest bet is to let them see me get punched on without punching back. I'm screaming to get everybody to calm down.

Finally my host at the guest house comes from around the corner and tells everybody to stop. To my amazement, everybody does. They even drop the rocks! He parts the crowd to get me and escort me back to his area. "What the hell happened?" I tell him the story from start to finish.

"Yeah, I heard about the argument the day before," he explained, "I told people not to be so violent on the court with you." *At least they listened to you today,* I thought, *otherwise I'd still be getting marshmallow body blows.*

I explain the whole thing to the authorities who insist I pay a fine and the medical bills for the guy's face. It all comes out to about 100 USD. I look at my host and ask him, *"Seriously, do I need to leave the island for my safety?"*

"Everybody knows your staying with me now," he says reassuringly. "I'm the most important man on this island; trust me. Nobody will bother you again while you're here. If anybody says a bad thing to you, then just tell me and I will have them thrown off the island until you leave." He promises me he will fix the court, but not until after I am gone.

I see a guy wearing my hat a few days later and I ask him if I can buy it from him. *I know I lost it.* He looks at me and says, "It's yours; I just found it." He hands it back to me. Wow....

Back to surfing, smoking and having fun for the remaining days. I met another model and her girlfriend on the island and have some fun with them. The model tells me about her experiences in Bali which seem to parallel mine. She did not enjoy guys pulling out their dicks in public and talking to girls this way. I thought it was just an isolated incident. She told me she saw it on 2 separate occasions and talked to a few girls who had the same experience. Like me, she was more shocked that the girls giggled about it than at the guys who yanked it. *Apparently girls like to be treated this way.* We just laugh over a couple of joints.

We discuss Milan and how 16-18 year old girls should never be brought there. The drugs and sexual activity of it all should not be subjected to young models. I'm surprised at her maturity. Were it not for the ugly, unsightly gashes in my leg, the encounter with the model and her girlfriend might have gone differently. As it was, we limited our intercourse to the verbal variety and thoroughly enjoyed each other's company.

Ten days expire and I am off to Bali to fly home. I miss being home, my girlfriend and some familiar creature comforts. For the last 2 months of my trip finding toilet paper was nearly impossible. I chose to forgo the whole thing, just using water and my hands to clean myself after toilet usage! It was actually cleaner after you got over the initial shock of handling your business this way.

Getting back to Bali was easy; finding out I had the wrong flight from Bali to Singapore was deflating. The capital of Bali is called Denpasar and the Bali Denpasar airport is actually in Borneo. I am in Bali and my return flight leaves from Borneo many miles away. "Right ticket; wrong airport." Having to scramble to get a flight out of Bali to Singapore was my only focus. No worries. The airlines can accommodate a traveler with American Express. In spite of a huge layover, I'm ok. I want to go home now and see my noogy. To be around people who actually know me will be like home at last.

CHAPTER 24

For the first time in all my travels I want to be home. It takes me two days to get there! My girl had a tough time getting adjusted to her Masters Program and is quite upset I abandoned her at this critical time for 6 months. We meet and she runs and jumps into my arms; boy, did I miss her so much. We spend some time playing catch up while driving from NYC.

I have already told her about my legs and how cut up they are. In fact, my last night I met a couple from the Midwest who let me use their fresh water shower and gave me some proper dressings for my legs. That works out very well since it was 2 days before I got home without iodine and wraps; I probably would have gotten an infection. It's funny – I always take a comprehensive first aid kit with me on all my travels. I've never needed one before. So when I was lowering the weight of this backpack before departure I decided to leave the first aid kit home. Lol! I actually needed it this time. I will never leave it home again.

At home I want my Playstation 3. I bought a PSP in Tokyo airport paying about 100 dollars less than the US. I also have to go out and buy my first computer. I want to start a blog and webpage for my travels. I have so many new contacts with whom to keep in touch that I have to upgrade into the internet world. My girl and I go shopping for the gear and I am reminded of the contrast with many of the areas of my recent travels.

I begin the search for a new apartment. Find some work and get my life together. I start working for my step brother's company. He is behind on his mortgage and the company is in debt a little. Since I'm off the books, I can save him about 60 dollars an hour. I get steady work and save my money for an apartment.

Arriving from 6 months in Asia takes major adjustments. From tropical Bali to a winter like you can't believe, I am frozen solid. It's below zero; my body is in shock. My girl and I have a few heated arguments, as well; things even get out of hand. It's hard when she is angry at me for everything and I'm still in shock from my trip, exhausted. It takes us about 3 weeks to get adjusted to being around each other again.

I have to soak my legs in warm water each night and let the wraps soak off on their own. The wounds need iodine and clean bandages again. They are very painful, very raw and exposed. The tendons and ligaments in the ankle are visible but are not severed or damaged. Wow! Am I lucky!

My girl is very upset at me being hurt, telling me my only job was to come back home safely and all put together. We plan a week of snowboarding up north. (FYI teaching girls how to snowboard is impossible. First women need all the info before doing anything. Example… She needs to know all the angles and all the variables before attempting anything. Where as a guy will just do what you say. After multiple fights some of which the chair lift attendees even say "I've seen ppl break up trying to teach snowboarding." I'm trying to explain to her that I know she is not trying hard enough. She screams at me telling me yes I am trying. I inform her that I know she isn't because she is not falling correctly, she is holding back. After she finally gets the curve and can actually snowboard beautiful s-turns. She comes up to me and says. "Shane your right I was not trying hard enough"). This begins the healing process for us. We have a week of fun and we're finally adjusted.

To show her how grateful I am that she helped me with flights along the way and for being there on my bad days, I plan a week on a cruise. It's a play cruise with a flow-rider on board. Since we both love climbing, I book the one with the climbing wall, too. I'm excited because she can finally swim. I'm really happy to take her snorkeling in a couple of different islands and take another catamaran ride.

We get our wrist bands the first day so we can do the sports activities: climbing, surfing, the ice skating rink. It's going to be fun. I purchase a full wine package for dinner so we can taste different wines to accompany our fine meals!

The flow-rider is harder than surfing. The board is so small that maintaining great balance is super challenging. I schedule a lesson because I love anything that floats on water and is fluid. Besides, one can accomplish anything one sets his mind to. The lesson is useful because we get to practice in private more than when the ride is open to everybody.

My girl is better than me on the ride! I'm jealous and happy for her. Next day I schedule a second lesson; hey, I want to be ok at this by the end of the week. They tell me there is a bigger board that I can request for the next time on the ride. *"Ha-ha! Now you tell me."*

The climbing wall offers a view of the ocean in the distance when you begin to climb up which is a little weird. The walls are more challenging than I expected with different degrees of difficulty! My girl and I are both 5.10 outdoor climbers. I can climb 5.13 indoors.

Every time the flow-rider is open for people and surfing- not boogie boarding, we get in line. It's a lot of fun in the morning before the drinkers wake up. If you don't need assistance loading yourself, then you can get in the morning line. Yeah, we both can load ourselves after the 2nd lesson. This became the focus of the cruise.

We did get off the boat for the activities we wanted. I got to show my girl a lion fish underwater on one snorkeling excursion. She is fully comfortable in the water now which I'm really excited about. All the hard work she did to learn has paid off; now we can have all sorts of water fun together. Snorkeling all day long on island days! Stopping at a water park in the ocean to play on and jump off tubes. Renting separate jet skis. She tells me she would rather be on the back of someone else next time. I just wanted her to ride her own. I am a good rider but I don't really like them. It's all cruise fun.

The meals are amazing. I have no problem wearing nice clothes every night. My girl is beautiful and I want to show her off. The food in the main dining is much better than the buffet style cafeterias. Getting back to land we head out to a waterpark to have fun for the last day. We stopped by Discovery Cove on the way in to test my girl's snorkeling skills and get her used to fish being around her. To see the dolphins and ride with them was a dream of mine. Once again I was very disappointed with the dolphin experience feeling like cattle during the whole time! The snorkeling and river routes are nice; feeding the stingrays and birds was fun.

When I arrive home, I find an apartment where doing some upgrades will net me a few months free rent. I choose this so I can go surfing somewhere for a few months and finally get my learning curve finished. I plan a winter trip to Hawaii with my girl. She is off to another school in the next year and I'm aware this could be the end of our relationship.

I've tried to give her the best of everything, teaching her there is more to life than school. She is brilliant and now is heading off to get her PHD in bioengineering. She has no student loans; her whole education was funded by scholarship.

With such a strict religious family upbringing that sheltered her from many things, I wanted her to see more, grow more, and find out what is out there; I wanted to give her a chance to explore, to learn and be more confident. I'm so glad she is my girl and I love her much more purely than I loved my wife.

I want to take her to Hawaii for 9 days and go surfing and hiking and see wild dolphins. We plan it and have a great week. She tries surfing and is successful at it for a first timer. We get to see the wild Spinner Dolphins jump out of the water around us. We take a cool crater hike off the tourist path! We watch the fireworks on the beach both Fridays we're there. We even go sky-diving on the last day. I'm so proud of her for wanting and being willing to try. I know it's scary but the view over the north shore is better than any other place you can drop. It's a go!

I always wanted to see whales breach with my own eyes. We got to see them breach many times during that flight up to our skydive elevation. (I did get to see one breach in Tahiti at a distance of 20 feet the day I snorkeled with them). We get picked up by a friend of hers who is in the military there. He shows us around some parts of the island.

We get back home and schedule another snowboarding week up north. There are many places I have yet to see still on my wish list: more of South America, Easter Island and Patagonia, for example. I really want to backpack the Middle East for 6 months.

But for now, my girl and I go our separate ways. She heads off to her PHD. I head back to Hawaii for the next 5 months to learn how to surf and skydive. I even manage to throw in 9 days in Tahiti. Alas this adventure is for another story.....

EPILOGUE

Jumping out of the plane once again, I try to control my body during free fall. Thinking to myself:

"This is a lot harder than I expected it to be."

Being a tall man my limbs are fighting against me. After my 4th failure, the jump master comes over with this blunt news.

"You're not allowed to go surfing for the next few days."

The body positioning of my legs while spending 6 hours a day, everyday struggling to gain my balance, and perfecting my technique to get up on my board and ride has adversely affected my ability to relax and place my legs in the proper position for free fall while skydiving.

He continues. "I can see you're working really hard on surfing. Take a break and concentrate on skydiving."

This is fine with me because for the last month I have been working very hard with frustrating results. Some days I even cry while lying on my board in the water.

I'm never going to get this am I?

I didn't think that the one thing that would cause me to be humbled would be attempting to surf and skydive for 5 months at the same time. At least the view from 14,000+ feet above the north shore of Hawaii for jump after jump after jump is beautiful!

If you're gonna learn how to surf, there's no better view than the Hawaiian coastline.

I've been such a natural athlete since learning how to play basketball. Failure is quite the foreign concept to me. Failure day after day after day! Such is the life of a 6'5" man learning sports that are balance related. Hey, everybody could use a little more humble pie.

One month to learn how to get up on my board. A 2nd month and I'm turning. The 3rd month and I'm carving it up.

It took me more than 20 jumps to enjoy doing flips and spins during free fall. Getting beyond the struggle of work! Finally enjoying the ride, having the control to enjoy the view, and play again.

23328061R00140

Made in the USA
Middletown, DE
22 August 2015